T0340084

Cambridge Introductions to Music
Serialism

Serialism, one of the most prominent innovations in music since 1900, is a key topic in the study of music. From Schoenberg to Boulez and beyond, serial composition has been attacked as mathematical and anti-expressive, defended as vital and visionary. Both responses result from an understanding of the relationship between serialism as something new and the existing, established traditions it appeared to challenge so wholeheartedly. Coming nearly a century after the first stirrings of serial thinking in music appeared, this introduction provides a basic outline of the compositional techniques that embody serial principles, and of the historical evolution of those techniques as composers responded to the wealth of social and cultural imperatives that impinged on them in the years after 1920. Following a broadly chronological path, the book demonstrates the variety and adaptability of a wide range of serial compositions, and explains the compositional techniques clearly and concisely.

ARNOLD WHITTALL is Professor Emeritus of Music Theory and Analysis at King's College London.

Cambridge Introductions to Music
Serialism

ARNOLD WHITTALL

CAMBRIDGE
UNIVERSITY PRESS

CAMBRIDGE
UNIVERSITY PRESS

University Printing House, Cambridge CB2 8BS, United Kingdom

Cambridge University Press is part of the University of Cambridge.

It furthers the University's mission by disseminating knowledge in the pursuit of education, learning and research at the highest international levels of excellence.

www.cambridge.org
Information on this title: www.cambridge.org/9780521682008

© Cambridge University Press 2008

First published 2008

A catalogue record for this publication is available from the British Library

Library of Congress Cataloguing in Publication data
Whittall, Arnold.
    The Cambridge introduction to serialism / Arnold Whittall.
        p.   cm.
    Includes bibliographical references and index.
    ISBN 978-0-521-86341-4 (hardback) – ISBN 978-0-521-68200-8 (pbk.)   1. Music – 20th century – History and criticism.   2. Serialism (Music)   I. Title.
    ML197.W536 2008
    781.3′3–dc22   2008020522

ISBN 978-0-521-86341-4 Hardback
ISBN 978-0-521-68200-8 Paperback

Contents

Preface   *page* xi
Acknowledgements   xiii

Chapter 1 Introducing the *Introduction*   1
Some initial questions   1
History and hindsight: an overview   6
A Webern analysis   6
Collection, mode, series, set   8
Notes and numbers   9
Back to Webern   10
Forms of post-tonal composition   12
Terms, techniques   13
Serialism in critical perspective   14
A personal perspective   15

Chapter 2 Schoenberg's path to the twelve-tone method   17
Interpreting transition   17
Tonal or post-tonal?   18
Twelve-tone technique in embryo   19
Ideals and practicalities   21
Post-war problems   22
Parallels and pitfalls: Hauer   24
Eye witness: Gerhard   27

Chapter 3 Serialism in close-up   31
From Bach to Schoenberg   31
Schoenberg as music   32
Serialism as music   35

Fixed and free	36
Op. 25: further details	37
A twelve-tone canon	40
Coda	43

Chapter 4 Schoenberg in the 1920s — **45**

1920–3	45
Making, meaning: Op. 23 No. 5	47
1923–4	50
Schoenberg on Schoenberg: the Wind Quintet	51
More on the Wind Quintet	53
The Wind Quintet's finale	54
1925–9	56
Op. 29 and after	58
Meaning, making	61

Chapter 5 Alban Berg: reverence and resistance — **65**

Wozzeck and transition	65
Personal space	66
Berg–Klein–Berg	68
Berg's Chamber Concerto	70
A first step	71
Series, cycles	72
Lyric Suite	75
Lyric Suite: finale	76
The final dialogues	79
Serialism in *Lulu* and the Violin Concerto	80

Chapter 6 Anton Webern: discipline and licence — **85**

Purity, anxiety	85
Beginnings	86
The route to independence	90
String Trio, Op. 20	92
The method perfected	93
Form and feeling	94
Symmetry and balance	96
Twelve-tone canons	98

Chapter 7 The later Schoenberg **101**
Laying down the law 101
Religion, politics and serialism 102
Exile and readjustment 104
'Good old tradition!'? The Fourth String Quartet 107
Models for form and style 109
Suspended tonality? 110
Grammar or gibberish? 111
Matters of quality 112
Ambiguous endings 113

Chapter 8 American counterpoints: I **117**
From method to system 117
Varèse 118
More pioneers 119
Krenek 119
Sessions, Copland, Perle 120
Babbitt: words 122
Babbitt: music 125
Babbitt: music, words and politics 131
Consequences and contingencies 133

Chapter 9 American counterpoints: II **135**
Stravinsky: a balance of tensions 135
Stravinsky: series and centres 137
Cage and Nancarrow 141
The Minimalists 142
The serial inheritance 144
Carter 145
Carter's practice 146
Gra: playing with sets 148

Chapter 10 European repercussions: I **151**
Facing both ways 151
Britten and the British 152
Shostakovich and the Soviets 155
Lutosławski and the Poles 157

Cold War and style wars: Dallapiccola   160
Nono: commitment to progress   163
Nono: *Il canto sospeso*   166

Chapter 11 European repercussions: II   **171**
From Messiaen to Boulez   171
Testing extremes   174
Structures   175
Hearing techniques   176
Behind *Le Marteau sans maître*   177
Serialism in *Le Marteau sans maître*   178
Stockhausen: Cologne, Paris, Darmstadt   181
Stockhausen and the piano   182
Gruppen   184

Chapter 12 European repercussions: III   **187**
Xenakis   187
Ligeti   189
Ligeti's techniques   191
Berio   193
Berio's transformations   197
Kagel   198

Chapter 13 European repercussions: IV   **203**
The later Boulez   203
Boulez as lecturer   204
Style and idea in *Incises*   205
The later Stockhausen   209
Serialism *in excelsis*   213
Kurtág   216

Chapter 14 European repercussions: V   **219**
The contemporary scene   219
Scandinavia: Nørgård   220
British serialism after 1950   221
Maxwell Davies: before 1970   223
Magic squares and serial structures   225

Maxwell Davies since the 1970s   227
From Manchester to Cambridge   228
Birtwistle   231
Ferneyhough   232
Knussen   235
An ending   236

Notes   239
Bibliography   259
Glossary   271
Index   279

Preface

Serialism is sometimes portrayed as one of the great lost causes of twentieth-century music. An initiative that began in the 1920s with attempts to prove its relevance as a means of both refreshing and preserving traditional compositional methods, it allegedly expired in the 1950s as a result of misguided attempts to radicalise its principles and divorce its compositional manifestations from accepted conventions. After 1960, according to this scenario, it was a spent force, its products rarely performed or recorded, and serving mainly as objects of study for those keen to learn about the various dead ends in reaction to which the serious music scene today has evolved.

'In reaction to which' – the phrase that crept into that last sentence – suggests a key to the alternative interpretation of serialism offered in this *Introduction*. One of the most authoritative overviews of the early twenty-first century[1] ends with contrasting a naïvely evolutionary hypothesis – tonality as the living language of tradition from Bach to Brahms being eroded, then decisively supplanted by the freer, truly democratic techniques of 'atonal' serialism – with a less crudely progressivist interpretation in which (since 1900) tonality has adapted and survived, to remain today the predominant mode of musical expression, both serious and popular. Nevertheless, as argued here, tonality's adaptation and survival are intricately bound up with serialism's adaptation and survival. In these terms, serialism is no more a lost cause than radio in the audio-visual age, but a crucial and often invaluable aspect of that age's culture.

The concerns and challenges confronted in offering an introduction to the phenomenon of serialism are outlined in the early stages of the main text below. Since no author could plausibly claim omniscient expertise over the entire range of the composers and compositions as well as the theories and practices relevant even to an outline introduction such as this, there is a strong documentary element in the text, where acknowledged authorities are cited, sometimes at length. Some of the more detailed technical aspects of these discussions can be bypassed, but the reader should note that it has not been possible to provide technical chapter and verse, with music examples, for all the composers referred to. Such materials are indicated in the Notes. Terms and associated concepts, highlighted in the text in **bold**, are explained in the glossary.

Finally, I want to offer my heartfelt thanks to those friends and colleagues who have devoted valuable time to reading all or part of my work, and for whose suggestions and, at times, complaints, I am enormously indebted. My special gratitude to Ian Bent and Jonathan Dunsby, and to Edward Campbell, Peter Dickinson, Jonathan Goldman, Peter T. Marsh, Carola Nielinger-Vakil, Philip Rupprecht, Ciro Scotto, Joseph Straus and Charles Wilson.

The Cambridge Introduction to Serialism is dedicated to the enduring memory of Mary Whittall, who witnessed its inception, but did not survive to see its completion.

Arnold Whittall
London, March 2008

Acknowledgements

The publisher acknowledges with thanks permission from the following to reproduce music examples in the text.

3.4, 3.5, 3.6: Schoenberg, Suite Op. 25 1925 © Universal Edition (London) Ltd; © Gertrude Schoenberg, renewed 1952. All rights reserved.

7.2: Schoenberg, *Moses und Aron* © Gertrude Schoenberg, 1957; Schott Music GmbH & Co. KG, Mainz, Germany.

8.3: Milton Babbitt, *A Solo Requiem* © C. F. Peters Corporation, New York. Peters Edition Ltd, London.

9.5: Elliott Carter, *Gra*, bars 1–9 © 1993 Hendon Music, Inc.

10.9, 10.10: Nono, *Il canto sospeso* © 1957 Ars Viva Verlag, Mainz, Germany. All rights reserved.

11.4a, 11.4b: Stockhausen, *Klavierstück VIII* © 1965 Universal Edition (London) Ltd, London/UE13675D. All rights reserved.

11.5: Stockhausen, *Gruppen* © 1963 Universal Edition (London) Ltd, London/UE13673. All rights reserved.

12.4: Berio, '*Points on the Curve to Find*' © 1963 Universal Edition (London) Ltd, London/UE13673. All rights reserved.

13.7a, 13.7b: © Karlheinz Stockhausen, Stockhausen Foundation for Music, Kuerten, Germany, www.stockhausen.org.

14.2a, 14.2b: Peter Maxwell Davies, Five Pieces for Piano © 1958 Schott Music Ltd, London. All rights reserved

14.3c, 14.3d: *Ave Maris Stella*, Peter Maxwell Davies © 1976 Boosey & Hawkes Music Publishers Ltd.

14.5b: Brian Ferneyhough, *Superscriptio* © Hinrichsen Edition, Peters Edition Limited, London.

14.7d: Knussen, *Two Organa* © Faber Music Ltd.

Chapter 1

Introducing the *Introduction*

Some initial questions

• *What is serialism?*

A way of writing music.

• *When did serialism first appear?*

During the 1920s: but preliminary forms of serialism can be traced back for several years before that. Those anticipations came about as Arnold Schoenberg and other composers increasingly turned away from the conventions of tonal composition, using major and minor keys, which had dominated its evolution since the seventeenth century. Serialism is therefore part of what has become known as **post-tonal** musical thinking.

• *Who invented serialism?*

Arnold Schoenberg (1874–1951) was the composer most decisively involved in devising and demonstrating the fundamentals of serialism. But other contemporaries were working along comparable lines, and it is clear that the establishment of serialism, as an instance of post-tonal thinking, was not the work of just one musician.

• *How many composers have adopted serialism?*

This book aims to introduce the music of all the principal serial composers, starting with Schoenberg and his pupils Alban Berg and Anton Webern. From the 1920s onwards serialism has been adopted and adapted by many different kinds of composer. Some, like Milton Babbitt and Pierre Boulez, have stressed its radical potential. Others, like Dmitri Shostakovich and Benjamin Britten, have used only those aspects of it which could enrich their much more traditional ways of composing. I am not aiming to provide a 'complete' history of the phenomenon: however, some indication of the range and flexibility of serial thinking can be given. I will also discuss the extent to which it remains a force within compositional thinking today.

• *What is serial music like?*

An initial indication of what serial music is like can be found in Arnold Schoenberg's reference to 'when I used for the first time rows of twelve tones in the fall of 1921'.[1] By 'rows of twelve tones' Schoenberg was referring to a linear ordering of the complete chromatic scale, an ordering which served as the source of all the pitch materials of the composition in question. This 'row' ('Reihe' in German) became known in English as a **series** – an ordered sequence of notes, as opposed to the raw, unordered material of the chromatic scale in its pure ascending or descending form (Ex. 1.1a). Ex. 1.1b shows the series for Schoenberg's Suite for Piano, Op. 25 (1921–3) in abstract form, written on a single stave and without any rhythmic values. Ex. 1.1c shows its use as the theme of the Trio section from Op. 25's Minuet.

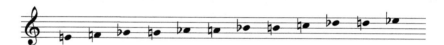

Ex. 1.1a Chromatic scale

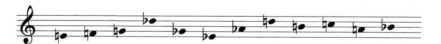

Ex. 1.1b Schoenberg, Suite Op. 25, twelve-tone series (P-0)

Ex. 1.1c Schoenberg, Suite Op. 25, opening of Trio section of Minuet

A series can therefore be thought of as a theme. Nevertheless, in generating all the melodic and harmonic materials of a twelve-tone serial composition, it represents an expansion of the function of a theme in earlier music. That more comprehensive quality is underlined by the convention of showing a twelve-tone pitch series as a notated sequence without rhythms, and with the assumption that the registers of the individual pitches are variable. For this reason, the notes shown in Ex. 1.1b are often termed **pitch classes**. This means that each such pitch class stands for every possible octave position of the pitch in question. It will be obvious that composers will not normally wish to confine themselves to the actual registers of a series notated as in Ex. 1.1b. Nor does Schoenberg do so in Op. 25, as Ex. 1.1c shows, and the analysis in chapter 3 will demonstrate in detail.

• *How does serial composition differ from tonal composition?*

Tonal compositions tend to rely more on the **functional** harmonic relations of tonality to provide structural principles than on the sequence of pitches and intervals present in any particular theme. As such, serial composition represents an alternative to tonal composition. Nevertheless, as the history of music since 1920 shows, serialism has not replaced tonality, but coexists and interacts with it.

• *Twelve-tone or twelve-note?*

As the basic terminology applicable to serialism migrated from German to English a certain diversity became apparent, especially between those two cultures divided by a common language, British and American. The British preference for 'twelve-note' persists, as the most recent edition of *The New Grove* (2001) confirms. Nevertheless, the professional consensus has moved fairly decisively in the direction of the American preference for 'tone' as general and 'note' as specific. 'Tone' seems closer to pitch class, and will therefore be used as the normal term in this book – except where quotations determine otherwise.

• *Are all serial compositions twelve-tone compositions?*

'Serial' is a much more general and comprehensive term than 'twelve-tone'. As this *Introduction* will show, a series of pitches can comprise fewer than twelve tones or, with repetitions, more than twelve tones. Similarly, a series can be devised for other musical elements, or **parameters**, such as rhythmic durations, dynamic levels and modes of articulation. Sometimes, as in Ex. 1.2a, these simply translate the

$pppp$	ppp	pp	p	$quasi\,p$	mp	mf	$quasi\,f$	f	ff	fff	$ffff$
1	2	3	4	5	6	7	8	9	10	11	12

Ex. 1.2a Series of twelve dynamic levels

Ex. 1.2b Series of twelve durations

sequence 1 to 12 literally, moving from extremely soft to extremely loud in the case of dynamics, or from very short to relatively long in the case of durational values (Ex. 1.2.b).

If used in actual compositions, such manipulations can give the impression of mathematical, mechanical routines seriously at odds with the inspiration and spontaneity usually seen as vital for valid works of art. In addition, attempts to work with series of twelve different dynamic or durational values have created immense problems for live performers. For this reason, composers have often used series of fewer than twelve elements for these secondary parameters, as well as, in many cases, for pitch itself.

• *Is it true that serial composition has little or nothing in common with tonal composition?*

As Schoenberg's preferred procedures for serial composition evolved and became more widely known, it was clear that the initial ordering of the twelve different pitches was only the starting point. With the conviction that any serious compositional process should be able to match the work of the great masters of the past in length as well as technical skill and artistic sophistication, Schoenberg recognised that only very rarely would it be sufficient simply to repeat or vary the single version of the twelve-tone series with which he had started. He therefore derived new versions of a single series from the original version, and the three basic ways in which he did this stem from techniques found in traditional harmony and counterpoint: **transposition, inversion** and reversion (retrogression).

The original version of the series is now generally known as the untransposed **Prime** (Principal) **form**: P-0 for short. Transposing this Prime successively onto the remaining eleven pitches of the chromatic scale creates twelve versions in total. Ex. 1.3a shows the P-6 version used by Schoenberg in the Trio section of Op. 25's Minuet: the first note is now B flat, six semitones above the '0', E. Turning all twelve

Ex. 1.3a Schoenberg, Suite Op. 25, P-6 form of series, and its use in Trio section of Minuet

Ex. 1.3b Schoenberg, Suite Op. 25, I-0 form of series, and its use in Trio section of Minuet

of those Prime forms backwards creates another twelve versions: the retrograde of P-0 is usually identified as R-0 or P-0^R, of P-6 as R-6 or P-6^R, etc.

Inverting the intervals of the Prime forms – that is, mirroring of the kind where an ascending interval of five semitones becomes a descending five semitones, and so on – creates a further twelve versions. Ex. 1.3b shows the inversion of P-0 – I-0 – as used in Schoenberg's Trio section, and the first tone is now written as F flat, rather than E natural: such enharmonic changes, for ease of reading, are common in post-tonal music. Again, retrograding the twelve inversions generates another twelve RI forms, shown for I-0 as RI-0 or I-0^R, for I-6 as RI-6 or I-6^R.

There are therefore forty-eight versions of Op. 25's series in all. What the consequences of this are for the composer will be considered in due course. But it will be clear at this stage that serial thinking is quite distinct from tonal thinking, even if the serial composer finds ways of responding positively to the challenge of building bridges between the new and the old (for example, the use of inversion and retrogression in tonal fugues and canons).

History and hindsight: an overview

One way for composers to seek to justify a move to serialism, and to persuade listeners that the results need not be impossibly difficult to follow, is to underline the similarities between old and new: for example, pointing out that thematic manipulations in tonal music from (at least) Bach to Brahms could well involve inverting or retrograding motives, as well as transposing them into different keys, or to different pitch-levels within the same key. It was no less important to demonstrate a degree of inevitability in the way twelve-tone serialism was felt to have evolved out of the freer and more flexible situation that existed early in the twentieth century as the old tonal certainties began to break down. For a disarmingly simple statement claiming a degree of such evolutionary awareness, we can refer to comments by Schoenberg's disciple Anton Webern, made during a lecture in Vienna in 1932, which were noted down by students at the time.

About 1911 I wrote the *Bagatelles for String Quartet*, Op. 9, all very short pieces, lasting a couple of minutes – perhaps the shortest music so far – here I had the feeling, 'When all twelve notes have gone by, the piece is over' . . . In short, a rule of law emerged; until all twelve notes have occurred, none of them may occur again. The most important thing is that each 'run' of twelve notes marked a division within the piece, idea or theme.[2]

In these remarks, Webern moved quickly from the idea of form defined by a single traversal of the twelve tones to one in which larger forms would be governed by multiple twelve-tone sequences. After all, by 1932 he had written some of his most sophisticated serial works, and was also familiar with some of Schoenberg's much larger and longer twelve-tone compositions. But Webern did not claim that his 1911 *Bagatelles* were serial, or twelve-tone, in this way. At most, in their concern to keep all twelve tones in circulation, and to unfold them in a relatively systematic manner, they were groping their way towards a basic principle, sometimes known as 'total chromaticism', whose full theoretical and practical consequences would be worked out over the next decade.

A Webern analysis

The fifth of Webern's *Bagatelles* Op. 9 (Ex. 1.4) is in most respects the simplest in rhythm and texture, and we can soon see how what happens in it relates to the composer's comments. Starting with four different pitches in bar 1 (C, C sharp, D sharp, E), Webern adds D in bar 2, B and F in bar 3, G flat and B flat in bar 4, G

Ex. 1.4 Webern, *Bagatelle* for string quartet, Op. 9 No. 5

natural and A flat in bar 6, and finally A natural in bar 7. Even here, then, there is more going on than is accounted for by the claim that 'When all twelve notes have gone by, the piece is over'. So it is not too surprising that scholars have looked more closely at the music, the better to understand the composer's most basic point, which was to argue that 'new laws' had come into force that had made it 'impossible to describe a piece as in one key or another'.

This was clearly the case in Op. 9 No. 5, even though the gradual unfolding of the twelve different tones between bars 1 and 7 involves a certain amount of repetition of those tones – sometimes in different registers. The extreme economy of the music excludes thematic elements of the traditional melodic kind: and even pared-down motives or thematic cells are not allowed to make their presence felt, not least because the extremely faint sounds required – very soft pizzicatos, playing on the bridge – ensure that actual pitches are barely audible at any point. Webern appears to be employing a degree of logic and consistency, as in the gradual opening out of notated pitch and register, a process begun when the first violin in bar 2 fills in the gap left by the other three instruments in bar 1. But he then does his utmost to ensure that any sense of asserting an inexorable logic should be undermined by the extreme reticence of what is actually heard. It would nevertheless be straining credulity to argue that the pitch formations and combinations in this music are arbitrary – aimed simply to achieve a sonic effect rather than to present a musical argument, however brief and basic. The piece moves in and out of various instrumental combinations, and the vertical alignments of two, three, or four notes are likely to have been as much the focus of the composer's attention as the individual, horizontal lines of the four constituent parts.

Collection, mode, series, set

Certain initiatives which can be viewed retrospectively as anticipations of serial thinking in music written well before 1920 have been identified by music historians. For example, the article on 'Twelve-note composition' in *The New Grove* begins with a reference to Skryabin's Piano Sonata No. 7 (1911–12) and the seven-note pitch **collection** (C, D flat, E, F sharp, G, A, B flat) on which it is based. This collection, or **mode,** can be deemed an anticipation of a twelve-tone series.[3] Yet in itself it has more of the aspect of a conjunct scale or mode than of an intervallically diverse series, ordered to highlight particular generative motivic or melodic materials. For this reason, music theorists have established a distinction between **set** and series, in which the defining characteristic of a set is its total content, without regard to order within the set, whereas a series is always ordered. As Joseph Straus has framed the distinction: 'a series is a line, not a set, of pitch-classes. A pitch-class set retains its identity no matter how its pitch-classes are ordered. In a series, however, the pitch classes occur in a particular [usually non-scalar] order; the identity of the series changes if the order changes.'[4] This interplay between series, where linear order is crucial, and set, where the total content is more basic, is one of the most significant features in many technical analyses of serial music. Perhaps the most spectacular consequence of the contrast between series and set is that, while there are many millions of ordered series possible – 479,001,600 twelve-tone series, for example – the total number of **normal order** pitch-class sets ranging in size from one to twelve pitch classes is a mere 224.[5]

Another respect in which the series/set distinction breaks down is that a set, like a series, can be transposed, inverted and reversed without changing its fundamental identity. In addition, not only can sets, of however many pitch classes, become series, but the compositional manipulation of a series tends to draw attention to the various **sub-sets** which can be derived from it. As will be seen in later chapters, there is evidence that during and after the 1960s composing systematically with all twelve tones, disposed in various modal or scalar formations, though not consistently ordered in true serial fashion, became a more attractive and widely adopted compositional technique than consistent, strictly ordered serialism. After 1950 the perception emerged – stemming mainly from the theoretical work of Milton Babbitt[6] – that twelve-tone series could usefully be thought of as ordered versions of a much smaller number of **source sets**. This has tended to reinforce the distinction between an attitude which regards the pre-compositional progress to ordering as primary, and the attitude that prefers to avoid such specific and consistently deployed orderings of source sets altogether.

Some detailed analysis of Schoenberg's Piano Suite Op. 25 in chapter 3 will show that, even in a composition based on an ordered twelve-tone series, textural and other considerations mean that in practice the fixed ordering of the series as a single line is compromised as often as it is confirmed. If, as most do, a serial composition involves the interaction of vertical and horizontal factors – harmony and counterpoint – then alignments between pitches will occur which are not the result of their immediate adjacency in the particular form of the twelve-tone series in use.

The *New Grove* example from Skryabin shows that, as scholars became more familiar with the exploratory works of the decade or so after 1908, they were increasingly inclined to interpret them in terms of characteristics shared with an overall development from tonal thematicism to post-tonal, motivically suffused serialism. In any case, from an early stage many twelve-tone works can be shown to have derived their twelve-tone resources from smaller groupings – collections of three, four, or six tones which tend to be related, as in the case of Webern's Concerto for Nine Instruments, Op. 24 (1934). Here the four clearly differentiated three-note groups, or **trichords**, with which the work begins (Ex. 1.5) all employ the intervals of the major third and minor ninth/augmented octave.

Notes and numbers

With the initiatives taken after 1945, particularly in America, by mathematically expert serial composers and theorists such as Milton Babbitt and David Lewin, the tendency to identify notes as numbers increased by leaps and bounds. After 1950 the study of serial composition often proceeded on the basis of **integer notation**, translating classes of pitch names and intervals into whole numbers, then arranging the resulting integers into consistently ordered sequences to facilitate the

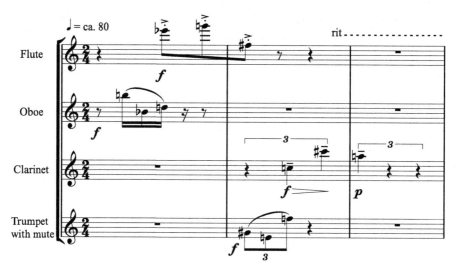

Ex. 1.5 Webern, opening of Concerto Op. 24

identification of relationships within the various motivic and harmonic materials drawn from the twelve-tone series itself.

Writing out forty-eight different version of a series on manuscript paper is a time- and space-consuming exercise, prone to error. It is much more economical to translate pitch-class letter names into integers signifying the distance in semitones between the pitch class in question and the initial '0' – especially when Primes and Inversions are then interlaced in the **matrix** form shown in Ex. 1.6 for the series of Schoenberg's Suite Op. 25. Technical writing on twelve-tone compositions may well use two integers to identify the pitch class in question: first, a number indicating the order position of the note in the series, with the first as '0': second a number indicating the distance of that note in semitones from the '0'. So, for the P-6 version of Op. 25 (as shown in Ex. 1.3a), the fourth note, G natural, is '3,3', and the seventh, D natural '6, 10'. (One final notational refinement: in order to avoid the double digits 10 and 11 in series tables and analyses, some writers use 't' for ten and 'e' for eleven.)

Back to Webern

Integer notation was a feature of pitch-class set analysis from the beginning, and this enabled comparison of post-tonal techniques to be made between music like the Webern *Bagatelles* and later, twelve-tone works. The trichord found on the first beat of bar 3 of the Webern *Bagatelle* discussed above – F, E, B – is an instance of

		E	F	G	Db	Gb	Eb	Ab	D	B	C	A	Bb	
P-0	E	0	1	3	9	2	11	4	10	7	8	5	6	Bb
P-11	Eb	11	0	2	8	1	10	3	9	6	7	4	5	A
P-9	Db	9	10	0	6	11	8	1	7	4	5	2	3	G
P-3	G	3	4	6	0	5	2	7	1	10	11	8	9	Db
P-10	D	10	11	1	7	0	9	2	8	5	6	3	4	Ab
P-1	F	1	2	4	10	3	0	5	11	8	9	6	7	B
P-8	C	8	9	11	5	10	7	0	6	3	4	1	2	Gb
P-2	Gb	2	3	5	11	4	1	6	0	9	10	7	8	C
P-5	A	5	6	8	2	7	4	9	3	0	1	10	11	Eb
P-4	Ab	4	5	7	1	6	3	8	2	11	0	9	10	D
P-7	B	7	8	10	4	9	6	11	5	2	3	0	1	F
P-6	Bb	6	7	9	3	8	5	10	4	1	2	11	0	E
		Bb	B	Db	G	C	A	D	Ab	F	Gb	Eb	E	

Ex. 1.6 Matrix showing series forms for Schoenberg, Suite Op. 25 in **integer notation.**

For **Prime** forms, read horizontal lines from left to right

For **Retrograde** forms, read horizontal lines from right to left

For **Inversions**, read columns from top to bottom – e.g. the third column, descending from G, represents **I-3**

For **Retrograde Inversions**, read columns from bottom to top – e.g. the final column, ascending from E, represents **RI-0**

the [016] set, representing the distance in semitones between notes 1 and 2, and then notes 1 and 3 (reading downwards in this case, because the smaller of the two intervals is at the top). The exercise in reduction and rationalisation which this **set-class** identity [016] represents is one in which all possible versions of this trichord are regarded as projections of an order which theorists deem the normal order. This is reached by a process of two or three stages. The two-stage process is relevant to situations like bar 3 of the *Bagatelle*, where the actual intervals in the music (semitone, perfect fourth, tritone) are the same as the **interval classes** of the pitch-class set (1, 5, 6). The three-stage process comes into play in bar 10 of the Webern piece. Reading the intervals of the trichord B, C, G flat in ascending order gives 1 and 6, and a normal order of [017]. If, however, we discount the actual registers used by Webern and think of the three pitches as pitch classes, it will be clear that the most concise arrangement possible is C, B, G flat, or [016].[7] As a pitch-class set the [016] trichord is one of a group of twelve trichords within the larger sequence of

Transcribing the entire pitch content of Webern's piece in this manner is a simple, systematic way of identifying and relating sonorities which are otherwise unclassifiable – the trichord in question is not an instance of any of the four traditional triad forms (major, minor, augmented, diminished). As a pitch-class set the [016] trichord is one of a group of twelve trichords within the larger sequence of

208 normal-order sets containing from three to nine elements. We shall see in later chapters how important such trichordal formations can be to the organisation of twelve-tone series as well.

Forms of post-tonal composition

There can be considerable appeal in an argument that perceptions about the aesthetic value of a new compositional principle for pitch organisation to replace (or complement) tonality evolved from the relatively simple, small-scale use of sets, or collections, of three or four notes towards its logical completion in the pervasive use – after 1920 – of an all-embracing twelve-tone series. It is true, theoretically, to say that all twelve-tone series are the same: that is, different orderings or permutations of the same twelve pitch classes of the well-tempered chromatic scale. But all three-note sets are not the same, even when differences of pitch such as are found in the Webern *Bagatelle* between the F, E and B of bar 3 and the F sharp, G and A flat of bar 6 are represented in integer notation, the difference between [016] and [012] cannot be further collapsed to the same basic scalar order in the way that, trivially but crucially, must be the case with any twelve-tone series (0, 1, 2, 3, 4, 5, 6, 7, 8, 9, 10, 11). However diverse the sequence of intervals might be between two given examples of twelve-tone series, the total pitch-class content will be identical.

That two manifestations of the same fewer-than-twelve-tones set need not contain exactly the same pitches is also shown in the *Bagatelle*, where the [016] trichord occurs on the first beat of bar 3 (F, E, B) and again in bar 10 (C, B, G flat]. In this case they have B, in the same register, in common. Describing them as examples of the same structural entity demonstrates the analytical concern to determine degrees of similarity and difference in the materials of a composition which is not subject to the laws of tonal harmony and counterpoint. On the one hand, according to the system designed to identify particular formations within the universe of pitch-class sets, they are identical: on the other hand, as deployed at different points in the piece, the differences, not simply of pitch content, but of musical character and formal function, cannot be ignored in any attempt to provide a fuller account of compositional character than that given by commentary on pitch-class set structure.

With respect to this kind of analysis, Allen Forte has made the important point that while 'pc [pitch-class] set analysis illuminates twelve-tone music ... the ordered set concepts of twelve-tone theory are only peripherally relevant to the study of music in which the unordered set is the basic structural unit'.[8] As already argued, Webern's *Bagatelles* (1911) are not serial compositions, if by 'serial' we understand the kind of consciously constructed, consistently ordered and all-determining kind of twelve-tone series used by Schoenberg and others after 1920.

Nevertheless, during the first two decades of the twentieth century there is evidence of an emerging consciousness – in Schoenberg, Webern, Skryabin and others – of non-traditional formations like the [016] trichord as valid formal elements in post-tonal music, and of that consciousness playing a fundamental role in the eventual arrival at the principles of twelve-tone serialism itself. Analysis can demonstrate degrees of common ground between the materials of twelve-tone compositions and other kinds of post-tonal music: it can also show that features most fully realised in twelve-tone serialism are far from irrelevant to other kinds of post-tonal music, from both before and after the relatively short period, from *c.* 1920 to *c.* 1960, in which 'pure' twelve-tone composition flourished.

Terms, techniques

A quick glance at a range of writings on serialism, from dictionary articles to full-length studies of particular composers or of the historical development of music since 1900, will indicate from an early stage that absolute consistency and uniformity of terminology is not to be expected. From (just in English) row, series, or set, the terms proliferate into **dyad, hexachord, tetrachord, trichord, sub-set, aggregate, array**, and on into broader concepts like **matrix, magic square, combinatoriality, complementation, hexachordal complementation, partitioning, permutation, derivation, rotation** and **multiplication**. No wonder that serialism appears to invite the damning dismissal, 'mathematical': though what this tends to imply is 'mechanical', and not so much the unavoidable presence of elements that – like individual pitches which, as vibrations in air – can be defined in terms of proportions or ratios. In this context, 'mathematical' implies a mindless dependency on calculation and pre-ordained processes which relieves the composer of any need to think, let alone respond to 'inspiration'.

It is certainly possible, if not essential, to discuss serial techniques in terms directly derived from such branches of mathematics as set theory and group theory. But serial music has the best chance of success when initial planning stimulates the composer to think afresh about the most fundamental of all creative enterprises: the tension and interaction between, and possible eventual intersection of, things which are (relatively) fixed and things which are (substantially) free. In this respect, the early defence of serialism mounted by Schoenberg and Webern – to the effect that they were still *composing*, and that this activity had a great deal in common with what pre-serial composers understood by the process – is entirely valid. Knowing how serial composition differs from traditional tonal composition might make it hard, at least to begin with, to get away from the assumption that while the latter can be inspired, the former is more likely to be arid and mechanistic. But one of the purposes of this book is to challenge that assumption, however sincerely held, and to challenge it by urging a reconsideration of what composition itself can and should be.

Serialism in critical perspective

Serial music is less prominent in concert programmes, or the schedules of record companies, than earlier classical composition or those types of music written since 1900 – from Debussy to John Adams – which remain most directly related to earlier tonal or modal techniques. Even with what is probably the most frequently per-formed and familiar serial composition, Alban Berg's Violin Concerto (1935), its twelve-tone compositional procedures will be irrelevant to the aural experience of most listeners, despite the vital role of those procedures in determining the nature of the music that is heard. Nevertheless, information about the serial processes underpinning the sounds has never been kept secret, and since the 1920s, when pitch serialism was first mentioned in print, controversy has raged about the consequences of giving cerebral manipulations of musical materials a more fun-damental role in compositional creation than they had had before – at least since the thirteenth century Ars Nova, described by Richard Taruskin as 'music for an intellectual and political elite'.[9]

   Another distinguished music historian has recently raised the issue of serialism's accessibility and viability in discussing the attitude of an important composer who 'converted' to serialism in the 1950s – Igor Stravinsky (1882–1971). Stephen Walsh quotes comments made by Stravinsky in 1936, describing Schoenberg as 'a chemist of music more than an artistic creator. His investigations are interesting, since they tend to expand the possibilities of auditory pleasure, but . . . they have more to do with the quantity than with the quality of music.' Walsh goes on:

> In 1936, Stravinsky had almost certainly not heard any of Schoenberg's serial music, but he had had it described to him, mostly by hostile judges . . . In the circumstances, his opinion is much what one would expect. Schoenberg had devised a method that involved taking the twelve different notes in the octave, arranging them in a certain order, then using that order – or series – as a fixed template for the melodic and harmonic material of an entire work. Put so crudely, it sounded about as pointless artistically as change-ringing. You could play the series forwards, backwards, or upside down, or the upside-down version backwards, and you could do all these things starting on any note you liked. Every music student has experienced that moment of despair on first hearing Schoenberg 'explained' in these terms, that feeling of disbelief that anyone would bother to write, listen to, or study music conceived in such a way.

Walsh then suggests that what Stravinsky's young American assistant, Robert Craft, did to promote that conversion to serial technique 'was simply what any sensible music teacher would at once see as necessary: he transmitted his own enthusiasm for the actual music and only then, when pressed, showed how the music and the method interacted – how this particular music came out of this particular set of procedures, exactly as one might do in analyzing a Josquin motet or a Bach fugue'. In this way Stravinsky was able to accept that one serial work which Craft was rehearsing at the time, Schoenberg's Suite Op. 29 (1925–6), was, 'from the very first chord, musically compelling. Stravinsky knew at once that it could not be ignored. And suddenly its method began to intrigue him.'[10] The 'chemist of music' was an 'artistic creator' after all: and it remains true for all of us that, if we do not find a serial composition 'musically compelling', then no amount of technical information about how it was written, or claims about its historical importance, will persuade us to take it seriously.

A personal perspective

It is in the nature of textbooks and introductions to over-simplify, to lay down the law, and this is never easier to do than when the subject-matter itself appears to be law-governed, rule-determined, to – for music – an unprecedented degree. Nevertheless, to introduce serialism is to outline something that resists generalisation. Just as with modality, tonality, or any other general category, the sense in which all serial compositions are similar may well seem of less moment than the ways in which they differ, and attempting to arrive at an understanding of serialism both historically and technically creates many challenges. How comparative can such attempts be, and what are the appropriate contexts for comparison? To what extent does serial music remake earlier forms and styles: to what extent does it reject them? And how far can such questions be considered by way of what you can expect to hear when a serial composition is performed, as opposed to what you can expect to see when you pore over the score, and its associated commentaries, for long periods of time?

It is fitting for an *Introduction* to ask these questions, even when the answers can be only partial and provisional. In one important sense this book is restricted to historical excavation. It is not an introduction to how to compose serially, though students of these pages who want to try out the techniques for themselves should acquire a fair idea of what is involved quite quickly. More crucially, however, it is an introduction in the documentary sense – less a sequence of dogmatic assertions by an all-knowing author, more an assembly of views from the vast amount of writing on serialism, both introductory and specialised, which has appeared in such profusion since the 1920s. Of course, dogma and authorial power-assertion are detectable in the choice of materials cited, and the interpretations of those materials offered. But I have attempted to filter my biases, enthusiasms and blind spots through as wide-ranging and evenly balanced a selection of composers and commentators as the format of the volume permits.

Serialism has often been paraded as the ultimate demonstration of that negative side of musical modernity, in which long-established, well-tried traditions based in nature and human aural sensibility are jettisoned in a misguided, arrogant concern to elevate the desperate ambitions of composers who desire to be thought original at all costs, and who dogmatically disregard as irrelevant what mattered most to their predecessors and precursors down the centuries. Attempts in recent decades to replace the negative term **atonal** (i.e. entirely lacking tonality) with the more constructive **post-tonal** have so far failed to provide a cast-iron defence of serial composition against its detractors. Small wonder, their argument continues, that classical music – even if not explicitly serial – has become increasingly devalued during the decades since the 1920s, and that those kinds of popular music rooted in emotional and technical directness are commonly seen as much more significant, both culturally and commercially.

Even as a word, serialism can have unpleasant associations, to do with obsessive behaviour, which can then be linked with the propensities of composers who prefer to work with arid calculation rather than expressive immediacy. Nor has it helped those disposed to argue that a serial composition demands to be judged aesthetically by listeners in the same way as any other kind of musical work, that prominent composers – Schoenberg and Pierre Boulez among them – have made triumphalist assertions about the phenomenon which can easily seem like the misguided idealism of the proponents of Esperanto as a linguistic solution for all the political, cultural and social ills of modern civilisation.

My object in the following pages is not to claim that serial composition in all its aspects deserves to occupy that aesthetic and theoretic high ground which most musicians, from critics and historians to performers, promoters, concertgoers and record buyers, have consistently denied it. Still less am I disposed to urge patience on my readers on the grounds that serialism's time is yet to come. While no future possibility can be totally ruled out, such a scenario is implausible, mainly because the history of serial theory and practice has had more to do with evolution and adaptation than with reinforcement of its strictest principles. Since, broadly speaking, serialism is not a style, but can be employed by composers whose works sound radically different from each other, it has always had the chameleon-like capacity to underpin very different kinds of music. An *Introduction to Serialism* that confined itself to what the author felt able to define as the most purely serial compositions only – ones in which no other technical principles played significant roles – would be very different from this one. Rather, my aim is to introduce readers to the ways in which a principle has impinged on so much music composed since 1900 that it might not be too extravagant to call the years 1900–99 'the serial century'.

Chapter 2

Schoenberg's path to the twelve-tone method

Interpreting transition

In 1921, when Schoenberg began work on the Suite for Piano, Op. 25, he was completing a long period of exploration and experiment. This had involved abandoning the late-romantic tonality of his earliest works (e.g. *Verklärte Nacht* for string sextet, Op. 4, 1899), then a preliminary post-tonal phase. As suggested in chapter 1, this phase – in which Webern and others were also involved – was not literally 'serial' in the twelve-tone sense. But it can now be seen to have anticipated some of the method's most significant features.

In Schoenberg's case, the exploratory years from *c.* 1908 to *c.* 1920 generated music which, by and large, gave such a high priority to freedom and innovation that – with occasional exceptions, like the use of canon and passacaglia in *Pierrot lunaire* (1912) – it sought to avoid those allusions to even earlier forms and textures which would become central to his twelve-tone compositions. The purest phase of the exploratory period was relatively brief: its principal achievement was the monodrama *Erwartung* (1909), an expressionistic case-study of a woman deranged by her husband's death, and by the possibility that she is guilty of murder. Yet even with *Erwartung* music-ologists have had some success in showing that the desire for freedom, coupled with writing the work very quickly, did not eliminate all recurrences of thematic and harmonic materials. This innovatory, post-tonal music was not devoid of all contact with the tonal, thematic past.[1]

Not even the independent-minded Schoenberg can be said to have worked in total isolation, though he was doubtless unaware of what other radical composers – as rarely performed as he himself was – were doing at the same time. But there was a distinct restlessness, focusing on the need for music to explore new means of construction and expression, which was particularly strong in such cultural centres as Berlin, Paris and New York, as well as Vienna. In his pioneering survey of post-tonal theory and practice, George Perle claimed that 'the twelve-tone system is not as insulated from other contemporary musical developments as it is sometimes assumed to be. Essentially, Schoenberg systematized and defined for his own **dodecaphonic** purposes a pervasive technical feature of "modern" musical practice, the **ostinato**.' On this basis, Perle was content to conclude that 'serial procedures have been employed not only by Schoenberg and his disciples but also, independently, by Scriabin, Stravinsky, Bartók, and others'.[2] By 'serial procedures', Perle is referring to the kind of pre-twelve-tone manipulation of pitch-class sets mentioned in chapter 1: and such manipulations have often been found in Schoenberg himself.

During the later decades of the twentieth century theorists and analysts explored the work not only of Schoenberg and Webern, who eventually became twelve-tone serialists, but also of post-tonal composers like Ives, Skryabin, Stravinsky, Bartók and even Debussy, whose music could be interpreted in terms of procedures involving pitch-class sets. Of these composers, only Stravinsky – after 1950 – eventually embraced twelve-tone serialism. But one important consequence of such interpretative exercises was to shed indirect light on the tendency of twelve-tone serialism itself to facilitate interplay between ordered series and unordered sub-sets. For example, if it is indeed the case that in Skryabin's later music, like the Piano Sonata No. 7 (1911–12), 'the relations among sets – especially those based on pitch-class invariance – are the primary determinants of structure',[3] and if this occurs in a context where 'functional [tonal] relations are totally suspended, at least for the overall structure', then a possible connection between the abandonment of consistently deployed tonality and the kind of 'set-class thinking' which has important links with serial thinking is made plain.

Tonal or post-tonal?

It is in the nature of transitional phases of musical history that the effect of new initiatives cannot be entirely separated from the persistence of long-standing conventions. For this reason, both post-tonal compositions involving pitch-class sets and twelve-tone serial compositions do not by definition lack all points of contact with the harmonic procedures of functional tonality. A good example of the contrasting, not to say conflicting, technical interpretations than can result was provided in 1981 when two very different studies of Schoenberg's Piano Piece Op. 11 No. 1 (1909) were published side by side.[4] Will Ogdon focused on what he saw as residues of tonality, despite the absence of triadic harmony and diatonic progressions. Allen Forte worked with his then-preferred mode of pitch-class set analysis, emphasising the role of larger, mainly six-note sets – hexachords – from which the vocabulary of tonal harmony, as well as traditional kinds of small-scale motivic working, were excluded.

That particular pairing of analyses illustrates an opposition often found in the interpretation of twelve-tone serial compositions as well. At issue is the possibility that Schoenberg's career did not involve a transition from tonal to post-tonal and serial composition in which the attributes of the former were totally overlaid by the novel features of the latter. Rather, the polarities of tonal and post-tonal defined a field of action within which Schoenberg would move with inspired freedom and resourcefulness for the rest of his life.

By allowing the post-tonal to exclude all consideration of the tonal, an analysis of pitch-class set structure in Op. 11 No. 1 is likely to make most sense as an indication of ways in which prefigurations of serial procedures can be detected. In particular, Allen Forte's focus, at this stage in his work, on the hexachord as structurally fundamental in pre-twelve-tone post-tonal music acknowledges the significance of such hexachords as source sets in twelve-tone theory, as determined in the 1940s and later by Milton Babbitt.[5] No less significantly, Forte-style pitch-class set analysis involves principles of **invariance** – the properties of transposition, inversion, retrogression and even permutation which can reduce a multiplicity of different formations to the same source set – which reflect the most basic procedures of twelve-tone serialism.[6]

Precisely for this reason, Bryan Simms claims that 'there is no persuasive evidence that Schoenberg used reordering, transposition, inversion, and complementation as part of a systematic composition method in the earlier [pre-twelve-tone] styles of atonality'.[7] For Simms, the transitional status of the Piano Piece Op. 11 No. 1 has little or nothing to do with the proto-serial manipulation of hexachords or other set classes. Nor, for that matter, is the possible survival of tonal harmonic routines particularly important. Rather, the piece 'begins to show an important change in Schoenberg's thinking about atonal music' [Simms prefers 'atonal' to 'post-tonal'], adopting that 'homogeneous, dissonant, and distinctly anti-romantic' manner' (63) from which twelve-tone serialism, as both technique and style, would eventually emerge: between the relatively tentative explorations of the unfinished symphony (1914–15) and the first completely twelve-tone work, the Suite Op. 25, of almost a decade later.

Twelve-tone technique in embryo

In terms of transition, or of change of emphasis within Schoenberg's ever-evolving musical language, the year 1914 was crucial. The particular importance of the incomplete draft of a symphonic scherzo which Schoenberg sketched, and is dated 27 May 1914 (Ex. 2.1), is stated by Simms: 'the principal theme is made from all twelve tones with none repeated, and it is subsequently varied, at least in part, by serial procedures that keep the twelve tones together as an integral unity, a tone row' (159). What is important about this, Simms argues, is not so much the twelve-tone

Ex. 2.1 Schoenberg, twelve–tone scherzo theme

theme itself: similar examples can be found as early as the beginning of Liszt's *Faust Symphony* (1854–7). What is genuinely innovatory in the Schoenberg scherzo is the use of 'a new concept of variation that approached an entire theme or phrase as an indivisible entity'. This innovation leads Simms to propose the concept of 'serialized variations', since the way in which 'the order of intervals in the original melody is retained in the later variant' clearly anticipates the systematic use of interval-order-identical transpositions, inversions and retrogrades in twelve-tone serialism 'proper'. As such, it is to be distinguished from the freer process of **developing variation** found in Schoenberg's earlier works, both tonal and post-tonal (160). It also means that analysis solely in terms of smaller pitch-class sets can begin to give way to analysis in terms of a twelve-tone series.

Simms sees the transition from free atonality to serialism in aesthetic as well as technical terms:

> at first Schoenberg's atonal music was touched by angst and spurred on by a need for liberation from the past; it erupted from the same energetic creativity [often termed 'expressionism'] that was evident in literature and painting in the years before World War I. But gradually it lost its spontaneous and emotional character, and came to rely on methodic controls in the fashioning of its materials. After about 1912 its explosive subjectivity dissipated in a more objective atmosphere; its expressive content had cooled by then to a level that could admit even parody and humor. (3–4)

It is clear from this that Simms regards analysis of that angst-touched, liberty-seeking post-tonal music in terms of the kind of 'methodic controls' appropriate to the later music as missing the point – even if Schoenberg himself, in the 1920s and later, did not actively discourage the idea that connections between the two types of post-tonal music might be important. As Simms accepts, 'in the first edition of the *Harmonielehre* [1911] Schoenberg had already alluded to the twelve-tone chromatic scale as the basic "conceptual unit" of ultramodern harmony, and by the early 1920s he was all the more inclined to suggest a connection between this twelve-tone element in his atonal works and twelve-tone composition per se' (9).

Ideals and practicalities

Consensus about precisely when Schoenberg arrived at a process that can unambiguously be identified with serial thinking, and how relevant pitch-class set analysis is to these transitional works, will probably never be reached, and certainly not on the basis of Schoenberg's own writings.

> In his writings Schoenberg associated 'composing with tones' with the early stage of twelve-tone composition. But reserving that term solely for proto-serial works like the Symphony [fragments drafted in 1914] and *Die Jakobsleiter* [text begun 1915, music begun 1917] obscures the degree to which he was already thinking in similar terms prior to those pieces. Closely related to the techniques Schoenberg described as 'working with the tones of the motif' are his procedures in [the short opera] *Die glückliche Hand* [1910–13] and other atonal works of establishing a contextually-defined referential collection of pitch classes which can function formally as a point of stability in passages of varying lengths and from which melodic and harmonic material may be derived.[8]

By a 'contextually-defined referential collection of pitch classes' Joseph Auner is identifying the kind of unordered collection that brings consistency and, in his terms, 'stability' to a particular passage, even if they do not provide the kind of all-embracing unifying force that an ordered twelve-tone series can bring. A very simple example would be the collection embodied in the six-tone chord that begins and ends Schoenberg's tiny piano piece, Op. 19 No. 6 (1911).[9] Elaborating and complicating the process of transition and evolution between such materials and fully fledged twelve-tone materials, as Auner does, helps to explain why that process was so extended, and why the more ambitious compositional projects that Schoenberg initiated along the way were, in the end, left unfinished. In the event, the earliest completed twelve-tone compositions, after 1920, were neither a symphony nor an oratorio, but smaller-scale piano and chamber pieces. Yet this does not mean that Schoenberg had become disillusioned with the spiritual or social aspirations that underpinned a grand, never-to-be-completed project like the oratorio *Die Jakobsleiter*. Rather, he seems to have become convinced of the need to separate the process of perfecting a technique from the creation of fully realised works in which his convictions about both music and the world might find adequate expression. To this extent, the inspired pragmatism of the born teacher, who was his own most adept pupil, won out over the aspirations of the would-be spiritual – and even political – leader.

There is a notable contrast between Schoenberg's difficulties with major projects during and immediately after the war years and the achievements of prominent contemporaries. For example, two German composers whose primary purpose was not radical technical innovation completed major operas whose content can be seen as powerfully symbolic of social, spiritual, and artistic values: Hans Pfitzner's *Palestrina* (1911–15), and Richard Strauss' *Die Frau ohne Schatten* (1914–17). More strikingly still, Stravinsky – living outside the war zone in Switzerland – followed up his searing study of pagan ritualistic sacrifice (*The Rite of Spring*, 1911–13) with an even more intense depiction of a wedding ceremony as both social and religious ritual (*Les Noces*, 1914–17, with later revisions, 1921–3). Had Schoenberg been able to complete *Die Jakobsleiter* during these years, it could well have confirmed his position as a legitimate heir of Mahler and Wagner. In the end, however, it was as if the images of perfection and redemption, of a truly heavenly life, which Schoenberg's oratorio dealt with, had first to be pursued in a more modest, even mundane manner, before the new technique's relevance to a very different religious topic – the earthly conflict between Moses and Aaron – could be tried and tested.

In this context, it is not surprising that Schoenberg – always paranoid about the capacity for pupils and associates to steal his ideas and pass them off as their own – should have been so outraged at what must have seemed to him the glib and pointless spiritual perspectives of his twelve-tone rival, Josef Matthias Hauer (1883–1959), whose work is discussed later in this chapter. Yet it was indeed the technical necessity of allowing for an 'earthly', gravitational dimension that enabled Schoenberg to find a workable serial method. As Jennifer Shaw notes, 'despite Schoenberg's comparison of his twelve-tone universe to a neutral Swedenborgian heaven, tonal system **tropes** permeate his twelve-tone sketches and compositions',[10] and study of sketches also reveals the persistence of tonal thinking in the tendency to label the untransposed form of the series as T for tonic, and the transposition (P-6) at the tritone as D, the 'dominant' form. Noting this feature in his earliest written comments on the new method (*c.* 1923), Schoenberg confirmed his reluctance to jettison aspects of tonal thinking, even conceding that, as experience of these new perspectives increased, 'a new kind of tonality may be found again. Triads would once again probably be possible.'[11]

Post-war problems

The reasons for Schoenberg's failure to complete the music for *Die Jakobsleiter*, or the symphony from which it grew, cannot be reduced to a series of purely technical or aesthetic problems; the privations of army service, and of civilian life in the aftermath of his release from the military in 1917, coupled with possible stresses relating to the fact that 'although officially still a convert to Protestantism, he had resumed considering himself a Jew in his work and in his thinking' could all have played a part. O.W. Neighbour tells the story.

By May 1917 the text of *Die Jakobsleiter* was ready. In June he began to compose the music. The time could scarcely have been less favourable. Food and the coal necessary to cook it were becoming desperately short in Vienna; money, at least in the Schoenberg household, was shorter still. Yet in the space of three months Schoenberg set the whole of the first part of the oratorio, and had it not been for a further period of military service between September and December 1917, more substantial progress might well have been made. Yet, according to Neighbour, 'to the oratorio the short spell of military service proved fatal. Despite constant efforts to pick up the thread, he had managed by 1922 to compose only about half of the interlude intended to link the two halves of the work, after which he added nothing more.'[12]

The path from symphony to oratorio has been traced in great detail by several commentators, and I have already cited Bryan Simms' comment that, as early as 27 May 1914, a draft for the symphony's scherzo has a theme which 'is made from all twelve tones with none repeated, and it is subsequently varied, at least in part, by serial procedures that keep the twelve tones together as an integral unity, a tone row'. This fits with the composer's own comments, made around 1948, about his 'plans for a great symphony of which *Die Jakobsleiter* should be the last movement. I had sketched many themes, among them one for a scherzo which consisted of all the twelve tones ... My next step in this direction – in the meantime I had been in the Austrian Army – occurred in 1917, when I started to compose *Die Jakobsleiter*. I had contrived the plan to provide for unity – which was always my main motive: to build all the main themes of the whole oratorio from a row of six tones – C sharp, D, E, F, G, A flat.'[13] And it is this hexachord, differently ordered, which is used as an ostinato at the start of the *Die Jakobsleiter* draft (Ex. 2.2).

Losing momentum when work on the oratorio had been flowing so smoothly must have been intensely frustrating for the composer. Nevertheless, 'in March 1918 Schoenberg turned away from his unfinished oratorio and sketched out the beginnings of two new compositions; a piano piece and a string septet'. This was the

Ex. 2.2 Schoenberg, opening of *Die Jakobsleiter*

moment at which Schoenberg decided to pursue his serial explorations in more modest genres and forms, and the experiments involve series of fewer than twelve tones, as well as more than one series at a time. Yet these initiatives also ground to a halt: 'it was not until 1920 that Schoenberg would have the luxury of uninterrupted time during which he could work out these ideas, experiment with them, and develop some of the techniques that would enable him to begin to see the compositional potential of serial organization.'[14]

Parallels and pitfalls: Hauer

Further evidence that the 'serial century', and the twelve-tone technique, were not entirely synonymous with Schoenberg's initiatives and influence is provided by the work of Josef Matthias Hauer (1883–1959). Hauer has been given considerable prominence in theoretical and historical accounts of twelve-tone theory on the grounds that he provided the very first published formulation of the technique (*Vom Wesen des Musikalischen*, 1920: revised as *Lehrbuch der Zwölftontechnik: vom Wesen des Musikalischen*, 1923). A little later still, in 1924,

> Hauer chronicled his August 1919 discovery of the twelve-tone idea, casting himself as desperately searching for some underlying objective principle, not only in his own atonal music up to that time, but also in the atonal music of Webern and Schoenberg. Driven by the hope that such a discovery would vindicate atonality against the criticisms of its many critics in Vienna at the time, he had discovered – or as he put it, 'uncovered' – an objective and eternal law of music: the notion of constantly circulating the aggregate.

As John Covach then observes, 'the work in which Hauer claims the break-through occurred, his piano piece *Nomos*, Op. 19 (1919) does indeed begin with five statements of the same twelve-pc series, articulated melodically in units of five pcs creating twelve five-note phrases. But the piece is not entirely dodecaphonic: twelve-tone sections mark out large-scale formal divisions, but many of the smaller sections seem to experiment with circulating collections of fewer than twelve pcs.'[15] Nevertheless, 'by the early 1920s, Hauer's music was entirely twelve-tone, and this turn toward the exclusively dodecaphonic is likely related to his discovery in late 1921 of the forty-four tropes … pairs of complementary hexachords that enabled Hauer to classify any of the 479,001,600 possible twelve-pc melodies into one of these forty-four types'. Hauer set out these materials in several later publications, and although many subsequent writers, notably George Perle, tend to emphasise the 'unordered' basis of Hauer's serial materials, Covach makes the useful point that 'the distinction often made between Hauer and the Schoenberg school – that the former's music is based on unordered hexachords while the latter's is based on an ordered series – is false: while he did write pieces that could be thought of as "trope pieces", much of Hauer's twelve-tone music employs an ordered series'. Equally, as we have already seen, the reliance of Schoenberg and his disciples on strict ordering was inevitably tempered by practical considerations: in effect, they worked on the basis of an interaction between ordered and unordered pitch collections.

It follows from this that the most essential distinction between Hauer and and at least some of the early Schoenbergians is aesthetic: their music is better than his. Though such a judgement is obviously a matter of taste, the general perception that Hauer's music is inferior probably has much to do with the rather cerebral consequences of his view that it was 'essential . . . to raise music to its highest, most spiritual level' (604). The beginning of the piano piece *Nomos*, Op. 19 (Ex. 2.3), shows a simple succession of short motives which run through untransposed forms of a twelve-tone series, and the whole point of the music seems to be to let the solemn, spiritually elevating principle speak as directly as possible, without aesthetic interference. The verdict of *The New Grove* on where Hauer went after *Nomos* is bleak:

> throughout a final period of 20 years, he wrote exclusively *Zwölftonspiele*, designated sometimes by number, sometimes by date; about 1000 such pieces were written, most of them lost. They reveal a still more throughly objectified and simplified technique [than that of his earlier works]: melodies are strictly athematic, the part-writing is undifferentiated, tempo and dynamics impose inarticulate medium values, and the scoring, whether for piano, quartet or chamber orchestra, is mostly interchangeable. The elaboration of the material is mere manipulation, the selection of fixed procedures from an imaginary catalogue – with such operations composition has become a game.[16]

Even so, in the 1920s Schoenberg – quick as ever to feel dismay at any apparent slight to his pre-eminence – took Hauer seriously enough to launch some brief broadsides against him in print. 'He sought his solution in the cosmos. I limited myself to the human brain available to me.'[17] By this Schoenberg suggests exactly that constructive spirit of compromise, with what to him were still-relevant musical principles and forms, which has proved the most controversial aspect of his serial initiative. It helps to explain why one other early theorist of twelve-tone composition, Herbert Eimert (1897–1972), whose *Atonale Musiklehre* (1924) not only stems from Hauer but foreshadows aspects of twelve-tone theory that were not fully worked out until after 1960, would eventually have a significant influence on at least one member of the post- and, to a degree anti-Schoenbergian generation of serialists, Karlheinz Stockhausen.

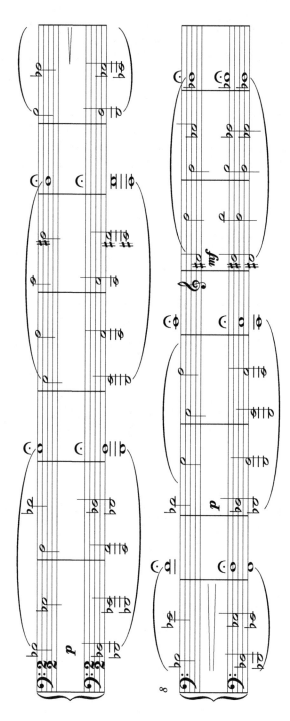

Ex. 2.3 Hauer, *Nomos* Op. 19, beginning

Eye witness: Gerhard

Before pursuing the compositional consequences of Schoenberg's establishment of the twelve-tone method, it is worth considering how the longer-term evolution of the serial principle was seen by a composer, close to Schoenberg, who was also involved in that evolution after Schoenberg's death.

Roberto Gerhard (1896–1970) has a rather special position in the history of serialism. Born in Catalonia of Swiss and French parents, he studied music in Switzerland, Munich and Barcelona before becoming a pupil of Schoenberg's at the age of twenty-seven. Gerhard then spent the years 1923–8 studying in Vienna and Berlin, after which he returned to Barcelona. At this stage, his compositions still reflected his primary commitment to Spanish idioms. It was only after the Civil War, and his permanent move from Spain to England, that he began to adopt thoroughgoing serial techniques: and it was not until 1951, the year of Schoenberg's death, that his first fully developed twelve-tone work, the Concerto for Piano and Strings, was completed. For the rest of his life his major concert works were consistently serial.

Between 1932 and 1961 Gerhard wrote a sequence of essays and lectures concerning Schoenberg and serial music which, more than any other writings by pupils or associates, provide vivid and unvarnished portraits of Schoenberg himself. They also trace with particular pertinence the evolution of the twelve-tone method between the 1920s and the 1960s – an evolution which can now be seen as part of the much broader evolution of post-tonal compositional thinking which spanned the entire twentieth century and continues today.

Gerhard's first essay, 'Schoenberg in Barcelona' (1932) offers an uncompromising vision of the newness in Schoenberg's then-recent work: 'the works of his maturity ... embody with absolute purity a concept of music that emanates from a spirit and sensitivity radically different from that encountered in the past.' As a result, there was no point in audiences expecting to 'hear' the techniques involved:

> one can't reach Schoenberg's music from the outside – to try and arrive through technical analysis. There is just one way: to listen and to listen; simply that. Until the veils drop from people's eyes; until the deafness of the internal ear ceases and starts to feel, despite its unprecedented novelty, Schoenberg's music; the beauty of its melody, the prodigious art of its structure, the superb clarity and soberness of its forms, the genius of its constructions, the greatness of its conception, its spirituality, its ineffable emotionality.[18]

A quarter-century later, when Gerhard himself was committed to serial techniques, a very different perspective is provided in his 'Reminiscences of Schoenberg'

(1961). In place of that radical difference from the past, we have the insight that 'the man who revolutionized contemporary music was nothing of a revolutionary himself ... Schoenberg felt a deep reverence for the masters of the past. Their works were his constant terms of reference, both in his own creative work and in his teaching' (107). In addition, 'it is difficult to think of any innovator who was less theoretical ... Paradoxically, the man who did in fact revolutionize the technique of musical composition, at the beginning of the century, was essentially intuitive and, what is more, an ingrained traditionalist' (112). By 1961, when these words were written, Gerhard was well aware that it was more important to defend Schoenberg from accusations of redundant conservatism than of intransigent radicalism; his own knowledge of how contemporaries like Pierre Boulez and Milton Babbitt thought of serialism led him to provide unusually sensitive explanations of exactly what the points of contact between Schoenberg's methods and more recent, more 'systematic' procedures, might be.

There was also an implied reproof to these younger thinkers in the comment that 'seldom can a great innovator have been less dogmatic than Schoenberg' (114). Nevertheless, Gerhard clearly believed that twelve-tone techniques needed to evolve, and do so by building on Schoenberg's own foundations, just as Schoenberg himself had claimed to build on the manifestations of developing variation found in Brahms and Wagner. It followed that, in an essay from 1952 with the provocative title 'Tonality in Twelve-tone Music', Gerhard moved from Schoenberg's own rejection of the term 'atonal' to explore ways in which a possibility he remembered Schoenberg referring to in conversation (in 1924!) might be brought about: 'our new musical language is in its early phase of development; promiscuity with elements of the older system at this stage could, therefore, only obstruct and delay its natural growth. But when it consolidates itself the time will come, no doubt, for the re-integration of many elements from the older system which for the present we must firmly discard' (119). This fits particularly well with Schoenberg's own comments about the possibility of a 'new kind of tonality' emerging through serial thinking, made at much the same time, and quoted earlier in this chapter.

Gerhard did not choose to argue that elements of such 'reintegration' were already present in the twelve-tone works that Schoenberg completed during the 1920s, but he understood that turning abstract tables of series forms into actual music inevitably involved negotiation between the order presented by single series forms in that abstract fashion and the more diverse orderings that tended to arise when series forms were combined, superimposed, or allowed to interact according to compositional imperatives. Just as in tonal composition, thematic–harmonic textures cannot usefully be reduced to a single ordering of the scales in question, even though such scales are usually thought of as having their origins in such single orderings, so in twelve-tone music, the basic order of the pitch classes in the series (with its possible sub-divisions into two hexachords, three tetrachords, four tri-chords, six dyads) can only provide a background. What Gerhard identifies in Schoenberg's twelve-tone practice (and he is clearly making use of Milton Babbitt's concept of the unordered source set in framing his argument in this form) is

> the acceptance of the principle of permutation (within antecedent and con-sequent) based on a recognition of the fact that beyond the actual series there is an ultimate ground, an abstract archetype – represented by the coupled hexachords – of which the individual series is only one *aspect*, that is, one of the possible permutations ... The identity of the series will be maintained in spite of permutation, provided that this takes place exclusively within the con-stituent units (hexachord, tetrachord, etc.), in other words, as long as these constituent units maintain *their* identity and place. (126)

It is not essential to accept Gerhard's ultimate conclusion from this point – 'this seems to me to confirm the view that the fundamental idea of the twelve-tone technique is in fact a new formation of the principle of tonality' (126) – to see its potential for that process of re-integration that Schoenberg himself not only foresaw but implemented, in ways which will be explored and explained below, and which many other later composers have developed in turn. It is now time to trace the serial initiatives of Schoenberg and his principal pupils in more detail.

Chapter 3

Serialism in close-up

From Bach to Schoenberg

The Musette (Gavotte 2) from J. S. Bach's English Suite No. 3 is an uncomplicated example of the dance genre in question, with a pastoral quality stemming from smooth rhythms and flowing upper parts over a drone or pedal bass. Bach's Musette is in an unambiguous G major, as signalled by the presence of a single sharp key signature, and the Musette's initial four bars (Ex. 3.1) move entirely around a G major chord – the tonic chord of the principal tonality.

The first four bars of the Musette from Schoenberg's first completely twelve-tone composition, the Suite for Piano Op. 25 (1921–3) has no key signature and, on first glance at least, none of the harmonic stability of the Bach (Ex. 3.2). Both Musettes employ sustained or repeated Gs to represent the drone. But whereas in the Bach the G major triad recurs on the third and first beats of every bar, none of the vertical sonorities on Schoenberg's first and third beats (or first and second if the metrical unit is the minim rather than the crotchet) are identical. They are not exactly unrelated, as far as shared pitches are concerned, but the impression is created that this is music which lacks the kind of universal harmonic principle that enables us to relate Bach's G major triad to major triads of all kinds and positions in thousands of other compositions which use tonality. As a result, it would be difficult to claim that the 'E minor triad in first inversion' which appears at the very beginning of Schoenberg's Musette has any genuine tonal identity or function.

Readers with relatively advanced musical training might already be tempted to ask for further refinements and distinctions in this discourse, such as that between Bach's diatonic tonality (all the notes belonging to the parent major scale) and what, in the Schoenberg, looks like the kind of 'chromatic' tonality in which there will be a principal note, or tonic (G in this case), but all the other notes of the chromatic scale, not just the seven diatonic notes, can be described as 'regional' satellites of that tonic.[1]

The most basic difference between Bach and Schoenberg is often equated with the contrast between tonal and post-tonal. In Bach's Musette the music proceeds on the basis of distinctions between fundamental consonance and incidental, or decorative, dissonance: try to reverse this pattern, so that the initial four-bar phrase begins and

31

Ex. 3.1   Bach, English Suite No. 3, Musette, bars 1–4

ends on the kind of dissonant, or less consonant sonorities found on the second and fourth beats, and the result would be strange in the extreme. The fact that music in keys was the only kind written for the best part of three centuries, from 1600 to 1900, means that there was time for a highly refined theory of harmonic practice to evolve around distinctions between consonance and dissonance, and composers after 1900 wishing to move beyond the harmonic practices of tonal music willingly accepted the loss of the functional differentiations on which it depended. That is certainly the case with Schoenberg's Musette. But does this mean that nonsense replaces sense?

Schoenberg as music

Even though we have not yet addressed the question of how the Musette from Op. 25 is serial, we can observe – with ears as well as eyes – that, like the Bach, the segment in Ex. 3.2 sub-divides into smaller one-bar units which repeat and vary the same rhythmic patterns and intervallic shapes in the three constituent voices or parts. Such repetitions of clearly differentiated cells of material indicate that, even if post-tonal, the music is not a-thematic. For example, if we take the first three notes in the upper line as a motive defined by interval and rhythm, the second group of three notes constitutes a simple motivic variant – starting again with an ascending semitone but then rising rather than falling a minor third to arrive on the same D flat. Turning now to the inner voice, the initial eight-quaver sequence (starting in characteristically allusive Schoenbergian fashion with the BACH motive – B flat, A, C, B natural) sub-divides into two four-note groups, which on repetition are inverted – until the very last interval, which is a descending diminished fifth in both cases: A flat/D in bar 1, G flat/C in bar 2.

Schoenberg's small-scale motivic development here is not so dissimilar to Bach's. But Bach derives his material from a major scale which he can use in whole or in part, with some notes repeated many times and others less often, all subject to the governing principles of tonal harmony and counterpoint. Schoenberg's material derives from a twelve-tone series, though exactly how this particular series was

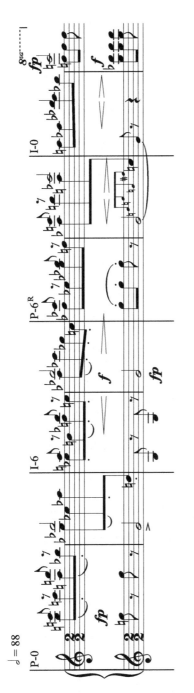

Ex. 3.2 Schoenberg, Suite Op. 25, Musette, bars 1–4, with series forms

33

Ex. 3.3a   Schoenberg, Suite Op. 25, twelve-tone series, three tetrachords

Ex. 3.3b   Schoenberg, Suite Op. 25, initial sketch for a 'polyphonic complex of tetrachords'

formulated in his mind has been the subject of detailed scholarly enquiry. Those who have studied surviving sketches and drafts have concluded that the Suite is a hybrid work, in the sense that only the last two sections, composed in 1923 – the Trio for the Minuet, and the Gigue – use the series in the particular, fixed linear sequence shown in Ex. 3.3a. The rest of the work uses what Ethan Haimo defines as a 'polyphonic complex of tetrachords'[2]: that is, three groups, each of four different notes, which are superimposed rather than arranged end to end in a single line (Ex. 3.3b). This produces an aggregate – a complete twelve-tone collection – but does not assign a linear priority to the three tetrachords in the way that setting out the pitch classes in a single line must necessarily do.

There are other refinements and complexities concerning the evolution of the twelve-tone material for Op. 25. But in terms of the overall development of Schoenberg's serial technique it is important to reject any suggestion that the 'tetrachordal polyphonic complex' is by definition a more primitive, compositionally less acceptable way of deploying a twelve-tone series than the single-line P-0 form. The relative flexibility afforded by the tetrachordal aggregate contrasts with the stricter ordering of the linear series: and since twelve-tone compositions usually involve the interaction of vertical and horizontal dimensions – harmony and counterpoint – an exclusively linear deployment of series forms is scarcely possible in practice.

Jonathan Bernard is one writer who has noted the tendency of twelve-tone composers to emphasise '*content* as much as *order*' when working with linear segments of twelve-tone series forms. Referring specifically to Schoenberg's Op. 25, Bernard observes that 'the order of the tetrachords, and even the order within the tetrachords, exhibit a certain freedom from what one would expect to be the strict dictates of the row. Such "collectional" treatment of row segments was a part of the twelve-tone method from the start.' As we will discover in chapter 4, a comparable point can be made about other works of Schoenberg's from this period: and it is precisely this interaction between degrees of freedom and strictness with regard to order within the series that provides the principal link with comparable 'collectional' tendencies, whether to completion of the twelve-tone aggregate, or to consistent set-class organisation, in both pre- and post-dodecaphonic composition from the post-tonal era. Such interplay between the ordered twelve-tone series and the unordered content of its various smaller segments was a positive way of adapting to the new situation in post-tonal music, where the functional differentiations of tonal harmony no longer obtained, and – in Bernard's words – 'the elements of a musical idea are partly incorporated in the horizontal plane as successive sounds, and partly in the vertical plane as simultaneous sounds'.[3]

Serialism as music

More detailed comments on the basic procedures of serial practice will follow, but at this stage it is more important to emphasise certain stylistic specifics evident from the musical surface of Op. 25. Rhythmically, Schoenberg's Musette is as dance-like as Bach's: but Bach's top line is certainly more song-like, fitting definitions of the musette genre which emphasise conjunct linear motion, and a pastoral quality, as primary generic properties. Schoenberg's writing is the result of a process, begun almost two decades earlier, of what he thought of as emancipation – freeing his music from the tired, no-longer-binding constraints of tonal counterpoint – important though these still were for students not yet mature enough to abandon traditional procedures.

The notion of 'the emancipation of the dissonance' is often found in histories of twentieth-century music,[4] referring to a change of perception in the century's early years when many composers no longer felt it necessary to resolve dissonances, or to retain the outmoded, repressively hierarchic distinction between (subordinate) dissonance and (superior) consonance. Along with this innovation, and the impulse to reduce if not entirely eliminate elements that were thought of as decorative or ornamental, came the even more radical impulse to erode the distinction between motive and chord. As music tended increasingly towards the post-tonal, so it could also tend increasingly towards all-thematicism, every tone in the texture contributing to the thematic process, and none being 'purely' chordal or harmonic. If chords could be constructed from any combination of intervals felt by the composer to be appropriate at that point, then one way to ensure a degree of control over the musical material was to think of chords as verticalised motives: to think of the compositional process, at least in part, as involving the interplay between horizontal and vertical forms of the same musical idea.

During the tonal era, only the contrapuntal forms of fugue and canon had tended towards the all-thematic: and even these would often use 'non-thematic' filling-out at points of climax or closure. But the new perspectives on musical space which the emancipation of the dissonance brought with it – especially the rejection of the idea that coherence was guaranteed by the presence of an all-controlling bass line – were felt to have brought a new intensity and richness to music. To this way of thinking the functional constraints of tonal voice-leading, with its categories of melodic embellishment – neighbouring or auxiliary notes, passing notes and so on – could be replaced by a more flexible and sophisticated sense of function, whereby developments or variations of motivic, thematic material permeated the music so imaginatively that even when occasional allusions to old-style features appear, as in the relatively conjunct writing at the start of Schoenberg's Musette, these might be sensed as having emancipated themselves from their earlier dependence on the conventions of tonal construction.

Fixed and free

Since the Musette from Op. 25 belongs to the polyphonic, aggregate phase of the work's evolution rather than the final, linear phase found only in the Minuet's Trio and the Gigue, detailed analysis proceeds best in terms of the tetrachordal content of the four series forms and their retrogrades on which the whole work is based: P-0/R-0, P-6/R-6, I-0/RI-0 and I-6/RI-6. But how do we decide which pitch class should be identified as '0'? With Op. 25, this is not such a difficult question, since the leading voice at the beginning of the first movement (Ex. 3.4) actually presents a complete linear series statement, moving between E and B flat. Study of Schoenberg's drafts, as well as internal evidence from analysis of the work as a whole, confirm that it makes sense to identify the pitch class E as '0'. However, it is often the case that the opening of a twelve-tone composition does not present such a clear-cut situation, and theorists and analysts uneasy with the tendency for the '0' pitch class to acquire some of the hierarchic attributes of a tonal tonic have preferred to neutralise the effect of integer notation as far as possible by the arbitrary convention of assigning the '0' to C, '1' to C sharp and so on. Consistency might be more convenient than flexibility: but there is much to be said for using a movable '0', since – as already noted in this text – many twelve-tone compositions do indeed

Ex. 3.4 Schoenberg, Suite Op. 25, Prelude, bars 1–3

acknowledge the residual role of hierarchic pitch relationships: and this tendency has increased as serial composition has evolved during the later twentieth century and beyond.

Op. 25: further details

At the beginning of the Musette from Schoenberg's Op. 25 (Ex. 3.2 above) the material is organised so that each sub-phrase or segment exhausts a single stream of twelve different pitches. In other contexts each of the three distinct textural lines might form the beginning of three different versions of the same series, but that is not the case in the Musette. Rather, a single twelve-tone stream is stratified so that the outer voices employ one four-note group (with the drone G in two different registers) and the inner voice has the remaining eight notes. The orderings applied in the two upper voices do not seek to avoid small-scale motivic correspondences: the inner-voice sequence A, B flat, G flat across the first bar line echoes the initial upper-voice shape (E, F, D flat) a perfect fifth below, and in turn that shape can be heard as a variant of the initial inner-voice three-note cell, B, C, A: ascending minor second/descending minor third becoming ascending minor second/descending major third.

The first series form, P-0 (see Ex. 3.3a), is employed in the stratified manner shown earlier (Ex. 3.3b). In the inner voice tetrachord c comes first, followed by tetrachord b, bringing B flat and G flat into a juxtaposition which they would not have if the 'correct' linear ordering of the series were being followed. As Ex. 3.2 also shows, the initial series form, P-0, is followed by I-6, beginning at the mid-point of the first full bar. The inner voice provides the main focus for motivic activity, and Schoenberg links I-6 to P-0 by keeping E flat and D in the same octave position. As already noted, the third tetrachord of I-6 precedes the second in the inner voice, while the first tetrachord (with the all-important G/D flat) provides the outer voices. The remaining series forms used in this four-bar extract are shown with Ex. 3.2.

In the later stages of the Musette (Ex. 3.5, bars 20–25) Schoenberg reorders the 'BACH' tetrachord to provide ascending and descending segments of the chromatic scale. This reinforces the point that at this stage his concern is less with establishing a fixed connection between a linear twelve-tone succession and a theme than to use the series to provide the basis for constant development and variation, as part of a compositional strategy in which exact repetition is not ruled out, especially when generic conventions demand it. The series cannot be equated with one theme, and it follows that its original, initial order is both fundamental and expendable, provided the processes of developing variation which predominate preserve at least some of the smaller-scale motivic features of that original, initial ordering. That is why a series, even when the surface of a composition seems to treat its pure linear ordering rather casually, cannot be equated with a tonal scale which, as a complete entity, will have no all-determining compositional ordering.

The beginning of the Suite's Prelude (Ex. 3.4) sets out as clearly as possible the twelve-tone material on which the whole composition will be based. As the right hand unfolds the form of the series beginning on E (P-0), the left hand starts with P-6 – the same sequence of intervals transposed onto B flat, six semitones above (or below) E. Beginning as a well-nigh canonic imitation of the right hand, the left hand proliferates into two lines after the first four notes, and while the upper line (C, A, D, G sharp) repeats the interval-sequence of notes 5 to 8 in the right hand, the lower left-hand intervals (ascending minor second, descending augmented second, ascending minor second) are not quite literally reproduced by the right hand's descending major seventh, descending minor third and ascending minor second. Variation is already at work, and as soon as the music deviates from simple linear presentations of series forms the emphasis – and interest – for the listener begins to shift from the ordered series itself to the materials drawn from it.

A twelve-tone composition consisting of nothing but linear statements of series forms, whether singly or in combination, would tend to provide too little opportunity for the kind of concentrated variation processes which Schoenberg valued so highly, since it was through these, rather than through the mere invention of serial material as such, that he claimed to be contributing to the continuation of hallowed traditions. As we shall see in due course, one of the main objections from later serialists such as Pierre Boulez to those of the Schoenberg generation was that this concern to preserve specific links with the ways in which earlier tonal composers in the royal line of Bach, Beethoven and Brahms conceived and deployed their musical ideas was misguided. In 1921, when work on the Suite Op. 25 was begun, Schoenberg was not a hot-headed twenty-something, but entering his forty-seventh

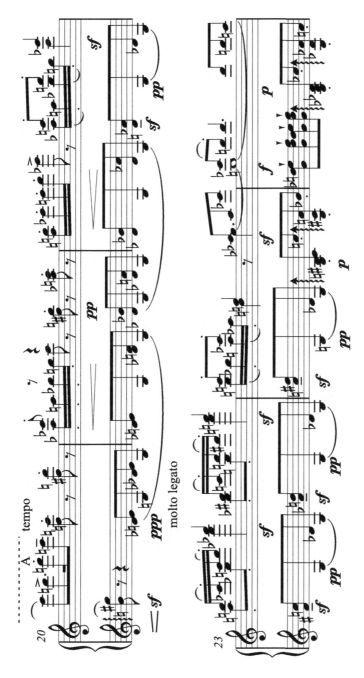

Ex. 3.5 Schoenberg, Suite Op. 25, Musette, bars 20–25

year. No doubt, to a twenty-something Boulez, this confirmed that true, visionary innovation was hardly to be expected.

A twelve-tone canon

It will be clear by now that analysis of twelve-tone music involves a particularly acute distinction between attempts to reconstruct and describe serial techniques, and interpretations of textural, thematic and harmonic features which are most likely to impinge on the real-time listener. In the sections of Op. 25 considered so far – the Prelude and the Musette – Schoenberg's use of his 'polyphonic complex of tetrachords' makes it even less likely than might otherwise be the case that real-time listeners could learn to detect distinct twelve-tone series forms as they pass in succession and combination. This is to some degree 'four-tone music', as much if not more than twelve-tone music. With the Minuet's Trio and the Gigue the emphasis shifts, and to the extent that they give greater prominence to the linear identities of twelve-tone series forms, they can be seen as providing a clearer demonstration of the nature of the twelve-tone method with respect to its capacity to work with ordered pitch sequences than the Suite's earlier movements do.

The Trio section Minuet (Ex. 3.6) is in binary form, with each half repeated, and is a two-voice canon by inversion at the tritone. The first section uses two pairs of series forms (see Ex. 1.6 for the complete matrix for Op. 25). In the leading (Dux) voice, P-0 (left hand, bars 1 and 2) and I-0 (left hand, bars 3 and 4); in the answering (Comes) voice, I-6 (right hand, bars 2 and 3) and P-6 (right hand, bars 3 and 4). As noted earlier, Schoenberg tended to think of the series form at the tritone transposition as equivalent to a 'dominant'. So it is mildly ironic that the effect of setting out the canon at the distance of one bar is that the first note in the answering voice, B flat, is heard against the E flat, and not the E, of the leading voice.

This raises the issue which is often seen as the most problematic in this kind of post-tonal **neo-classicism**: do the intervallic relationships between the two canonic voices in bar 2 obey any general contrapuntal principles, as they would certainly need to do if the canon were tonal? It is difficult to see any positive principle at work, beyond that of rhythmic characterisation, ensuring that the two voices are adequately distinct, as contrapuntal convention dictates. Apart from that, the fact that all of the vertical intervals, with the exception of the first, are (according to convention) dissonant, could suggest that all that matters to the composer is avoiding the kind of consonant–dissonant successions that would bring the music closer to what he wishes to avoid – traditional voice-leading. All well and good, yet in bar 3, on the last two quaver beats, we have precisely the kind of succession – minor sixth/perfect fifth, minor third/major second – which (at least in isolation)

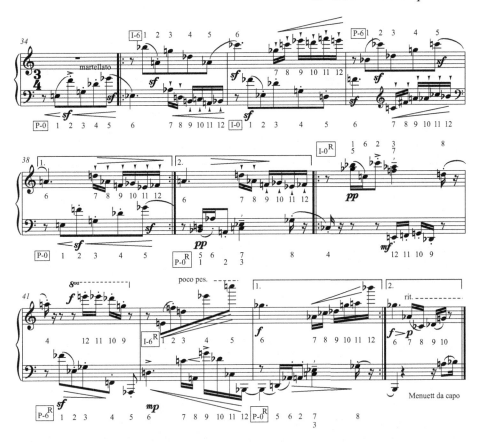

Ex. 3.6 Schoenberg, Suite Op. 25, Trio section of Minuet

seem either to relax the principle established just before, or else to fail to recognise its existence.

Some would argue that the whole point of Schoenberg's emancipation of the dissonance was to render traditional voice-leading criteria redundant. What matters here, not least because the music is moving at a rate where single vertical intervals are rarely sustained for very long, is the contrapuntal interplay and polarity of the two canonic voices. The focus of compositional craft is on managing the interaction of similarity and difference. For example, in the leading voice the octave positions of four of the first six notes of I-0 (left hand, bars 36–37) are the same as they are in the preceding statement of P-0 (bars 34–35): an instance of invariance which helps to focus aural attention. Nevertheless, Schoenberg's commitment to developing variation means that he is always concerned to balance similarity, with its potential to become mechanically predictable, against difference – the kind of variation that has an element of the spontaneous about it. And so the one thing the composer does not do is to continue the canon with neatly stratified exchanges between the ordered series forms, paired as they are at the outset.

In bar 39, the leading voice (left hand) has music that seems very different from the original continuation of the theme (left hand, bar 35). It is more as if it is intended merely to accompany the thematic continuation of the leading voice (right hand, bar 39). Apart from anything else, Schoenberg briefly abandons single-line writing, filling-out the left hand with two thirds before writing what seems like a conventional cadence figure linking bar 39 with bar 40. So the question is: has the composer's newly honed twelve-tone technique broken down under the pressure of compositional imperatives? How does the left-hand part in bar 39 relate to that in bar 40?

If we consider the first six notes of bar 39 (left hand) as a group, we can see that it is drawn from the second and third tetrachords of P-0. All six notes have the same octave positions as they were given in bar 35 (left hand), but the order has been changed. It can then be seen that the next six notes in the left-hand leading voice, from the G flat in bar 39 to the D flat in bar 40, are the same pitch classes (in different registers, and reordered) as those of the first hexachord of P-0. As a linear entity, then, the series form can be labelled as P-0^R.

Schoenberg has reordered the successive hexachords of P-0^R for his leading canonic voice in bars 39 and 40, and the answering voice (right hand, bars 40 and 41) follows suit for the hexachords of I-0^R. The compositional rationale for this is not simply the need for variety, but to promote an interesting asymmetry between the balanced pair of thematic statements in the Trio's first part and the compressed recapitulation of the second part, beginning with the leading voice in bar 41 (left hand). For the second part of the binary form to mirror the first half as literally as the series forms in use could imply would be too predictable, and betray the sophisticated heritage of the great masters of the past of which Schoenberg was always so conscious.

This moment of change between the parts of the binary form nevertheless creates a few problems. In bar 39 the sustained right-hand A is briefly doubled two octaves lower by the left hand, and the two G flats are also very close together. These might seem like tiny, trivial details, but Schoenberg was greatly concerned about the effect of octave doublings in post-tonal music, and sought in principle to avoid them – a search that would soon lead to his preferred procedure for combining or super-imposing series forms whose parallel hexachords avoided common pitches; to **combinatoriality**.

Variation affects the rest of the Trio, in that the final statement of the canon theme in the leading voice (left hand bars 41 and 42) uses a new series form, the retrograde of P-6 (R-6 or P-6^R). This is answered by RI-6 (or I-6^R), with registral variation in the final group of semiquavers. Then the lead-back to the repeat in the following voice (bar 43) varies the registers of the reordered second hexachord of P-0, while in the final second-time bar (44) the following voice reorders the second hexachord of RI-6, the last two notes providing a link back to the repeat of the Minuet.[5]

Coda

Blow-by-blow verbal analysis of serial music is probably no more enthralling than detailed technical accounts of tonal fugues or recitatives. But it is useful – even necessary – from time to time, to give a sense of the kind of possible thought-processes that led the composer to make some of the decisions reflected in the completed work. Composers would surely have not persisted with serial technique if they were not stimulated – even inspired – by the possibilities and challenges it creates. Serialism is indeed a way of writing music. Yet its principles become musically meaningful only if they generate aesthetic responses. One can have such responses without understanding the principles. Yet understanding – being informed about – the principles can enhance the responses. The next stage of this *Introduction* is therefore to show how Schoenberg's own understanding of the new method's potential laid down crucial precedents and challenges during the 1920s.

Chapter 4

Schoenberg in the 1920s

1920–3

1920–3 were the decisive years for the establishment of the twelve-tone method. In July 1920 Schoenberg wrote what would become Nos 1 and 2, as well as part of No. 4, of the Five Pieces for Piano, Op. 23: music which displays aspects of serial thinking without being fully twelve-tone. The following month, August 1920, he began a large-scale chamber work, the *Serenade* Op. 24, which also includes examples of serial thinking, notably in the twelve-tone vocal line of its Petrarch Sonnet setting. (The *Serenade* was eventually completed in April 1923.) Meanwhile, in July 1921 Schoenberg wrote the Prelude and part of the Intermezzo for what would be the fully twelve-tone Suite for Piano Op. 25. Then, in February 1923, he returned to Op. 23, finishing it that same month with its fully twelve-tone Waltz: he then completed the Suite in March.

As the detailed discussion of parts of Op. 25 in chapter 3 has indicated, it is often possible to distinguish between serial composition based on an ordered twelve-tone series and serial composition which works more directly either with smaller segments of a twelve-tone series, or with collections of different sizes in which overall content is more salient than any single ordered presentation. In Schoenberg's case, this flexibility is one result of the extended consideration of new possibilities that had occupied him since at least 1914. Ethan Haimo, after close study of various sketches and drafts surviving from this period, has concluded that

> far from displaying a decisive, sudden break with past methods of composition and setting out boldly and immediately in a new direction, Schoenberg's compositional activities of the years 1920–23 reveal a far more gradual process of change. Techniques and methods characteristic of his earlier compositional style persist, coexisting side by side with the new ideas: it took some time for Schoenberg to solve a series of compositional problems and to begin to understand the potential of serial organization.[1]

Simply because Schoenberg had been trying out potentially serial techniques for so long, establishing genuine distinctions between preliminary and fully fashioned procedures took some time. Op. 23 shows how this distinction was beginning to emerge. No. 1, as Bryan Simms explains, is an example of that 'composing [or working] with tones' which, Schoenberg claimed, he had 'used for 2 or 3 years (before discovering the ultimate necessity of the twelve)'.[2] But it is not always easy, in the set of pieces as a whole, to establish what type of series is in use, and how all-embracing that use actually is.

Kathryn Bailey's monograph on Op. 23 is especially useful in demonstrating the resourceful flexibility of Schoenberg's techniques during these years: for example, 'in Nos 1 and 2 the rows grew out of the music, whereas in Nos 3 and 5 ... the row was the first thing composed'.[3] But Haimo and Simms provide the most detailed accounts of the longer-term emergence of the twelve-tone method, including the case of the Variations movement from the *Serenade* Op. 24, in which 'almost every note can be understood as part of a set statement'. Here, therefore, 'Schoenberg attempted to structure the development entirely in serial terms'.[4] A no less significant event occurred between 24 and 29 July 1921, when Schoenberg composed the Prelude of the Suite Op. 25, along lines indicated in chapter 3. Yet it is clear that, at the time, he was still reluctant to abandon his large-scale, grandly conceived earlier projects for something as modest and traditionally structured – even as neo-classical – as that Prelude seemed to imply.

Schoenberg accordingly returned to *Die Jakobsleiter* in July 1922, perhaps expecting that the relatively restricted exercises he had recently been concentrating on would translate constructively onto the larger scale and make completion possible. As Haimo sees it, Schoenberg's subsequent abandonment of the oratorio was brought about by his attempt to preserve its earlier qualities despite his changed circumstances: 'in order to finish *Die Jakobsleiter* and keep it stylistically consistent he would have had to suspend his serial development for quite some time'.[5] Alternatively, Schoenberg might have hoped that his new technical discoveries could have been transferred to the oratorio without conflicting inappropriately with what had gone before. If so, any such hopes were soon disappointed.

It is possible to align Schoenberg's arrival at a definitive form of the twelve-tone method with a decisive move away from (if not total abandonment of) the more expressionistic idiom that had been so important to his style in the earlier post-tonal years. Referring to the March movement from Op. 24, written in September–October 1921, Bryan Simms claims that Schoenberg 'refashioned his compositional experiments in a style filled with broad allusions to traditional music. This was what Stravinsky had done in his *Piano-Rag-Music* [1919], but Schoenberg leaves behind enough grotesquerie to make it plain that his essay in "new music" was in large part a critique of the new taste, not just an imitation of it.'[6] To no small degree, the flow of twelve-tone compositions that followed the completion of Op. 25 in March 1923 constitutes Schoenberg's constructive but radical critique of his own earlier manner and methods.

Making, meaning: Op. 23 No. 5

In the Waltz, Op. 23 No. 5, composed in February 1923, the ordered sequence of the series (Ex. 4.1), which is used throughout without inversion or transposition, serves to stimulate the composer's sense of the kind of dialogue between discipline and spontaneity which, arguably, always underpins true composition in any style or genre. The piece is an early demonstration of how this dialogue works in twelve-tone composition, and a suitable context is outlined by Kathryn Bailey. She highlights questions of order, writing that she has

> made a point of emphasizing the serial aspects of those materials [in Pieces 1–4] that other writers have tended not to see as serial; specifically the whole of no. 4 and . . . the second theme in no. 2 and the second group in no. 3. These materials have been widely treated as unordered sets, not only because of their texture, which is frequently complex (the notes do not unfold in a linear way) but more particularly because their contents are slightly reordered on occasion. But exactly these two things are true of the pitch material throughout the fifth piece, which has been universally recognized as a twelve-note serial piece . . . These irregularities are not signs of a system that has been incompletely formulated; on the contrary, they will continue to be features of Schoenberg's twelve-note music.[7]

The twelve-tone series for Op. 23 No. 5 generates material which responds to the generic conventions of the movement's title, Waltz: a genre, that is, to which such non-twelve-tone aspects as rhythm and texture are fundamental. Schoenberg has sometimes been mocked for his naïvety in promoting the idea that to combine a radical new technique with a well-established musical genre was a positive step forward. Why invest so much time and energy in devising ways of moving beyond traditional melodic and harmonic formulae if all you do in the end is to 'compose as freely as before'[8] – at least as far as everything except pitch organisation is concerned? Yet composing as before *in a new way* was precisely the attraction of twelve-tone serialism for Schoenberg and his pupils, and this rich and stimulating old/new conjunction extended into harmony itself: hence Schoenberg's dislike of the word 'atonality', with its negative aura of rejection. His preferred alternative, **pantonality**, has not achieved comparable ubiquity, perhaps because it embodies too paradoxical

Ex. 4.1   Schoenberg, Piano Piece Op. 23 No. 5, twelve-tone series

a concept.[9] The potential presence of all tonalities, which pantonality implies, not only seems to require an obsessively self-absorbed kind of listening, but could also suggest the absence, or suspension, of any specific, singular tonal identity. Nevertheless, from Schoenberg's perspective, it was perfectly natural to propose a positive conformity between the circumstances which made twelve-tone technique desirable, and the evolution from diatonicism through late-romantic chromaticism to a harmonic world in which allusions to multiple tonal possibilities (**suspended tonality**) replaced the straightforward diatonicism and unambiguously singular modulatory schemes of early compositional styles.

Given that diatonic major or minor scales use more than half of the available chromatic total, composers wishing to devise a twelve-tone series that unambiguously excludes any conceivable tonal allusions will always have their work cut out: and even though those allusions can be rendered more tenuous by the actual compositional use of the series, they will not automatically be eliminated completely. Nor, as conceded by Schoenberg in his early statement of twelve-tone principle cited earlier, will the composer necessarily wish to eliminate them. It is rather ironic that the least tonally allusive twelve-tone succession is probably the unordered chromatic scale, ascending or descending: and even this can conceivably be used in such a way that, for example, the polarity of 'tonics' and 'dominants' can be emphasised at the expense of less diatonic allusions.

Many serial composers relish the range of possibilities: even though traditional functional harmony is by definition excluded, the ability of the ear to recognise allusions to such functions, alongside alternatives to them, can be tolerated, and even exploited. To take a simple example from Schoenberg's Waltz Op. 23 No. 5 (Ex. 4.2a): in bars 22–23, there is the kind of motion from A via G sharp to E in the bass which can suggest an enriched version of the motion from tonic to dominant in A major. This tendency to 'A-ness' might be inferred from the basic form of the series: in its first hexachord (C sharp, A, B, G, G sharp, F sharp) only the G natural is not diatonic to A major. Yet this means that, by definition, the second, complementary hexachord will emphasise 'non-A' pitches; it would therefore be naïve to regard the devising of a twelve-tone series as a kind of substitute for, or expansion of, a single diatonic scale. Schoenberg's Op. 23 series can be thought of as in constant, pantonal evolution between an initial allusion to A, through a central allusion to F sharp and on to a quite different region – F major? – at the end. This evolution then generalises into the kind of alternation and interaction between relatively sharp and relatively flat sides of the extended tonal spectrum which bars 22–23 and the balancing phrase in bars 24–25 can be heard to propose. (For the piece's most explicit allusion to a diatonic cadence in A, see bars 77–79, Ex. 4.2b.)

Ex. 4.2a Schoenberg, Op. 23 No. 5, bars 22–23

Ex. 4.2b Schoenberg, Op. 23 No. 5, bars 77–79

As suggested earlier, learning to hear this music in terms of a constant floating around allusions to specific tonalities is the kind of recondite activity which probably has far less appeal than learning to follow the evolutionary adventures of particular ideas, shapes, or motives. Even in tonal music, this is what most listeners probably do. So a fundamental reason for the employment of traditional genres in twelve-tone compositions is to facilitate the identification of thematic elements. The initial four-bar phrase of Schoenberg's Waltz sets out a twelve-tone melody (Ex. 4.3). The close rhythmic similarity between bars 1 and 2 is an early indication of the importance of rhythm as an aid to the perception of thematic process in a serial composition: and Schoenberg reinforces this by evoking such traditional techniques as sequence (bars 10–14, Ex. 4.4). Allusions to traditional waltz form as a rather complicated ternary or even sonata design (A, 1–28 + B, 29–43: C, 44–67: B + A^1 with coda, 68–113) are fundamental, too: and we should not underestimate the satisfaction for a composer wishing to communicate new discoveries to audiences familiar with the achievements of Bach and Brahms in discovering that the new did not require the total exclusion of the old.

Ex. 4.3   Schoenberg, Op. 23 No. 5, opening twelve-tone melody

Ex. 4.4   Schoenberg, Op. 23 No. 5, bars 10–14

1923–4

Schoenberg's completion in March 1923 of his first fully twelve-tone composition, the Suite Op. 25, inspired one of those bursts of creative energy through which he compensated for intensive periods of planning and experiment. During the next six years he wrote five large-scale compositions: the Wind Quintet Op. 26 (April 1923–August 1924), the Suite Op. 29 for three clarinets, string trio and piano (January 1925–May 1926), the String Quartet No. 3, Op. 30 (January–March 1927), the Variations for Orchestra Op. 31 (May 1926–August 1928) and the one-act opera *Von heute auf morgen* Op. 32 (October 1928–January 1929) – as well as two sets of choral pieces, Op. 27 and Op. 28 and the short Piano Piece, Op. 33a. For some commentators, these compositions consolidate a natural conjunction between the anti-expressionist, constructivist impulse that underlies large-scale use of the twelve-tone method and a neo-classicism manifest in the connection Schoenberg willingly made between the new technique and old compositional principles and formal outlines. Yet 'connection' – as implying a smooth transition between tonal and twelve-tone works in sonata form – does not exclude elements of tension, of conflict, as the fundamental differences between old and new refuse to be erased. Discussion of the opening of the Wind Quintet will demonstrate some aspects of this dialogue between tradition and innovation.

Schoenberg on Schoenberg: the Wind Quintet

In his essay 'Composition with Twelve Tones (1)' (1941), Schoenberg uses the Wind Quintet as an example of how diverse themes can be drawn from the same twelve-tone series, and he also mentions in passing the traditional generic forms which he employed, such as scherzo and rondo. Before illustrating the themes themselves he states a general principle in which an analogy with the hierarchies of tonal structuring is made explicit: 'while a piece usually begins with the basic set [BS] itself, the mirror [inversion] forms and other derivatives, such as the eleven transpositions of all the four basic forms, are applied only later; the transpositions especially, like the modulations in former styles, serve to build subordinate ideas.'[10] He then quotes three forms of the Quintet's series (P-0, I-0, I-5) without further comment. But the implication is that these comprise a group whose collective significance is indeed more basic than subordinate: and the first actual theme illustrated, 'the main theme of the first movement' (Ex. 4.5), is said to use 'for its first phrase the first six tones, the antecedent; for the second phrase, the consequent of the BS. This example shows how an accompaniment can be built. As octave doubling should be avoided, the accompanying of tones 1–6 with tones 7–12, and vice versa, is one way to fulfil this requirement' (228). Schoenberg cheerfully accepts the analogy between the time-honoured phrase-structuring principle of antecedent–consequent and the division of the series into two complementary halves – a division that has particular resonance in Op. 26, since the second hexachord of P-0 is an almost exact transposition of the first onto its 'dominant' (the perfect fifth above, that is, not the tritone): only the final interval is different, since an exact transposition would involve repeating the G natural from the first hexachord.

As noted earlier, it is always conceivable that a serial composer could emphasise the pitches diatonic to a particular tonality within any twelve-tone series and thereby suggest connections between tonal and twelve-tone modes of construction: in the case of Op. 26, this would involve treating E flat, G, and C from the first hexachord and B flat, D, A flat and F from the second as structural pitches decorated or prolonged by the remainder. Schoenberg would have had little patience with such naïve literalness. But there is plenty of evidence that he enjoyed the irony of suggesting the kind of dialogues between old and new that become audible when that initial E flat is made the focus for larger-scale motions of convergence and divergence: procedures that simultaneously evoke and resist the goal-directed motions and imitative conventions of tonal voice-leading. The circle that had to be squared in twelve-tone composition as Schoenberg conceived it was between the presence of thematic statements and developments on the one hand and the absence of functional harmonic support on the other. So he reconceived the polarity of

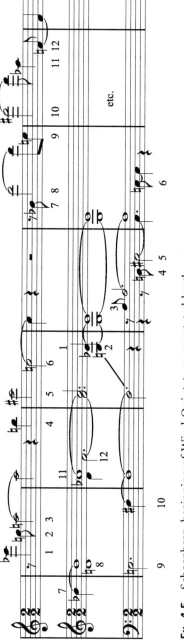

Ex. 4.5 Schoenberg, beginning of Wind Quintet, as annotated by the composer

theme and accompaniment (or subject and countersubject) as a dialogue between complementary segments of the basic series itself, generating a superimposition of thematic strata which balanced the competing claims of similarity and difference.

More on the Wind Quintet

In the published score of Op. 26 (but not in Schoenberg's 1941 example) the flute's initial statement of the first hexachord of P-0 is marked as the **Hauptstimme** (principal voice). Divided into two trichords, this already employs the balancing antecedent–consequent effect of traditional thematic structuring, and although it is not one of Schoenberg's more arresting thematic inventions, it confirms the hexachord's central succession of whole tones as its principal non-diatonic component. As accompaniment, the second hexachord is divided between horn, oboe and clarinet, in such a way that what could have been homophonic – two three-note chords (E, D, B flat moving to F sharp, D, A flat) – is more like three independent contrapuntal lines, two of which pick out the most frequently used interval class of the series. The horn extracts a descending whole-tone from the hexachord (B flat, A flat: notes 1 and 5), the clarinet an ascending whole-tone (E, F sharp: notes 3 and 4), leaving the oboe with the minor third D to F: notes 2 and 6, pitches which encircle the E flat to which the oboe moves as the pitches of the first hexachord return.

A tonal composer aiming to provide an effective, contextualising accompaniment to an initial theme would be expected to attend to the vertical conjunctions in relation to some principle of harmonic organisation, primarily to do with the correct preparation and resolution of dissonances. The only principle Schoenberg mentions in his 1941 essay is that 'octave doubling [between melody and accompaniment] should be avoided' (228). This fundamental tenet – not just of the twelve-tone method, but of all post-tonal thinking – indicates that pitch-complementation (superimposing segments of the series with different pitch contents) is the primary factor, even if the composing-out of the complementary pitch material echoes or imitates the motivic elements of the principal voice. Whether the result is in any sense analogous to the integral balances of tonal voice-leading depends on how structurally one hears the latter. But since tonal and twelve-tone works begin from different locations, hearing one consistently 'in terms of' the other is not a realistic option.

As we have seen, long before the twelve-tone method emerged, Schoenberg and others had freed music from the constraints of functional tonal harmony, and from its roots in the voice-leading orthodoxies of strict counterpoint. Schoenberg's most far-reaching radicalism lay in deciding that music did not also need to be free of textural and formal features that had grown up with those now-rejected constraints, and that the kind of graded employment of materials that goes with the idea of hierarchy could be as relevant to serial composition as it had been to tonal and modal writing. Schoenberg's Wind Quintet is no more a parody of a tonal symphonic composition than his *Verklärte Nacht* (1899) is a parody of an orchestral symphonic poem. In both cases, generic conventions are transformed through the power of positive rethinking. Twelve-tone harmony simply centres on one aspect of harmony in tonal composition – its ability to create an appropriate context, setting off but also interacting with the thematic processes that work out the central idea of the composition.

The Wind Quintet's finale

Discussing the Quintet's rondo finale in 'Composition with Twelve Tones (1)', Schoenberg again concentrates on thematic diversity, with the important point that 'while rhythm and phrasing significantly preserve the character of the theme so that it can easily be recognized, the tones and intervals are changed through a different use of BS and mirror forms' (230). This expresses Schoenberg's view that comprehensibility is mainly conveyed through thematic character – the expressive nature of a theme, and the way it behaves, rather than through thematic structure, as represented by the shape of its successive intervals. That is, the rondo theme (Ex. 4.6) and its recurrences are recognisable primarily by way of the combination of a very clear-cut rhythmic profile with predominantly large intervals (of more than an octave), offset as this is at the beginning by busier, more narrow-intervalled patterns in the supporting voices. The analytical interpreter might note a formal analogy between this opening and that of a traditional fugal exposition: there is a subject, starting on E flat, supported by two countersubjects, then an answer (flute, bar 5) starting on the 'dominant' B flat, accompanied by countersubjects that derive from the originals. The complex contrapuntal character of the writing is reinforced by a further entry of this answer, also on the dominant, in the bassoon (bar 8), and the canonic continuation of this strengthens the perception that Schoenberg's thinking is governed by traditional contrapuntal processes, despite the fact that close analogies with fugue are short-lived.

Even first-time listeners to this movement should spot the difference between those passages which are dominated by this principal theme and those which feature contrasting material – the rondo's episodes. Schoenberg's commentary makes a point of showing how one such episode, or 'subordinate theme' – that from bar 117 – is also derived from the basic series, though by way of 'a more complicated procedure. At first a transposition of the retrograde is used three times in succession to build melody and accompaniment ... The principal voice, the bassoon, uses three tones in each of the four phrases; the accompaniment uses only six tones, so

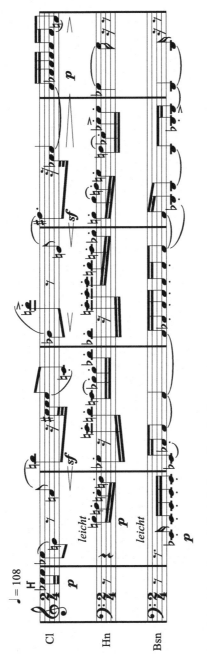

Ex. 4.6 Schoenberg, Wind Quintet, Rondo, bars 1–5

that the phrases and the sets overlap each other, producing a sufficient variety' (230). But why should Schoenberg bother to present this analysis when all the listener is likely to hear is the contrast of character between this more flowing idea and its bolder, more brittle superior? He is indeed 'composing as before', inventing a theme with an antecedent and a consequent, each further sub-divisible so that the similarity of character between the four three-note segments, with their complementary ascents and descents, is clear.

Schoenberg's analysis confirms the significance of the twelve-tone method for him, as something strictly ordered yet flexible: a stimulus, able to cooperate constructively with spontaneous inspiration, rather than merely a constraint, and providing a more clearly defined background idea for him to work with than the 'unordered' chromatic scale, or a nexus of differently sized sets, could do. Indeed, there is a particularly witty moment near the end of the rondo where Schoenberg makes play with those 'unordered' segments of his ordered series, provided by the central whole-tone tetrachords of both hexachords (G, A, B, C sharp; D, E, F sharp, G sharp). He does this as part of his final reinforcement of the hierarchic pre-eminence of the fundamental, ordered pair of series forms, P-0 and I-0, and of the distinction between thematic and accompanimental figures that is essential to any rondo design (Ex. 4.7: see the oboe part). In Op. 26 Schoenberg had still not quite arrived at the method for determining hierarchy within the twelve-tone system that he would use consistently later on. But there can be no mistaking the relish and resourcefulness with which he worked through the possibilities his system provides for playing off freedom against constraint.

1925–9

Schoenberg's euphoric prediction – to his inner circle – that the invention of the twelve-tone method ensured the future of German music for the next century soon rang hollow. Performances of early twelve-tone works did not arouse great enthusiasm in a decade when musical pace-making seemed to be in the hands of neo-classicists in general and Stravinsky in particular, and when the cultural practice associated with the Weimar Republic increasingly favoured the sardonic, and the jazz-derived music of Hindemith, Krenek and Weill. As we have already seen, Schoenberg himself could not be regarded as anti-classical, or as incapable of being sardonic. Nevertheless, at the time the gulf between his Wind Quintet and *Von heute auf morgen* on the one hand, and Stravinsky's Octet for Winds and Weill's *Die Dreigroschenoper* on the other would have seemed extreme.

Schoenberg left vivid evidence of his own sense of this gulf in the last of his *Three Satires* Op. 28, completed in December 1925 – a 'little cantata' called *Der neue*

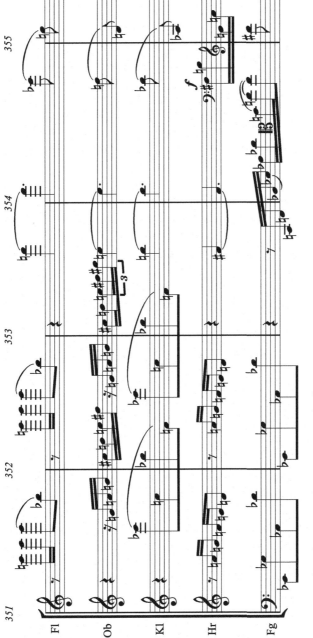

Ex. 4.7 Schoenberg, Wind Quintet, Rondo, bars 351–355

Klassizismus. Schoenberg had been irritated by 'the attacks of some of my younger contemporaries', and decided to hit back at 'all those who seek their personal salvation by taking a middle road ... those who nibble at dissonances ... the quasi-tonalists ... those who pretend to aspire "back to" ... the folklorists'.[11] To him, the difference between himself and 'der kleine Modernsky' was total: in contrast to his own creative continuation of tradition, all Stravinsky and his acolytes could offer was – allegedly – distorted mimicry of tradition. Ironically, a quarter of a century later, we will find Pierre Boulez and other post-war radicals describing Schoenberg's music of the 1920s in very much this way – and just at the time when Stravinsky was becoming the very model of a post-Webernian serialist.

Even if *Der neue Klassizismus* itself is intended as a textbook demonstration of the difference between distorted mimicry and creative continuation, the two opposites do tend to converge. The instrumental introduction presents the basic series in the form of simultaneous scales of C major (viola) and D flat (cello), and scale-like motives are the most obvious unifying factor in what follows. As for the concluding fugue, it might be more obviously chromatic than the coda to the finale of Stravinsky's Octet, but both can be heard as offering post-tonal angles on C major. Overall, it was probably Stravinsky's folklorism that alienated Schoenberg more than his neo-classical, parodistic allusions to traditional genres, forms and harmonic structures. To use basic ideas that did not just derive from the modes found in folk music but retained the rhythmic, text-inspired character of that music could be regarded as the most regressive, primitive form of nationalism: and if Schoenberg saw *The Rite of Spring* as casting a long shadow even over those works by Stravinsky from the 1920s which seemed so different from it in musical character, he was being extremely perceptive.

Op. 29 and after

It can be argued that Schoenberg's most considered musical satire on folklorism was not *Der neue Klassizismus* but the third movement of the Suite Op. 29, written before the little cantata during the summer of 1925. The theme that is the subject of four variations and coda is not twelve-tone but an artless E major tune in folksong style by Friedrich Silcher (1789–1860), called 'Ännchen von Tharau'.

Schoenberg's initial presentation of Silcher's theme seems to have been designed to demonstrate the incompatibility of tonal and twelve-tone (Ex. 4.8a). Though both tune and accompaniment are marked 'dolce', there is a very strong difference in character between the flowing, purely diatonic melody in the bass clarinet and the jaunty, wide-ranging piano accompaniment. Schoenberg pursues the idea of incompatibility into the rhythmic domain: the tune would be most naturally notated

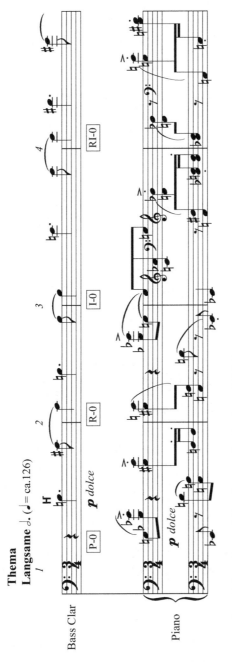

Ex. 4.8a Schoenberg, Suite Op. 29, beginning of third movement

Ex. 4.8b Schoenberg, Suite Op. 29, third movement, series forms used in bars 1–4

in 6/8 (at least until bar 6), but letting it drift against the active 3/4 patterns of the piano tends to characterise it as fecklessly innocent and other-worldly. The successive pitches of the tune are drawn from the piano's sequence of twelve-tone series forms: Ex. 4.8b shows the series forms used in the first four bars, with stems attached to the bass clarinet's melody notes. At the beginning of the movement, Schoenberg might appear intent on offering a lighthearted lesson on the extent to which twelve-tone serialism can highlight the incompatibility of tonal and pantonal. Yet the movement proceeds by dissolving the tune's tonality into the more explicit post-tonal characteristics insisted on by the succession of the twelve-tone series forms. After this ironically stratified opening, the variations and coda seem more concerned to show how such an alien musical phenomenon as the folk-like tune can be absorbed into the new twelve-tone world, exercising a ghostly, ambiguous influence over the character and material of the music but making no attempt to maintain its distinctive identity.

Schoenberg felt that folk music was fine in its proper place – in January 1929 he would produce tonal settings of four folk songs for women's voices: but allowing it to underpin the all-important generative materials of serious symphonic works was for him as blasphemous as the worship of the golden calf in the Old Testament story. In this way, Schoenberg revealed an impeccably functional aesthetic: settings of folk poems, orchestrations of Bach and Brahms, even amplifications of concertos by Handel and Monn, were legitimate if the categories to which they belonged were unambiguous. But such exercises had the function of complementing the true new world of twelve-tone composition, not of undermining it.

Schoenberg's belief in the significance of the new order he had brought about gave it a spiritual aura. Satire was all very well – and he even pandered to Weimar-style fascination with the shallowly new and the (allegedly) smart in his one-act opera *Von heute auf morgen*, ending as this does with a child asking the innocent question, 'Mummy, what's modern people?' Modern people, for Schoenberg, were those who had the capacity to embrace his challenging new musical world. Even so, through failures of leadership and their own innate weaknesses, they inevitably preferred soft options and superficial art. So it is no surprise to find that, late in 1928, Schoenberg made the first draft of the libretto for what would become the opera *Moses und Aron*, the work which more than any other served to focus the creative achievements and frustrations, as well as the spiritual beliefs and socio-political ambitions of the rest of his life.

From this perspective, it is understandable how galling it should have been for Schoenberg to realise that, for some listeners at least, 'mathematical' twelve-tone music sounded just like such nightmarish, expressionistic, 'freely atonal' compositions as *Erwartung*. Perhaps with this in mind, he wrote as follows about the first movement of the String Quartet No. 3 (1927):

> As a little boy I was tormented by a picture of a scene from a fairy-tale, The Ghostship, whose captain had been nailed through the head to the topmast by his rebellious crew. I am sure that this was not the programme of the first movement of the Third String Quartet. But it might have been, subconsciously, a very gruesome premonition which caused me to write this work, because as often as I thought about this movement, the picture came to my mind. I am afraid a psychologist might use this story as a stepping stone for premature conclusions.[12]

It would, then, be 'premature' to conclude that the character of the quartet movement is programmatic, representing the gruesome events of The Ghostship story. Though Schoenberg does not deny that the association with the story provides 'an illustration of the emotional background of this movement', he then asserts that 'it will not furnish enlightenment of the structure'. In this way, contrast and tension are brought into the centre of experience and understanding, and make an all-pervading integration and synthesis by way of the twelve-tone method that much more difficult to achieve.

Meaning, making

In claiming that 'Schoenberg's real conviction that the way something is made and what it means are two sides of the same thing', Carl Dahlhaus issued a salutary warning to commentators against the assumption that 'cracking the code' of a twelve-tone composition says everything that can or should be said about (or heard within) that composition.

Dahlhaus went on to argue that this 'conviction ... is to be understood as a system of poetics', and also as an attempt 'to mediate ... between the demand for convincing expressivity at every moment on the one hand and for total inter-relatedness of the musical events on the other. In Schoenberg's scheme of things the essence of a musical idea is that it both emanates from a need for expression, which can virtually assume the character of an imperative, and also has formal conse-quences and establishes far-reaching connections instead of exhausting itself in a momentary effect.' In other words, 'the intelligibility of the individual feature depends on the logic of the whole'.[13]

The value of Dahlhaus' discussion lies in the way it strengthens the case for claiming that the impulse behind and within twelve-tone serialism was not just to promote a radically new compositional method, but had to do with the special expressivity and comprehensibility of compositions in which that notably logical method was employed. While considerable scepticism has often attended Schoenberg's specific claim that 'you use the row and compose as you had done it previously', with 'the same kind of form or expression, the same themes, melodies, sounds, rhythms as you used before',[14] his notorious impatience with requests for the code-breaking type of information – 'my works are twelve-note *compositions*, not *twelve-note* com-positions'[15] – is certainly more baldly oppositional than it need be. The twelve-tone aspect and the compositional aspect merit more equal billing in any serious critical study of the serial phenomenon, and the real challenge to the analyst lies not in providing the basic information about the identity of the series and listing the various versions of it used in any particular movement or section. Rather, the challenge is to construct an adequate narrative around the process of deriving material and processes from the series. In John Covach's words, 'Schoenberg's poetics of music ... would require one not only to account for the static structure of a twelve-tone work, but also to account for the dynamic unfolding of materials'. And Covach proposes a meth-odology which involves 'shifting the emphasis of what we hear and say about Schoenberg's twelve-tone music to elicit an account that tends to hold the static and dynamic dimensions in a more openly dialectical relationship'.[16]

Covach then provides an outline analysis of one of Schoenberg's most elaborate twelve-tone works, the *Variations for Orchestra*, Op. 31 (1926–8) that distinguishes the structuralist from the poetic: the family of eight series forms around which the initial thematic statement is based is 'an important underlying *structural* component of the entire work. That such a group of rows can exist in a work depends upon the structure of the row and the constraints of the twelve-tone method; that such a group of rows is articulated through a dynamic process that favors development from simple to more complex formulations is a product of the poetics' (321). One of Covach's most important conclusions is that 'the twelve-tone method creates a wealth of potential relationships, a background upon which a dialectic between static and dynamic aspects of musical structure can be played out. The poetics dictates that some limited set of relationships should be developed according to a scheme that generally prefers a progression from closer to more complicated and remote variants' (332).

This is not necessarily a poetics that can be applied to all twelve-tone compositions by all twelve-tone composers – although the extent to which modernist or modern-classic compositions all involve some dialogue (which can be more like juxtaposition or alternation than progression) between the opposite poles of relatively simple and relatively complex treatment of ideas indicates that it has the capacity to be adapted and transformed in ways which suggest a wide-ranging relevance.[17] Because the 'making', pre-compositional aspect of twelve-tone serialism is so different from earlier compositional methods, the 'meaning' aspect is inevitably affected. All the more reason, Schoenberg seems to have believed, to ensure that the meanings of twelve-tone compositions should be seen as intensifying and refining those of earlier compositions, not striking out into wholly uncharted expressive territory – if such a thing were conceivable. Hence the convergence of twelve-tone techniques and pre-existing generic and textural features from the very first (as in the Waltz from Op. 23) offers the prospect of a new phase in which expressivity as well as form are enhanced through the new perspectives they cast on their own older manifestations. But it was the expressive need, not the structural inventiveness, that came first.

Chapter 5

Alban Berg: reverence and resistance

Wozzeck and transition

Alban Berg (1885–1935) finished his formal studies with Schoenberg in 1910, and for more than a decade thereafter he remained very much under the shadow of a master he held in awe. Then, in December 1925, at the age of forty, he had a major success with the première of his opera *Wozzeck*, written between 1917 and 1922 – a time when Schoenberg was still grappling with the new possibilities of serial thinking and the twelve-tone method. *Wozzeck* is not twelve-tone, but it anticipates aspects of serial technique as part of an essentially pluralistic kind of compositional method that Berg would adapt to twelve-tone principles rather than completely abandon.

Like his fellow Schoenberg pupil Anton Webern, Berg had followed the master into the brave new world of post-tonal total chromaticism as a student, as his 'graduation exercise', the String Quartet Op. 3 (1910), reveals. A few years later, his setting of aphoristic texts by Peter Altenberg for soprano and large orchestra (1912) has a twelve-tone series as its first theme (Ex. 5.1): in addition, the last movement is a passacaglia which uses two series, one of twelve tones, the other of five. As George Perle describes it, 'the finale of the *Altenberg Lieder* anticipates, as early as 1912, the twelve-tone passacaglia theme of the scene in the Doctor's study in *Wozzeck*', while 'the opening and closing bars of the third song present a vertical twelve-tone set, anticipating the twelve-tone chords of *Wozzeck* and *Lulu* [1929–35]'.[1]

As far as *Wozzeck* itself is concerned, Anthony Pople has provided a succinct account of the opera's plurality, explaining how tonal and post-tonal tendencies interact through Berg's use of pitch formations which can be variously defined as scales (tonal, modal), sets (particular unordered collections of different sizes, mainly between three and six pitch classes) and series which use all twelve pitch classes in an ordered sequence.[2] As Pople shows, the opera's pitch materials – its motives, melodies, chords and harmonic successions – are best elucidated by analysis in terms of scale/set/series interactions using the kind of systematic structuring and graphic economy provided by the integer notation of pitch-class set theory, as outlined in chapter 1.

Ex. 5.1 Berg, *Altenberg Lieder*, twelve-tone series

Ex. 5.2 Berg, *Wozzeck*, cadence chords

At the same time, in keeping with the style of the music, it is appropriate for the description of material components to be multiple, not singular. Given that, as Patricia Hall argues, 'Berg's concept of atonality ... relies on hierarchy',[3] it is inadequate to describe the pair of cadential chords fundamental to the materials of *Wozzeck* solely as projections of the pitch-class sets to which they can be reduced and to ignore their presentation as enrichments of triadic formations, with G as root as D as fifth (Ex. 5.2). Of their very nature, set classes, when laid out as abstract strings of pitch classes, reveal nothing about the degrees of emphasis on one or more of the pitches which might result from a particular compositional presentation. Such abstractions can therefore provide only the starting point for analytical interpretation – verbal, graphic or (most probably) both. The importance of balancing the contrasting claims of tonal and post-tonal tendencies in the technical interpretation of a work like *Wozzeck* is all the greater given the tendency for such interactions – as between the promotion of and resistance to hierarchy – to remain salient in many examples of consistently twelve-tone work.

Personal space

'Tonal oder atonal?' begins Schoenberg's text for 'Am Scheideweg' (At the Crossroads), the first of his *Satires for Mixed Chorus*, Op. 28 No. 1 (1925). Schoenberg sets it, tongue in cheek, as a twelve-tone fugue subject (Ex. 5.3): and although he was exasperated by the crassness of the bald, unreal alternative the question embodied, he found it hard in practice to separate his ideal, synthesising concept of pantonality

Ex. 5.3 Schoenberg, 'Am Scheideweg,' Op. 28 No. 1, twelve-tone fugue subject

from a practical reality in which tonal and post-tonal were either dramatically at war, provoking each other to ever more extreme feats of extravagance and sarcasm, or insidiously, seductively compatible, constantly on the look-out for new ways of engaging and interacting. This state of affairs is clear from the fact that, soon after completing Op. 28, Schoenberg added three canons in C major 'to demonstrate the twelve-tone system's possibilities for the seven diatonic notes'.[4] And this seems to have encouraged Berg, in a letter of 27 June 1926, to confess to feeling reassured: 'all the more, since a movement of my 2nd quartet [the *Lyric Suite*], on which I am now at work, is an attempt to write strict 12-tone music with a strong *tonal* element'.[5]

Schoenberg's response to this is not known, although an essay written in 1926, 'Opinion or Insight?', reaches the open-minded if also rather forbidding conclusion that 'to use the consonant chords [in a twelve-tone context] is not out of the question, as soon as someone has found a technical means of either satisfying or paralysing their formal claims'.[6]

Perhaps aware of his mentor's thinking on this point, Berg wrote again on 13 July 1926 with more details about his current work in progress, 'a suite for string quartet, that is, in six movements, of a rather more lyrical character'. With the letter, Berg included 'a sheet of staff paper' on which 'I have taken the liberty of making a note of my experiences with "composition with 12 notes" in this project (as well as earlier). Gradually, even I am becoming adept in this method of composing, and that is very reassuring. For it would have pained me dreadfully if it had been denied me to express myself musically this way. And I *know*, aside from personal ambition (and idealism), that from now on … no one will **be able** to compose in **any other way**.'[7]

This letter is a remarkable document. Despite Berg's recent success with *Wozzeck*, a work whose character and qualities marked him out as a very different creative personality from Schoenberg, he seems to have been driven to write to his former master as if he were still a pupil, perpetually adolescent and deferential. Yet the relation of Berg's music to Schoenberg's is complex in quite different ways, not deferring abjectly to the master's every stylistic and technical nuance, but exploring an intricate blend of connection and independence. Even if the tremendous achievement of *Wozzeck* was possible for Berg in part because Schoenberg himself was composing relatively little during those years, the work demonstrates a powerful creative impulse and a capacity for original invention which, in the end, must have been more decisive for Berg than questions of Schoenberg's approval or disapproval. On the one hand, he writes in such a modest, rather grovelling way – 'even I am becoming adept in this method of composing' – as if he would be the last person in the world Schoenberg would expect to be competent in the employment of his own, personal, way of 'composing with 12 notes'. But on the other hand, in the appended analysis, Berg shows that he is already taking a quite distinct line, in which 'notes' are less significant than 'intervals'.

Berg–Klein–Berg

Berg is quite clear that he is not taking one of Schoenberg's own twelve-tone series as his point of departure. Rather, with apparently unconscious irony, and without mentioning the highly pertinent topic of 'Tonal oder atonal?', he writes that 'for my first attempts I chose the row discovered by Klein' (Ex. 5.4).[8] Fritz Heinrich Klein (1892–1977), had studied with Berg and, apart from being a composer of modest attainments, had prepared the vocal score of *Wozzeck*. The series shown in Ex. 5.4 is laid out in such a way that its succession of intervals exhausts all eleven possibilities from within the octave – minor second, minor sixth, minor third, minor seventh, perfect fourth, tritone, perfect fifth, major second, major sixth, major third and major seventh. Another property is that while the first hexachord, with its 'minor' intervals, has pitches diatonic to F major (as well as C major and A minor), the second hexachord suggests G flat major (as well as C flat major and E flat minor). So a fundamental harmonic polarity is suggested which might be especially attractive to a composer seeking to preserve tonal qualities within a twelve-tone context.

Klein was an early experimenter with twelve-tone methods, and among his compositions is *Die Maschine: Eine extonale Selbstsatire*, Op. 1 (1921), 'which he proclaimed for decades to be "the first work in which a *twelve-tone Grundgestalt* appears, together with *retrograde, inversion, mirror forms, transposition etc., etc.*"'. Arved Ashby has concluded that 'Klein's twelve-tone works and theories apparently did originate [like Hauer's] independently of Schoenberg's and his frequent changes of compositional style and persistent claims of having preceded Schoenberg in his twelve-tone discoveries conspired to exclude him from the Schoenberg circle – and from most histories of twelve-tone music'.[9]

Berg's acknowledgement of Klein's work has encouraged the assumption that it was Klein's *Variationen* for piano, Op. 14 (1924) which directly affected Berg's

Ex. 5.4 Klein all-interval series

methods in his first twelve-tone compositions, the short song 'Schliesse mir die Augen beide' (1925) and the partially serial *Lyric Suite* (1925–6). 'Klein's eleven-page analytical preface to his *Variationen* is at once an analysis of his composition, a description of his research methods, and an ambitious twelve-tone manifesto. It clearly indicates that Berg's debt to his pupil went far beyond the simple borrowing of a row for his first twelve-tone works ... Klein's innovative ideas spurred Berg on to eleven years of his own discoveries in the area of row derivation': and Ashby argues that 'Klein's twelve-tone techniques differ from Schoenberg's in much the same way as Berg's do' (76). Ashby is also unequivocal in declaring that 'it now seems clear that F. H. Klein's system represented to Berg a prototype more relevant, more inclusive, more aesthetically satisfying than either Schoenberg's or Hauer's' (102).

Ashby nevertheless acknowledges certain similarities between Klein's techniques and Hauer's, and a later commentator, Neil Boynton, has claimed that Ashby 'perhaps overstates Klein's contribution to Berg's technique; conversely, the significance of Hauer in general is understated'. But Boynton also accepts that 'the degree to which it is possible to segregate individual contributions from the common theoretical knowledge of the time, as well as the significance thereof, is by no means certain': and he concludes that it is right 'to place emphasis on what Berg did with the knowledge that was available to him rather than where he got it from'.[10]

Considerations of indebtedness can also impinge on Schoenberg himself. Would the teacher who, in 1911, had proclaimed in the epigraph to his *Harmonielehre* that he had 'learned' the book from his pupils, learn anything about serial composition from Berg, Webern, or other students? As we shall see later, Schoenberg's own compositional concerns, especially after his move to America in 1933, were absorbing enough to make it unlikely that he found study of his students' compositions particularly stimulating or provocative. If certain types of convergence can be observed – the devising of series with explicit triadic or diatonic features, for example – this could have been more the result of shared concerns prompting similar conclusions than of 'influence' as cause and effect. As Schoenberg's comments in 'Opinion or Insight?' suggest, Berg's rather individual capacity for aligning the systematic with the backward-looking was something that Schoenberg was not going to reject out of hand. What Berg described as the main advantage or attraction of the Klein series, apart from its use of all the possible intervals from within the octave, was a 'symmetry' rooted in white-note and black-note hexachords. As Berg suggests, it produces a 'resultant tonal tendency towards A minor and E flat minor, that is, F and B [major]'.[11] This could well have provoked the Schoenbergian riposte that such thinking was taking the grand ambition to 'compose as before' rather too literally, as if the traditional 'formal claims' of triadic tonality could survive undamaged within the new, twelve-tone world. Berg's words were surely too unequivocal for the Schoenberg who, in Op. 28, mocked 'der kleine Modernsky's' neo-classical tonality, and who – as noted in chapter 4 – was plotting to demonstrate in the Suite Op. 29 that the only way a folk tune and twelve-tone technique could be made compatible was through the suspension, if not literally the dissolution, of diatonicism within total chromaticism.

Berg's Chamber Concerto

According to George Perle, the large-scale Chamber Concerto (1923–5), undertaken soon after the completion of *Wozzeck*, was 'the first work in which Berg attempts, in his own way, to establish a more or less continuous and consistent circulation of the totality of pitch classes'.[12] This work was intended both as a tribute to Schoenberg on his fiftieth birthday and also as a coded celebration that among those 'good things' that come in threes could be counted the composing triumvirate of Schoenberg, Berg and Webern. If, as is widely believed, Schoenberg and possibly Webern too made reference to a musical transliteration of Schoenberg's name in their earlier post-tonal pieces, then Berg was reviving that tradition. 'In the opening bars of the first movement, the segment of the "motto" that is derived from the German pitch-class names contained in the name of **Arnol**d **Sch**ö**nberg** is prefixed by the "missing" notes of the semitonal scale to form a thematic twelve-tone row' (Ex. 5.5a). Then, 'the two remaining segments of the motto are similarly derived from **A**nton **W**eb**e**rn and **A**lban **B**er**g**' (Ex. 5.5b). Perle believes that there is no case for calling 'the Chamber Concerto, or even any section of the Chamber Concerto, an example of anything that can reasonably be called "twelve-tone composition"'. Yet he argues that the differences between its procedures and those of Berg's largest twelve-tone work, his second opera *Lulu*, are best thought of as 'a difference in the *degree* to which twelve-tone elements play a role, rather than fundamental differences in the technical character of the two works'.[13]

As Berg's twelve-tone compositions show, he was perfectly capable of following Schoenberg into the kind of serialism in which particular pitch centres could be brought into focus from time to time, especially at cadence points. In addition, however, Berg went further down the path of incorporating triadic and tonal

A D S C H B E G

Ex. 5.5a Berg, Chamber Concerto, twelve-tone material

Ex. 5.5b Berg, Chamber Concerto, beginning

identities, not necessarily with the aim of dissolving tonal into serial, but relishing the juxtaposition of radically different musical materials: popular music and expressionistic music drama in *Lulu*, the religiosity of a Bach chorale and the erotic sensuality of his own idiom in the Violin Concerto (1935). This, we can safely infer, is not what 'Opinion or Insight?' had in mind. While, even in Op. 29's variation movement, Schoenberg preferred to allude to features of style and genre which might be deemed incongruous from the twelve-tone perspective without under-lining differences in what could appear a dramatic, if not melodramatic fashion, Berg relished the drama of the explicit. He never lost the excitement of showing what the expressive results of two essentially different musical worlds in direct confrontation might be.

A first step

As indicated above, Berg's interest in Klein's twelve-tone series preceded its adoption in the *Lyric Suite*. During 1925, he used it for his very first exercise in twelve-tone serialism, and this crucial step forward was also, in one sense, a step back. Berg returned to the poem by Theodor Storm, 'Schliesse mir die Augen beide', which he had set during his student years in 1907 (that composition remained unpublished until 1930) and produced a new setting, extending over just twenty bars.

The poem consists of eight lines, and a sequence of 8–7–8–7–7–8–8–7 syllables, making sixty in all. Since Berg sets the texts syllabically, he uses just five statements of his basic series, P-0, with no immediate note-repetitions, and the varied line-lengths ensure that the text-phrasing never coincides with the basic series divisions[14] (see Ex. 5.6). On its own, the vocal line might be heard as migrating between the tonal poles of F major and B major, though simple perception of this polarity is undermined by the line divisions, leading rather to a sense of suspended tonality from which F segments and B segments emerge from time to time. A piano accompaniment could be devised to support these tonal qualities, but Berg's does not do so to any degree that suggests a consistent policy of such support on his part. In essence, the accompaniment is too elaborate to lend itself to strong suggestions of any single tonality. Rather, a detailed analysis of the song has concluded that its pitch structure embodies an 'essential ambiguity'.

Craig Ayrey declares that 'the work is both serial and tonal, and the relative weightings of the two systems of pitch relationship fluctuate throughout'. Indeed, the song might even be in a technical sense more sophisticated, more integrated, even more Schoenbergian, than those more extended and familiar instances in Berg of tonal/serial juxtaposition and interaction. As Ayrey suggests, 'the piece . . . stands as a more ambiguous, more closely integrated tonal–serial structure than the chorale-variations of *Lulu*'[15]: and that could be because it is a preliminary to Berg's larger-scale twelve-tone compositions rather than a model for those compositions. As will become clear, *Lulu* uses a reordering of the Klein series as its basic twelve-tone material.

Series, cycles

Trends in theory-based studies of Berg's music have favoured the kind of position taken by Dave Headlam, who – building on the foundations laid by George Perle as both theorist and composer – argues that 'the underlying cyclic basis of Berg's music transcends surface distinctions of "tonal", "atonal", and "twelve-tone" periods, terms which, although used as chronological guidelines, should be regarded as signifying differences in degree rather than kind'.[16] By 'cyclic', Headlam is not referring to cyclic form, but to a manner of pitch structuring in terms of interval cycles – ordered series forms, traversing the total chromatic according to the outlines shown in Ex. 5.7 (14): the first series cycles interval-class 1, the second

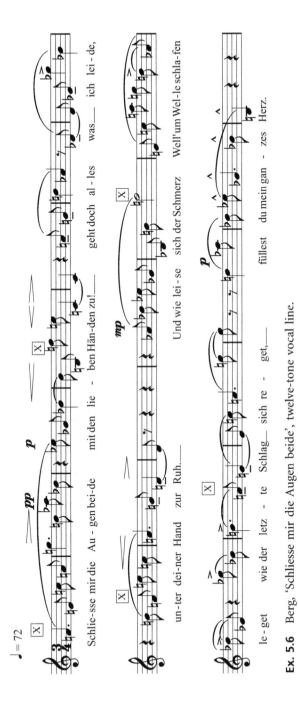

Ex. 5.6 Berg, 'Schliesse mir die Augen beide', twelve-tone vocal line. X marks where series statements (first note F) begin

73

Ex. 5.7   Twelve-tone interval cycles, 1–6

interval-class 2 and so on, until the sixth cycles the tritone, interval-class 6. (Cycle 6 is inevitably different from the others in that the core interval-class is interleaved with ic5: if this did not happen, a twelve-tone collection with six tritones would not be possible.)

When it comes to Berg's twelve-tone works, Headlam's most radical contention is that the twelve-tone series themselves 'are not central . . . Although [Berg] often carefully related derived materials to the original row, the use of row-derived materials in non-row contexts, the reordering of row segments, and the free addition of non-row-derived notes suggests that the basis of the language is not the rows but the smaller derived and non-derived materials, which are mostly, as in his atonal music, cyclic-based collections' (197–8).

Headlam moves from this to the assertion that 'since musical coherence does not depend on the row as the main referent, no requirement exists for a consistent treatment of the rows': with respect to the 'apparent juxtaposition of twelve-tone and tonal elements' in the Violin Concerto's use of a Bach chorale harmonisation, 'the chorale appears without disrupting the musical coherence because its tonal progression and the rows intertwined around the voices of the chorale are both underlaid by the cyclic collections that govern the entire piece'. Even though 'the chorale ['Es ist genug', 'it is enough' – referring to Christ's willing acceptance of death on the Cross] maintains its symbolic, extra-musical associations, which exceed the bounds of the piece . . . its tonal language seamlessly emerges from and dissolves into the surrounding cyclically-based passages' (200).

I would question the generic context and expressive aura created by Headlam's reading, as well as some aspects of the technical processes he employs. The problem lies not so much in Headlam's prioritising of interval cycles over other twelve-tone operations, as in his resistance to the modernistic tensions that the method's propensity for juxtaposing tonal and post-tonal examples of cyclic processes – especially in the Violin Concerto – provides. If Berg's language does indeed remain consistent in this sense throughout his career, the possibility that he liked the idea of using such dramatic oppositions in non-arbitrary but still potentially disorientating ways should not be rejected out of hand. 'Differences in kind' continue to have a vital role to play, and even if this means that such differences are regarded as of relatively superficial structural significance – subject to 'correction' by integrative man-oeuvres in the 'background' – the dialogue between modernist disjunction and the more classical organicist thinking that they imply is itself a far from superficial musical quality.

Lyric Suite

With the *Lyric Suite* we enter the fully Bergian serial world of hybrid forms and techniques, where the kind of ambiguities and allusions of which Schoenberg might have been expected to approve are themselves contextualised by those more urgently personal associations, preoccupations and references which were Berg's main way of distancing himself in his music from the musician to whom he owed so much. Like the Chamber Concerto, the *Lyric Suite* is to no small extent founded on coded allusions to people and, by extension, to their shared emotions: though this time it is lovers, not a master and his pupils, who are involved. Also, the differences between its twelve-tone and non-twelve-tone sections are of degree, not fundamental: just as discussion of the Chamber Concerto's post-tonal procedures and characteristics stems from the explanation of its coded materials, so with the *Lyric Suite* the revelations – emerging long after Berg's death – about its covert content, place the analysis of serial and non-serial interactions in a very special context.

Berg deviously obscured the suite's true content by way of a dedication to Schoenberg's 'master', Alexander von Zemlinsky, the conductor of *Wozzeck*'s pre-mière, whose own *Lyric Symphony* (1922–3) could be regarded as a precedent for the suite, especially when Berg quotes a phrase from that work near the end of his fourth movement. Not until 1977 did George Perle discover a copy of the suite whose annotations by the composer made clear that the piece was written 'in spite of the official dedication', for Hanna Fuchs-Robettin, for whom Berg felt 'a passionate but unfulfilled love'.[17]

Perle's account of this remarkable and fascinating story should be read in full, and although the revelation that the suite's finale is a hidden setting of a poem by Baudelaire is not directly relevant to an account of its serial technique, it certainly helps to explain why Berg contrived to make passing reference to the opening of Wagner's *Tristan* within his serial design. As with the Chamber Concerto, the pitch materials, which start out from the Klein series, allude directly to some of the musical letters in the names of Hanna Fuchs and Alban Berg – B natural, F, A, B flat: a technique which shows not simply life initiating art, but life, and love, determining twelve-tone technique. Berg's numerological obsessions provide an additional, constructivist stratum, helping to generate the work's design – number of bars in sections or movements as multiples of ten or twenty-three as well as metronome markings. All this is further evidence that intellectual contrivance, even of unambiguously mathematical origins, need not result in music of emotional reticence or aridity. What is reinforced by all these discoveries and interpretations is that the creative results of biographical and technical secrets can be heard, and appreciated, even when the very existence of such secrets remains unsuspected.

Lyric Suite: finale

The forty-six-bar finale of the *Lyric Suite* (Largo desolato) unfolds a principle of dialogue in several distinct ways: as already pointed out, there is the duality (which is now common knowledge, however unhappy Berg might be to know that the secret was out) between the suppressed poem and the musical setting of it.[18] There is also dialogue in the sense that the movement uses two twelve-tone series, the second derived from the first which in turn derives from the series used in the first and third movements (Ex. 5.8). This first series shares the overall F–B span of its predecessors, but the second confines the F–B span to the first hexachord (the second could have been ordered to span A–B flat).

Readers are recommended to study Headlam's discussion of this movement in order to see to what extent his preferred vocabulary and focus on cyclic pitch design sheds special light on the music's twelve-tone elements. The expressive intention of the movement's freely imitative opening – all four series forms starting on F (Ex. 5.9a) – seems to be to evoke the 'dead' landscape, the 'deepest abyss' from which the 'cry' of the first violin (bars 6–8) suddenly 'rises up'. This melodic form of

Ex. 5.8 Berg, *Lyric Suite*, finale, the two twelve-tone series

Ex. 5.9a Berg, *Lyric Suite*, finale, bars 1–9

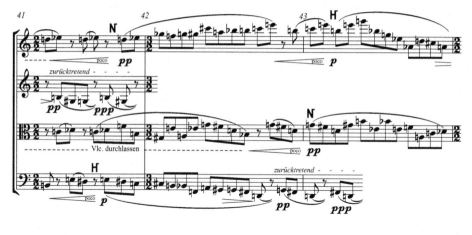

Ex. 5.9b   Berg, *Lyric Suite*, finale, ending

Series 2 is complemented from bar 10 in the cello by a melodic form of Series 1: and the hypothetical reconstruction of the vocal line provided by Perle confirms the sense in which the movement continues this dialogue between two related but distinct entities, not dissimilar to the way in which *Lulu* would differentiate character in part through series derivations. At the end, when the vocal line has fallen silent, the accompaniment unwinds, the two final strands formed by the first violin (Series 1), and the viola (Series 2) (Ex. 5.9b). As Headlam observes, the final series form in the viola was also the first series form for the vocal melody (viola, bars 12–14), and Berg marked the fading end in his annotated score, 'dying away in love, yearning, and grief' (283). In the published score, that personal gloss is replaced by the instruction that on no account should the fading repetitions of the major third in the viola end on the D flat. F (for Fuchs-Robettin) should be the last sound heard.

The final dialogues

Berg's last pair of twelve-tone compositions, *Lulu* (1929–35, orchestration of Act 3 unfinished) and the Violin Concerto (1935), are in all probability the most frequently performed of all partly or wholly serial works to date. To be sure, this says more about the degree to which the musical style in both works is perceived as moving closer to 'mainstream' late-romanticism, especially as found in Mahler's symphonic music, than about the fact that serialism is involved. Equally, pointless speculation about whether Berg would have written a *Lulu* opera and a violin concerto had he not adopted the twelve-tone method can be turned more productively into the evident truism that his adoption of the method did nothing to prevent him from writing these particular works, and from showing that serial technique was neither in principle nor in practice something to stand in the way of direct expressive appeal to an audience.

Few today would claim that such appeal was bought at the price of actually betraying the serial principle as Schoenberg (and Webern) conceived it, or that those apparent alignments with aspects of tonality and traditional textures and genres which distinguish Berg's version of serialism were the result of a simplistic, half-hearted response to the serial principle itself. Even Pierre Boulez, once the scourge of all that smacked of selling-out to neo-classicism and worn-out conventions in Schoenberg and Berg, came to celebrate 'the complexity of Berg's mind: the number of internal correspondences, the intricacy of his musical construction, the esoteric character of many of his references, the density of texture, that whole universe in perpetual motion revolving constantly around itself'.[19] Boulez here was writing of the Chamber Concerto rather than one of the more directly serial works. Elsewhere, speaking with admiration of the *Lyric Suite* as achieving 'a rare equilibrium, which was not to be maintained in the works which followed',[20] Boulez revealed his long-standing unease with the 'collage' aspect of *Lulu* and the Violin Concerto, where juxtapositions between different musics seem more important than any possible synthesis between less obvious common factors – the kind of thing which, as already mentioned, Headlam claims for the concerto.

Later developments in serial composition are deeply involved with the contrast between what might be categorised as modernist and **modern-classic** compositional principles. To the extent that this is a useful distinction, Berg's later works belong to the former category, since the kind of integrative impulse pertaining to classicism is resisted, if not entirely suppressed. That is not to concede that these works lack any kind of 'equilibrium', however: and it could be argued that Boulez could only distinguish between this quality in the *Lyric Suite* and its alleged absence later by deciding to attach less significance to the allusions, quotations and sheer stylistic and technical diversity in that work than is justifiable. As already suggested, Berg's use of the twelve-tone method in the opera and the concerto constitutes an elaboration and refinement of that already deployed in the second Storm setting, the *Lyric Suite* and the concert aria *Der Wein* (1929). George Perle's point that 'Berg's twelve-tone practice ... though historically derived from Schoenberg's concept of twelve-tone composition, must be distinguished from the latter in several fundamental respects'[21] can be matched by the suggestion that there are no less fundamental differences between the character of the operas and concertos by the master and the pupil.

Berg's second setting of Storm's 'Schliesse mir die Augen beide', as another covert gesture of devotion to Hanna Fuchs-Robettin, consciously echoed the dedication of his first setting to his wife Helene. This underlines the extent to which Berg's works are implicated in the 'secrets' of his private life (*Lyric Suite*, Violin Concerto): also, as especially in the case of *Lulu*, they explore a fascination with darkness and decadence from which little that is redemptive or spiritually ennobling can be derived. In a penetrating commentary, Douglas Jarman has noted that the difference between the 'luxuriant, elegiac music' with which *Lulu* ends 'and the events on stage' – Lulu's murdered Lesbian lover dying after singing a brief, ecstatic elegy for the murdered Lulu – 'produces an emotional disorientation that is deeply disturbing'. But, Jarman goes on, 'it can also, if we respond to the music and are prepared to give these characters the understanding and compassion that the humanity of Berg's score demands, be humanly restorative'.[22] Few would dissent, and it might even be argued that Berg's compassionate decadence is not so utterly different in its musical intensity from Schoenberg's struggle to evoke a spiritual transcendence beyond the mundane, fetishistic worship of images, in *Moses und Aron*, and elsewhere – even if, in the end, the Schoenberg/Moses admonition to 'purify your thinking' was taken more seriously by Webern than by Berg.

Serialism in *Lulu* and the Violin Concerto

The basic twelve-tone series forms for both *Lulu* (Ex. 5.10a) and the Violin Concerto (Ex. 5.10b) demonstrate the continuing importance for Berg of what Anthony Pople has called 'the embedding of tonalistic figurations' in serial music.[23] Pople summarised the ways in which Berg generated the mass of diverse musical materials needed for a full-length opera from this series (Ex. 5.11a–d). For example, he derives series to identify different characters by such mechanisms as choosing every seventh note from a sequence of Prime forms (Alwa) (Ex. 5.11b) or every third note for the Schoolboy (Ex. 5.11c). In a more complicated case – the series for Dr Schön (Ex. 5.11d) – Berg proceeds by skipping one, then two, then three notes from the Prime, then three, two, one, and repeating this process to complete the twelve.

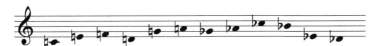

Ex. 5.10a   Berg, *Lulu*, basic twelve-tone series

Ex. 5.10b   Berg, Violin Concerto, basic twelve-tone series

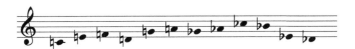

Ex 5.11a   Berg, *Lulu*, basic twelve-tone series

Ex. 5.11b   Twelve-tone series for Alwa, every **seventh** note of Ex. 5.11a

Ex. 5.11c   Twelve-tone series for Schoolboy, every **third** note of Ex. 5.11a

Ex. 5.11d   Twelve-tone series for Dr Schön

Such **sieving** is used in various other ways as well, ranging from the obvious to the arcane. Patricia Hall has provided a wealth of evidence from sketches and drafts to confirm her argument that, although Berg seems to have gone to great efforts to derive all the materials for the opera from the original series, such derivations were contrived 'in far too hidden (or, if you will, sophisticated) a manner' to make all the connections clear.[24] For Berg, there seems to have been a special pleasure to be derived from the dialogues between difference and similarity which function as a kind of emotional complement to the violent and irrational feelings with which the opera's music deals.[25]

The technical dialogue between tonal allusion, or quotation, and twelve-tone processes in the Violin Concerto did not require the derivational proliferations appropriate to the opera. In the concerto the 'tonalistic' series seems to have been suggested by a variety of ideas – the violin's open strings, or a chorale melody, beginning with the whole-tone sequence that ends the series, which suited the concerto's role as an instrumental requiem for the eighteen-year-old daughter of friends, Alma Mahler and the architect Walter Gropius. There was also the possibility of alluding to an Austrian folk tune as well as to (Viennese) waltz-like music. As a result, purely serial analysis comes far less close to the actual character of Berg's music than the more intricate melding of serial and tonal described in Anthony Pople's study. 'The analyses of thematic and motivic material ... illustrate the Schoenbergian function of the series, as a *Grundgestalt* which, in an essentially intangible way, binds together not only all the thematic material of the work ... but also underlies the other contrapuntal and harmonic elements of its textures.' Yet the familiar circumstance in which 'a series may be defined not exclusively by the order of its notes, but rather by its segmental pitch-class content' leads Pople to use pitch-class set designations as well as or in place of twelve-tone series labels.[26]

Ex. 5.12a, b are two of Pople's simpler analytical demonstrations, for *Lulu* (Ex. 5.12a) and the Violin Concerto (Ex. 5.12b), respectively.[27] In both compositions the musical style has strong links with the hyper-expressiveness Berg admired in Mahler and early Schoenberg, and it can seem paradoxical that Berg should derive such apparently backward-sounding music from such complicated twelve-tone manoeuvring. In the *Lulu* extract, what Pople terms 'the recycling of C major scale fragments', shown at the bottom of Ex. 5.12a, is drawn from, and combined with, the totally chromatic series forms P-9 and I-0. With the melodic line from the second movement of the Violin Concerto – known as the *Klagegesang*, or lament – two different series forms are again combined, in a way which would probably defy analytical decoding without the help of the composer's sketches. RI-5 begins on G and runs through to F, while P-3 is rotated to begin with its concluding whole-tone tetrachord, thereby coinciding exactly with RI-5's initial tetrachord.

Ex. 5.12a Berg, *Lulu*, serial structure of opening of Act 1 duet for Lulu and the Painter, see Pople, *The Cambridge Companion to Berg* p. 212

Ex. 5.12b   Berg, Violin Concerto, twelve-tone basis for lament melody (*Klagegesang*)

In both cases, there is a potent alliance between modern constructivism and traditionally shaped expressive gestures. This quality in Berg's work led to him being rather slighted during the early post-war years in which systematic strictness was valued over and above allusive ambiguity. Later on, however, as we have seen, even Boulez came to value the Bergian spirit, and the kind of derivational and tonal/post-tonal intersections central to all his serial works have proved mightily influential on later composers, including Dallapiccola and Peter Maxwell Davies. Most such composers also admire Berg's frankly hedonistic aesthetic. Spirituality is not a Bergian topic – which makes his use of Bach's harmonisation of a chorale whose text looks forward to eternal life with God in the Violin Concerto a controversial choice. Cynical? Sentimental? Sometimes it is possible to feel that it is only the knowledge that this was Berg's last work, completed just before his early and unexpected death when barely fifty, that saves it from condemnation as intolerably mawkish and opportunistic. Yet admiration for the piece has survived revelations about its particular secrets: on the one hand, it has always been known that the 'angel' in whose memory it is inscribed was Manon Gropius: on the other, it has only emerged more recently that Berg couldn't resist alluding, by way of a Carinthian folktune, to another young female, Marie Scheuchl, with whom, as a teenager he had a brief affair, and a child. That Berg saw nothing incongruous or distasteful in such associations, or for that matter in those presumably ironic allusions to the motto of a right-wing political group indicated on sketches for the concerto,[28] is something which can be accepted, and even ignored, by those for whom the experience of the music transcends such biographical specifics. Above all, Berg provided incontrovertible evidence that the 'mechanics' of twelve-tone technique need not inhibit the kind of intense and personal musical expression that maintained recognisable and positive links with the expressive gestures of pre-serial composition.

Chapter 6

Anton Webern: discipline and licence

Purity, anxiety

It is easy to see why, as Schoenberg pupil and serialist, Anton Webern (1883–1945) should be thought of as everything that Berg was not: more radical than romantic, the composer who obeyed Moses' injunction to Aaron to 'purify your thinking', while Berg remained defiantly, guiltily 'impure'. Webern's twelve-tone compositions, at least from the Symphony Op. 21 (1928) to the Cantata No. 2 Op. 31 (1941–3), are even 'purer' than Schoenberg's from the same years in distancing themselves from classical or romantic forms, textures and traditions. Here, despite the fact that even Webern could not entirely escape the lure of traditional formal designs, from canon to variation and sonata, was an appreciation of the innovative potential of the twelve-tone method that, to some composers of later generations, was far more significant than Schoenberg's more cautious approach.

The very neatness of this portrait of Webern renders it ripe for critique, from historians ready to argue for a less clear-cut separation of new from old, and from critics convinced that Webern's radical initiatives created an aesthetic dead end, which even his disciples, from Stravinsky to Boulez and beyond – Kurtág being a significant exception – were forced to reject as the limitations of his musical world became clearer. And even if many aspects of the story of Webern's life serve to underline the differences between him and Berg, that story could never be plausibly narrated in terms of a total absence of conflict or tension, of unAaron-like obedience to the laws laid down by Moses. Biographical accounts open to the seductions of Freudian psychology have made much of Webern's obsessiveness, if not with numerology, as in Berg's (and also perhaps Schoenberg's) case, then through an Oedipal attachment to his mother, as revealed in annotations to compositional sketches that lay bare explicit poetic and pictorial contexts for purely instrumental and orchestral compositions previously regarded as entirely abstract.[1]

Webern was even more dependent on Schoenberg's quasi-paternal approval than Berg, while his inability to develop an independent life as a conductor, despite evident talents in that direction, made it easy to characterise him as displaying the classic symptoms of failure to grow up and achieve independence of his teacher–parent, even after he had married and become a parent himself. Other aspects of Webern's desire to relate life and work, such as the connection revealed in sketches and writings between his later works and Alpine flora and fauna, were not inconsistent with the idea of purity of technique and serenity of atmosphere. Yet the revelation that he expected his Variations for Piano Op. 27 (1935–6) to be played with considerable expressive freedom and intensity, after the tradition of Chopin and Liszt,[2] strengthens the impression of a creative personality riven by conflicts between emotional and intellectual extremes – the kind of extremes also reflected in a double commitment, to Roman Catholicism and to right-wing politics.

Another reason why Webern's serial compositions tended to be categorised *en bloc* as chastely, classically pure and controlled was the attractive symmetry this interpretation established with his highly expressionistic post-tonal compositions from the years before 1924. Here could be located the origins of his ability to outdo Schoenberg in drawing progressive conclusions from the sense of the old order breaking down, lapsing into impotence and decay. Placed side by side, two of Webern's works for string quartet – the *Bagatelles* Op. 9 (1913) and the three-movement Quartet Op. 28 (1936–8) – do indeed appear to belong to very different technical and aesthetic worlds. But the effect of elevating comparisons of this sort into a general principle was to squeeze out any sense of transition or interaction between post-tonal expressionism and twelve-tone modern-classicism. Hence the particular value of the initiative taken by Anne C. Shreffler, whose study of sketches led her to conclude that 'Webern's adoption of the twelve-tone system is better seen not as a gradual development or "path" (as he himself would later describe it), but instead as a period of broad experimentation, during which he alternately rejected and embraced the new method'.[3]

In proposing this not-unBergian sense of turmoil, of trial and error based on a complex mixture of attraction and repulsion, Shreffler aimed to show that 'in adopting the method, Webern drew from it radically different consequences than Schoenberg had drawn. While Schoenberg valued above all the unifying force of serial operations, Webern's transitional and early twelve-tone works, almost all for voice, seem deliberately designed to prevent the perception of unity. With these pieces, which are among his least systematic, Webern 'created the most complex, even disordered, musical surface of any of his works up to that time': and Shreffler adds the critical point that 'though his later serial works show a more ordered face, some of the consequences of this early struggle with twelve-tone technique remain' (276).

Beginnings

It is not necessary to accept all elements of the contrast between Webern and Schoenberg proposed by Shreffler to see the force of her argument. As will be argued in chapter 7, the modernist capacity for resisting the unifying force of order and system was no less relevant to Schoenberg himself. Yet the fact that Webern, after he began to try out twelve-tone techniques in 1922, 'produced some of his most irrational and disorganized' as well as 'least accessible' works, reinforces the point that this commitment to Schoenberg's precepts 'required a major rethinking of his compositional habits and seriously disrupted what had been a reasonably steady flow of work' (277–8).

According to the chronology established by Shreffler, the first piece which Webern intended to be twelve-tone was the vocal setting, made in July 1922, of 'Mein Weg geht jetzt vorüber' (eventually Op. 15 No. 4): and at this date Schoenberg's own serial practice had not advanced beyond the Prelude of Op. 25. Possibly because Webern was aware of the dangers of getting ahead of a master who expected to be followed, and who made his secret methods public only because he feared that Josef Matthias Hauer (however inferior his music) would steal his thunder, this movement was ultimately completed 'in a free atonal style'. Webern did not resume his serial explorations until the later months of 1924, 'completing the *Kinderstück* for piano and the song Op. 17 No. 1, each of which is based on a single twelve-tone series. Only after completing the second of the *Three Songs* Op. 18, in October 1925, did Webern admit feeling comfortable with the technique.' He even felt able to write confidently to Berg (perhaps as a result of having seen Schoenberg's Piano Suite Op. 25, as well as the large-scale Wind Quintet Op. 26) that 'twelve-tone composition is now completely clear to me' (278).

The extent to which Schoenberg, Webern and Berg compared notes and even studied each other's sketches at this crucial time will probably never be known for sure. All three used terminology suggesting that they needed to project the new developments against a tonal background: as noted above, they tended to refer to the Prime, untransposed series as 'T' (tonic), and the transposition of the basic series at the tritone – not at the perfect fifth – as 'D' (dominant). It was in February 1923 that Schoenberg had outlined his new method to various friends. But this was two years after the completion of the Prelude to the Piano Suite: as Shreffler claims, 'the evidence is overwhelming that Schoenberg did indeed share his discoveries with several friends and students, including Webern, before his formal announcement in February of 1923' (286). She concludes that 'when Webern found out about the twelve-tone method, he did try to imitate Schoenberg ... and Schoenberg's influence ... is apparent on every page of the sketches for op. 15 no. 4' (298–9). The results of Webern's attempts at emulation were to provoke degrees of anxiety and bitterness in Schoenberg which were still rampant in his last years, after Webern's death, when he accused his devoted student of committing 'many acts of infidelity with the intention of making himself the innovator' (281). Schoenberg even claimed to have tried to keep Webern in ignorance of the nature of the twelve-tone method, on the grounds that he 'immediately uses everything I do, plan, or say, so that by now I haven't the slightest idea who I am' (286).

One can only guess at the tensions that afflicted Webern as he came to feel that the principle of twelve-tone composition was necessary for him, too, since the immediacy and intensity of Schoenberg's own early demonstrations of the method were often on an intimidatingly large scale, as well as in genres from which Webern felt more distant.

Shreffler explains the failure with Op. 15 No. 4 as follows. 'Webern's sketches for "Mein Weg" embody a clash between two fundamentally different modes of musical thought: the earlier one, in which the piece grew out of a direct response to the poem, and the later, in which the composition is governed by a twelve-tone row' (301). Webern was eventually able to find his way back to composition, in the Op. 16 Canons (1924), by using 'serial techniques such as transposition, inversion, and invariance within a firmly non-dodecaphonic context' (302) – and Shreffler relates this to Schoenberg's own methods in the Op. 25 Prelude. Nevertheless, Webern's earliest examples of completely twelve-tone composition were hardly twelve-tone 'versions' of the kind of writing found in the Op. 16 Canons. On the one hand, the extreme brevity and simplicity of the *Kinderstück* for piano indicate that it was intended for children with limited technical skills to perform, and not just to suggest images of childhood to sophisticated adults (Ex. 6.1a). With just six statements of its untransposed series, this seventeen-bar piece is in many ways a textbook demonstration of the kind of variety in unity that serial thinking makes available, even in the absence of traditional thematic processes. By contrast, 'Armer Sünder du' (Op. 17 No. 1, 1924–5), while equally brief, is not only more expressionistic in style but fractures the series (Ex. 6.1b) in an 'essentially a-thematic' texture (318) (Ex. 6.1c).

In this way, it might appear that Webern was thoroughly disorientated by his advance into such a new musical world, feeling that nothing was safe or secure, once the disguise or impersonation of childish insouciance was set aside. Shreffler proposes that Webern could proceed with twelve-tone composition only when he felt able to distance himself from Schoenberg, shunning any rapprochement with the thematic processes and textural features of baroque suite or classical sonata design, and embracing the idea that 'the mere presence of a twelve-tone row could provide a subconscious unity for the whole piece. Musical gestures could then be freed from their previous role of ensuring surface comprehensibility' (280). But, as we have seen, Webern – at least at first – also regarded the new technique as encouraging the restoration and intensification of those expressionistic aesthetic qualities which had been so important to him almost twenty years before, when tonal traditions were first abandoned. Webern's early twelve-tone works are not just 'the radical culmination of a previous complex atonal practice' (280) but the refocusing of

Ex. 6.1a   Webern, opening of *Kinderstück* (1924)

Ex. 6.1b   Webern, twelve-tone series for Op. 17 No. 1

Ex. 6.1c   Webern, Op. 17 No. 1, bars 1–5

expressionistic composition to an extent that would soon retreat, only to be revived again by a younger generation after 1945. Ironically, some signs of such a revival would be found in Schoenberg's own late works, written after Webern's death.

'In the songs opp. 17 and 18 and the choruses op. 19 [1924–6], Webern attained extremes of complexity that he would never again reach, yet paradoxically the twelve-tone technique in these works is quite "rudimentary" in terms of the number of row forms and transpositions used. After the String Trio, op. 20 [1926–7], he began to retreat from this extremist position by finding ways to organize the surface again; to this end, he employed canon and traditional forms such as sonata and theme and variations' (280). Crucially, however, Webern did so in ways that cemented his distance from Schoenbergian and Bergian perspectives on such traditions: and this was because the spiritual topics, and the psychological context, which permeate the texts of the transitional and early twelve-tone works carry forward into the fully personal and mature serial compositions. As Julian Johnson summarises the specific psychological aspect: 'in these pieces [Op. 12–Op. 19] one may well find a coming together of the apparently disparate, or even antithetical, areas of Webern's musical enterprise – the maternal construction of nature and the paternal imperative for syntactical order'.[4]

The route to independence

Webern's progress from his first forays to full maturity as a twelve-tone composer spans the period from the later months of 1924 to the summer of 1928. The completion of the Symphony Op. 21 seems to have brought to an end the years of uncertainty and instability which saw him wavering between the Schoenbergian manner of the *Klavierstück* 'Im Tempo eines Menuetts' (probably written in late August 1925) and the more personal expressionism of the various vocal pieces. There was a similar simplicity of serial practice in both styles, however: the *Klavierstück* deploys nineteen statements of its series, starting in the monodic manner of the *Kinderstück*, then proceeding to textures in which various chordal groupings emerge, but without using related transpositions and inversions along the lines of Schoenberg's Op. 25. No less 'primitive' (though at the same time highly significant in terms of the development of serial practice in later years) are the successions of unordered twelve-tone collections, or fields, as distinct from ordered series forms, found in Op. 17 No. 1. As Kathryn Bailey describes this piece, 'there are nineteen of these fields, all complete but the fourth and fifth, both of which lack the note A'.[5] Bailey's analysis shows that the lack of fixed ordering does not preclude the use of cellular repetitions (often ostinato-like) – the kind of invariant formations that bring a degree of harmonic stability and comprehensibility to music which avoids larger-scale motivic correspondences.

It was in Op. 17 No. 2 (actually the third of the set to be written, in July 1925) that 'all the parts are ordered strictly according to the series for the first time' (34). But there are still no transpositions, inversions, or retrogrades: just twenty-two statements of P-0, one after the other. 'All the notes appear in the correct order, with the exception of the clarinet's written B flat on the second beat of bar 14, which, as note 11, is one semiquaver early. In most cases the ends and beginnings of adjacent rows overlap (exceptions are in bars 12, 15, 16 and 19), but there is no elision.'

The twelve-tone series for Op. 17 No. 2 (Ex. 6.2a) demonstrates a feature that would be crucial to Webern's later works: as a linear event, interval class [ic]1 is particularly prominent, and although the vocal line is not confined to the minor seconds, major sevenths and minor ninths which are the main projections of this ic, they provide a significant degree of invariant stability. Although no transposed series forms are included, Webern avoids any serious suggestion that C sharp, the first pitch class of P-0, is some kind of tonic substitute; even though it is given spectacular emphasis in bar 18 as the highest and most prominent note in the vocal line (Ex. 6.2b), the accompanying instrumental counterpoints are more notable for balancing highly diverse pitch formations than for evoking the hierarchies of extended tonality. The character of the individual lines is nevertheless still quite close to that found in Webern's earlier post-tonal works.

Ex. 6.2a   Webern, twelve-tone series for Op. 17 No. 2

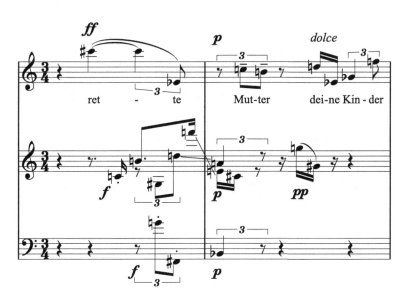

Ex. 6.2b   Webern, Op. 17 No. 2, bars 17–18

Webern's progress after this point is charted in Bailey's detailed and admirably clear narration. By the time he completed the three vocal settings of Op. 18 (October 1925)

> Webern clearly has the basic technical aspects of the row well in hand. He has moved from fields of twelve unordered notes to rows of twelve ordered notes, on to permutations of this order [inversions, retrogrades and retrograde-inversions of the untransposed Prime], and finally to simultaneous combination of permutations. In Op. 19 [*Zwei Lieder* for mixed chorus with celesta, guitar, violin, clarinet and bass clarinet, composed between December 1925 and July 1926] all these techniques are employed, as well as limited transposition [P/I 6, as in Schoenberg's Op. 25]. And, for the first time, both songs are generated by the same row. (35–6)

String Trio, Op. 20

With the String Trio (1926–7), Webern completed his years of transition. His serial technique is now more confident and sophisticated: 'here for the first time transpositions are used freely (forty-four of the forty-eight possible forms appear in the course of the two movements)' (40). One can therefore begin to sense his awareness of the systematic implications (and relatively abstract relations) of the total collection of series forms, as embodied in a matrix (Ex. 6.3). And the increasing

	A♭	G	D	C♯	F♯	F	A	B♭	E♭	E	C	B
A♭	0	11	6	5	10	9	1	2	7	8	4	3
A	1	0	7	6	11	10	2	3	8	9	5	4
D	6	5	0	11	4	3	7	8	1	2	10	9
E♭	7	6	1	0	5	4	8	9	2	3	11	10
B♭	2	1	8	7	0	11	3	4	9	10	6	5
B	3	2	9	8	1	0	4	5	10	11	7	6
G	11	10	5	4	9	8	0	1	6	7	3	2
F♯	10	9	4	3	8	7	11	0	5	6	2	1
C♯	5	4	11	10	3	2	6	7	0	1	9	8
C	4	3	10	9	2	1	5	6	11	0	8	7
E	8	7	2	1	6	5	9	10	3	4	0	11
F	9	8	3	2	7	6	10	11	4	5	1	0

Ex. 6.3   Webern, String Trio, Op. 20, twelve-tone matrix

For **Prime** forms, read horizontal lines from left to right

For **Retrogrades**, read horizontal lines from right to left

For **Inversions** read vertical columns from top to bottom

For **Retrograde Inversions,** read vertical columns from bottom to top

interest in invariance – how different forms of the twelve-tone series can be related through the smaller pitch-class collections (or sub-sets) that they have in common – began to suggest ways of giving priority to certain pitches or pitch collections from within the total range of twelve-tone materials. In addition, although the musical style of the Trio is fractured and expressionistic, to some extent even intensifying the idiom of the immediately preceding vocal pieces, examples of imitiative pattern-making are part of Webern's response to formal designs which are modelled on rondo and sonata, respectively. Although the first movement 'is not a typical rondo', it, no less than the second movement's sonata, 'adheres closely to the external requirements of the form' (238). Indeed, the second movement follows 'the classical format in a literal way that would not occur again' (155) – another indication of Webern's determination to throw away his Schoenbergian crutches as soon as he had persuaded himself that he had paid the master due homage by trying them out in all good faith.

With the homage to Schoenberg comes a no less significant homage to Beethoven. 'T4 [the Prime form of the series beginning on C] functions as a tonic metaphor in the first movement of Op. 20. The relationship between that transposition and the untransposed rows that act as a tonal focus in the second movement clearly corresponds to the third-relations between movements preferred increasingly by Beethoven' (162): and Bailey goes on to detail other Beethovenian features. Webern's later, more confidently personal twelve-tone compositions would relate to formal aspects of tradition more profoundly and more imaginatively than is the case with Op. 20. But the Trio is far from negligible, and with its completion Webern began an eighteen-year period which produced his most individual and influential achievements as a serial composer.

The method perfected

The richness of those achievements can be gauged from the range of commentaries devoted to the works from Op. 20 to Op. 31. For Kathryn Bailey, interested primarily in the twelve-tone technique, it makes sense to distinguish between the instrumental and the vocal compositions, and to discuss the instrumental works not as a chronological sequence but in terms of four basic formal prototypes: sonata (Opp. 20/ii, 21/i, 22/i, 24/i, 27/i), variation (Opp. 21/ii, 24/iii, 27/iii, 28/i, 30), rondo/ternary (Opp. 20/i, 22/ii, 24/ii, 28/ii, 28/iii) and binary (Op. 27/ii). This categorisation depends on traditional formal templates: and there have been as many complaints about Webern (like Schoenberg and Berg) failing to realise the radical formal potential of the twelve-tone method as there have about serial composers down the years betraying the true tradition in which both thematic material and formal design were generated by tonal and harmonic processes. Bailey's scheme nevertheless has the advantage of highlighting Webern's resourceful solutions to the challenge of interpreting such formal conventions by way of the twelve-tone technique.

Form and feeling

A rather different approach results when Julian Johnson considers the moods and materials of the twelve-tone compositions in relation to expressive as well as technical archetypes. With the Symphony Op. 21, for example, Johnson starts from the point that 'Webern's first plan for the work (November–December 1927) was not purely formal: I. Rondo; lively – sun. II. Variations – moderately. III. Free form: very calmly – moon.' Here there is a startlingly direct, even naïve, conjunction between the work, as form, and the world, as dependent on its 'parental' symbols of night and day: and Johnson's narrative shows that the variations, which were written first, but became the second of the Symphony's two movements, present 'a series of clear topics which not only permeate the late works but ... make clear links to much earlier pieces by Webern'. For example, 'the opening Thema has the quiet, calm lyricism of Webern's slow movements associated with his parents' gravesites'.[6]

Johnson's discussion of the Symphony's first movement, while not ignoring technical aspects, also emphasises the Mahlerian resonance of the opening, where 'the prominence of the horns' suggests 'the archetypal musical symbols of distance and wide alpine spaces' – Webern's favoured landscape. In this way, Johnson supports his claim that 'Webern's landscapes of the mind are profoundly shaped by a way of seeing real landscapes'.[7] Adopting the twelve-tone method did not mean that Webern abandoned the real world of nature and humanity for a purely abstract mental construction within which he could move untroubled by the kind of feelings and associations that his pre-twelve-tone music had embodied in abundance. On the contrary, it seems clear that Webern was able to embrace serialism whole-heartedly only when ways of connecting it to his own experiences, and to his earlier music, became clear to him.

One word – already prominent in a quite different context with Berg – can suggest the necessary connection between calm expression and twelve-tone technique: symmetry. As Webern himself declared in lectures from 1932–3, 'considerations of symmetry, regularity are now to the fore'. Nevertheless, just as feelings of calm and serenity are not unvaried, untroubled, in the music, so the idea that 'considerations of symmetry' in serial music might require entirely new, unprecedented formal and textural procedures was immediately contradicted by the continuation of this statement:

> considerations of symmetry, regularity are now to the fore, as against the emphasis formerly laid on the principal intervals – dominant, subdominant, mediant, etc. For this reason the middle of the octave – the diminished fifth – is now important. For the rest one works as before. The original form and pitch of the row occupy a position akin to that of the 'main key' in earlier music; the recapitulation will naturally return to it. We end 'in the same key!' The analogy with earlier formal construction is quite consciously fostered: here we find the path that will lead us again to extended forms.[8]

There could hardly be a clearer statement of the way in which an analogy between old and new, between perfect fifth-based hierarchy and diminished-fifth-centred symmetry, implies tension as well as balance. Hence the importance of Bailey's comment that, while the Symphony Op. 21 is 'perhaps ... the most eloquent expression of symmetries in all of his *oeuvre* ... perfect reflections are continually thrown out of focus by a variety of means' in order to achieve a 'perfectly judged ... balance between identity and variety'.[9] Not only do the forms used in both movements approach the perfect symmetry of literal palindromes, but the work's basic series (Ex. 6.4) is also symmetrical to the extent that the interval classes of the second hexachord mirror those of the first. This is a neat demonstration of invariance at work within twelve-tone composition: since P-0/R-6 and P-6/R-0 (and equivalent transpositions) are identical, the number of different series forms available is reduced from forty-eight to twenty-four.

Nevertheless, such pre-compositional planning of unity and connectedness simply sets the musical result in more dramatic relief. As I have noted elsewhere

> both movements of the symphony display a fine control of the tension between underlying symmetry and continuous, evolutionary change. In both there is a return to the set-forms from which the movement started out, but this degree of parallelism serves purely as the basis against which the foreground variants

Ex. 6.4   Webern, Symphony Op. 21, main series forms

are composed. The more concentrated, the more dependent on inversion and retrograde the local motivic interplay in a Webern movement becomes, the more important it is that the overall form, while logical and well-proportioned, should not be naïvely predictable or obviously predetermined.[10]

Symmetry and balance

In August 1928, soon after the completion of the Symphony, Webern showed a clear understanding of the rewards and challenges of aspiring to such a delicate balance in a letter to the poet Hildegard Jone, whose landscape-evoking, intensely spiritual writings would become the inspiration for all his later vocal compositions: 'I understand the word "Art" as meaning the faculty of presenting a thought in the clearest, simplest form, that is, the most "graspable" form ... That's why I have never understood the meaning of "classical", "romantic" and the rest, and I have never placed myself in opposition to the masters of the past but have always tried to do just like them: that is to say what it is given me to say with the utmost clarity.'[11]

Webern's conviction about this 'clarity' was matched by his belief that serialism was far from the unnatural distortion of 'real' musicality portrayed by its opponents. Johnson argues that Webern's practice suggests an 'equivalence' between 'the idea of nature as organic proliferation and development and the idea of a music that fulfils the same "natural" pattern'.[12] Yet simply because that music 'resists abstraction through the persistence, albeit in transformed versions, of representational topics of late Romanticism'[13] the organicist ideal is challenged, or at the very least destabilised, by the presence of those tensions and interactions that represent the dialogue between late-romanticism and modernism. In detailed discussions of Op. 27 and Op. 30 elsewhere I have suggested that 'the tragedy-sensing human presence in Webern is ... as salient as the idyllic, pastoral response to nature and belief in the angelic maternal presence', and that 'even those apparently Apollonian later works embody a natural unease and sense of transience in sound and time'.[14]

The special transparency of Webern's serial compositions means that the relations and interactions between ordered twelve-tone series and smaller, unordered pitch-class sets become particularly striking. For example, the ordered series for the Concerto Op. 24 (1931–4) is used at the beginning of the piece in a way that underlines how the twelve tones sub-divide into four motivic trichords, each of which presents a different ordering, transposition and rhythmic as well as dynamic characterisation of the same unordered pitch-class set [014] (Ex. 6.5a, b). A similar

Ex. 6.5a   Webern, Concerto Op. 24, twelve-tone series

Ex. 6.5b   Webern, Op. 24 series as four [014] trichords

Ex. 6.5c   Webern, Cantata No. 1, Op. 29, twelve-tone series

Ex. 6.5d   Webern, Cantata No. 1, Op. 29 series as four [014] trichords

kind of 'three-tone method' is used for the Cantata No. 1, Op. 29 (1938–9): again the source trichord is [014] (Ex. 6.5c, d).

Webern's awareness of this basic property is suggested by the decisions he makes about combining different forms of the series, and about how those combinations are to be managed contrapuntally – which means, also, harmonically. To put the matter trivially: if a twelve-tone composer wants to convey maximum consistency and unity in four-part harmony, he can simply superimpose four different prime forms, with the result that all the chords will be simple transpositions of each other. At the entry of the chorus in the first movement of Op. 29 (bar 14), Webern avoids such a mechanistic process by combining one of each series type: soprano, P-6, alto, R-0, tenor, RI-9, bass, I-3 (Ex. 6.6a). Translated into pitch-class sets in integer notation (Ex. 6.6b), the five chords embody a polarity between degrees of similarity (chords 1 and 3; chords 2 and 5) and difference (chord 4) which is compositionally more rewarding to Webern than absolute identity or complete and utter difference. Such sensitivity to degrees of similarity and difference is also to be found in the music's all-pervading dialogues between homophonic and contrapuntal materials.

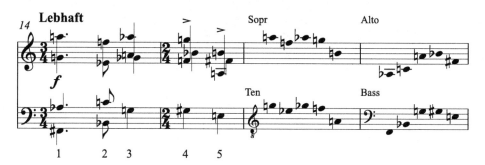

Ex. 6.6a   Webern, Cantata No. 1, Op. 29, first movement, initial choral homophony

Ex. 6.6b   Webern, Cantata No. 1, the five chords as normal order pitch-class sets

Twelve-tone canons

Although Ex. 6.6 gives only the smallest indication of how Webern proceeds in Op. 29, it shows some essential fundamentals at work. Dialogues between ordered and unordered, invariant and variant elements underpin the textural interplay of harmony and counterpoint, in which canons by inversion are often prominent. Webern's use of such time-honoured contrapuntal procedures might be regarded as evidence of pallid historicism, even neo-classicism, and as contradicting the progressive aspirations of his twelve-tone technique. Yet using the canon as a device to generate form and texture underlines the modernistic confrontation between tradition and innovation: between modes of musical thinking that are predicated on tonal distinctions between consonance and dissonance, and post-tonal thinking, which is not.

As Webern the musicologist knew well, the post-tonal canon loosens the bonds of the kind of literal strictness that would result if he had simply set out a homophony by superimposing four prime forms of the series. But it also prevents the total and seemingly random fragmentation that **integral serialists** after 1950, such as Pierre Boulez, were to embrace – if only in a spirit of experiment – as they sought to outdo Webern's concern to move radically away from earlier methods. Webern's achievement was not to struggle with unrealistic attempts to eliminate all the fundamentals of tradition – the modal/tonal principle of centredness, for example.

Ex. 6.7a Webern, Cantata No. 1, Op. 29, third movement, final choral homophony

Ex. 6.7b The five chords as normal-order pitch-class sets

But by focusing, often, on symmetrical chordal elements – like pitch-class set [0257] – he shifted centricity away from the functional principle of roots and a harmony-governing bass line into the literal centre of the texture. The over-riding quality of his music is that of a positive but thoroughgoing interrogation of the most essential principles of compositional thought and expression: not to impose rigid and impersonal laws, but to reveal the understated dramatic intensity that becomes possible when ideal and actuality interact.

The basic alternation of chorale and counterpoint shown at the start of Op. 29 returns at the end, with two brief choral statements followed by polyphony, the solo soprano accompanied by the orchestra. Here again, the texture is built from four series forms, one of each type, and in the first choral statement the chords – all symmetrical – form the tetrachords [0358] and [0156], and the trichord [027] (bars 65–66), this last the result of alto and tenor coinciding on the central A. The final choral statement (bar 70) uses the two symmetrical tetrachords again, differently transposed (Ex. 6.7a, b).

These comments convey little of the subtlety with which Webern creates his finely judged equilibrium. Nor has it been possible to show how Webern responds to the challenge of controlling the interaction of voices within post-tonal canonic textures.[15] As far as Op. 29 is concerned: even if you dislike the rather precious mystical language of Hildegard Jone's text, the strength of the musical expression is undeniable. The ludicity and originality of Webern's twelve-tone compositions helped to win him approval and admiration among post-1945 composers seeking for a new start and, from Dallapiccola and Stravinsky in the 1950s and early 1960s to Kurtág in later decades, the aphoristic concentration and purity of his works has offered an inspiring model. Even so, the early admiration, coupled as it often was with disdain for what was seen as Schoenberg's compromising pseudo-classicism, was destined to erode as leading thinkers about serialism came to conclude that the future of radical compositional thought lay elsewhere. Milton Babbitt preferred to build on Schoenberg's combinatorial model, while Boulez began to speak disparagingly of music which he viewed as offering too little. 'It is like a picture by Mondrian. You can see its perfection and it is very striking, being stripped down to the absolute minimum – a truly austere kind of perfection; but when you see it again at a later date, it offers you nothing further.'[16]

In these terms, the accusation is that Webern developed too narrow a commitment to twelve-tone technique as law – perhaps in conformity with Schoenberg's position, coming 'to see that the Jewish concept of law – as mediation between an unknowable God and the task of constructing a meaningful social existence – offered a parallel, on a grand scale, for his efforts to devise a method of pitch organization that could mediate between the idea of a piece ... and the listener's need to follow a musical argument over time'.[17] Yet even if there is some truth in such notions, Boulez's talk of austerity neglects the glowing intensity and uneasy serenity which, as a conductor, he has done so much to make evident in Webern's music. Repeated encounters with a work like Op. 29 might offer you 'nothing further' in terms of technical understanding: but they can, and should, be the source of unlimited aesthetic refreshment and illumination.

Chapter 7

The later Schoenberg

Laying down the law

'Webern's rarefied twelve-tone compositions exuded the atmosphere of a solitary alpine peak.' This is the view of Richard Taruskin, who sees danger in what he perceives as any artistic retreat from engagement with the earthly world of public, social music-making and appreciation. Taruskin therefore moves from the judgement that Webern's aesthetic was ' "dehumanized" and impersonal' to this claim:

> it is not hard to connect Webern's artistic vision, in the context of the turbulent 1930s, with the Utopian or Arcadian (futuristic or nostalgic) cravings that dominated European social and political thought ... Webern's musical Utopias, the most orderly and disciplined worlds of music ever to have been conceived and realized by that time, seem in their tidy beauty of conception and their ruthlessly exacting realization to broach a theme that was on the mind of every artist then alive – ominous to some, inspiring to others – of art and totalitarianism.[1]

Taruskin is particularly disturbed by Webern's appropriation of the BACH monogram (B flat, A, C, B) as a symbol of a perfection projected through repressively nationalistic thought-processes: and he makes a connection with Schoenberg's most explicit use of the same musical symbol in his Variations for Orchestra Op. 31. 'Bach, for Schoenberg, was above all a German, indeed the greatest of Germans and the fountainhead of German musical art; hence the special venom with which Schoenberg derided "Franco-Russian" attempts to appropriate him. Schoenberg's neoclassicism was uniquely laced with nationalism – the particularly embittered nationalism of a defeated and resentful nation.'[2]

Schoenberg's own embitteredness and anguish during the inter-war decades grew more acute as German nationalism turned against aliens in general and Jews in particular. Hence the strand of critical commentary that associates his commitment to the serial principle with an ambition not only to ensure the on-going supremacy of German music but also to establish certain parallels with Judaism as Schoenberg understood and promoted it. According to William E. Benjamin, 'his adoption, after 1920, of a conscious and extremely rigorous compositional technique was ... an act of self-abasement, and ultimately of worship'.[3] Yet Schoenberg's invention and adoption of the twelve-tone method can equally well be seen as an act of self-assertion, a way of validating his own identity as teacher, prophet, creator.

None of the compositions which apply that 'conscious and extremely rigorous compositional technique' engages more directly with issues affecting contemporary Judaic principles and practices than the opera *Moses und Aron* (1930–2, Act 3 not set to music): and commentators have not been slow to propose that, in Schoenberg himself, a 'Mosaic' quality was uppermost, which might well have been consciously cultivated. As Edward Latham states the case, '*Moses und Aron* ... can be seen as the ultimate statement of Schoenberg's personal creed'[4]: but that 'ultimate statement' was part of a long-lasting commitment to the exploration of the connections between religion, politics and art. 'In politics, he, like Moses, actively pursued a plan to lead the Jewish people into the wilderness toward a new home. In his artistic life he favored uncompromising idealism, turning increasingly to religious subjects for his texted works from 1915 onward, subjects that dealt specifically with Mosaic issues.'[5] Schoenberg clearly did not believe that the twelve-tone method should be used only for compositions with sacred texts or religious subject-matter. Joseph Auner is right to argue that he was no less concerned with 'the social function of art'. He sought to 'stake out a new terrain that would preserve an individualistic idea of art while responding to its changing social situation',[6] and to link this with attempts to bridge the gap between the twelve-tone and the tonal, as in the Six Pieces for Male Chorus, Op. 35 (1929–30). The religious aura and message of *Moses und Aron* were uncompromising. Yet Schoenberg must surely have felt that purely instrumental compositions using the twelve-tone method were not only able to embody the same ethical spirit: they positively needed to do so.

Religion, politics and serialism

The subject-matter of *Moses und Aron* could hardly have been more different from the contemporary domesticity portrayed in his lighthearted opera *Von heute auf morgen*, first performed in Frankfurt on 1 February 1930. But this work served as a significant precedent, showing the composer's increasing confidence at handling twelve-tone processes on a large scale, and allowing himself to treat pitch order within the hexachords of his chosen series forms with a certain freedom.[7]

Schoenberg's libretto for *Moses und Aron* comprises three acts, and the first two were set to music quite quickly, between May 1930 and March 1932. Some sketches for Act 3 were made, but – despite periodic attempts at resuming work on the opera – it was never completed, leaving commentators to argue about whether or not Acts 1 and 2 form a sufficiently satisfying whole.

Ex. 7.1   Schoenberg, *Moses und Aron*, combinatorial series forms: P-0/I-3

The general verdict is that they do. The existence of just two complete acts fits neatly with the focus on two characters, and with a use of twelve-tone technique in which the 'combinatorial' pairing of complementary set forms is fundamental.[8] This pairing is of P-0 with I-3 (Ex. 7.1), and not the more usual P-0/I-5 that Schoenberg had already tried out in the Variations for Orchestra and would use consistently in his later pieces. The role of combinatorial pairings in facilitating large-scale harmonic control, and with certain analogies to tonal structuring and modulation, has encouraged theorists to refer to the 'area' associated with particular pairings in terms of the Prime transposition level in question. Thus, 'A-0', in *Moses und Aron*, implies the combination and interaction of P-0 and I-3, A-1 is P-1 with I-4 and so on.[9]

From the musical point of view, *Moses und Aron* is especially significant for its resourceful application of traditional generic models, with thematic and textural recurrences, when dramatically relevant, suggesting parallels with Wagnerian musico-dramatic techniques. The fact that Moses uses the imprecise pitches and intervals of *Sprechgesang* (speech-song) almost throughout vividly evokes his relative remoteness from the predominant mode of expression of the world in which he finds himself – a world, in the opera, dominated by precisely notated musical ideas. As Milton Babbitt comments, by the time we reach the final scene of Act 1 'by-now-familiar musical materials or clear derivations from them are shaped into an intricate formal mosaic of cross-references to preceding events and within the scene itself'.[10] Pamela White makes the analogy with Wagner quite explicit: 'In both Wagner's operas and in *Moses und Aron*, the tonal scheme is related to the motivic plan of the opera, because certain motives are, at least initially, identified strongly by the ear with a certain key or row. For example, the rolling opening E flat chord of the Rhine in the *Rheingold* which belongs to a family of "nature" *Leitmotive* in E flat may be compared to the opening chords of *Moses und Aron* with P-0 and R-10 as their proper pitch level.'[11]

This emphasis on thematic, motivic identities reflects Schoenberg's concern with the musical characterisation of the opposed yet interdependent personalities of the brothers Moses and Aaron. What we know of Schoenberg's own religious and political beliefs encourages the conclusion that he himself identified more with the tragic, even pathetic image of Moses defeated and in despair at the end of Act 2 than with the sinful and carefree Aaron-led majority. But the opera would not work if both aspects were not represented with equal effectiveness, just as, in other vocal and instrumental forms of all kinds, a balance needs to be struck between opposing forces, their potential for convergence as well as divergence. A short example from the opera's final scene can give some sense of this. In their climactic confrontation the argument between the mellifluous Aaron and the craggy, melody-deprived Moses comes down to whether 'the people', or the 'idea' that should drive and determine the people's destiny, matters more (Ex. 7.2).[12] The soaring orchestral lines that entwine themselves with Aaron's melody underline the sheer magnetism of his personality, while brittle plunging figures and block chords depict the implacable strength of Moses' will.

If Schoenberg's serial works are interpreted primarily as successful, exclusive embodiments of his religious and political ideas, we get conclusions like those of Bluma Goldstein about *Moses und Aron*. She argues that Schoenberg's 'troubling ... antidemocratic and authoritarian predilections and solutions' are as 'blatantly apparent in Moses's autocratic rule over the Israelites' at the end of the opera, as they are in 'the authoritarian organizational structure' he planned for his 'Jewish Unity Party'.[13] From this, it is a short step to finding associations between serial 'rigour' and the totalitarian nationalism whose alleged presence in serial music so troubles Richard Taruskin. However, by shifting the emphasis away from religious politics to philosophical aesthetics, a richer, more ramified interpretation is possible. If, as is now widely acknowledged, Schoenberg's music results from the conviction that conflict is central to the creative process itself,[14] then it is the musical representation and projection of conflict that is at the forefront of his works, string quartets as much as operas, concertos as much as cantatas. It is in working consistently and lucidly with the tensions and accommodations of pairs of series forms superimposed in complementary combinatoriality that Schoenberg's most fruitful technical legacy as a twelve-tone composer resides: and this musical law had a flexibility and a viability not remotely matched by his proposals for a Jewish Unity Party.

Exile and readjustment

In January 1933 Hitler became Chancellor of Germany. On 31 October, Schoenberg and his family arrived in America, where he would remain for the last eighteen years of his life. Aged fifty-nine, he was forced to make a new beginning, but that new start did not lead him to turn against the compositional method he had once connected to the future – and continued superiority – of German music. While Schoenberg was

Ex. 7.2 Schoenberg, *Moses und Aron*, Act 2 Scene 5, bars 1015–1022

perfectly prepared to write non-twelve-tone pieces on occasion, and to return to tonality (as he did in 1939 in order to complete the Second Chamber Symphony, begun in 1906 and abandoned in 1916) his primary enterprise as a composer was to continue along the twelve-tone path as mapped out in the pioneering works of the years spanned by the Suite for Piano and the two acts of *Moses und Aron*. He continued to explore the compatibility between the new method and traditional forms and genres in such works as the concertos for violin and piano and the Fourth String Quartet. Yet there was also a significant group of more freely structured pieces in which his late-romantic, expressionist heritage was shown to be as vividly alive as the more classical side of his inheritance was in the symphonic works.

Two works from this period, the *Ode to Napoleon* (1942) and *A Survivor from Warsaw* (1947), are particularly important for the polarity they embody between the discipline of twelve-tone technique and the mode of vocal presentation that generally avoids specific pitches – speech-song. As with *Moses und Aron*, Schoenberg seemed to regard this melodramatic style of declamation as more appropriate for the urgent communication of ideas and attitudes than the warmer, more lyrical qualities of song. Both works have strong narrative qualities, the *Ode* setting Lord Byron's poetic account of the narrow line between enlightened leadership and tyrannical oppression, *A Survivor from Warsaw* (Schoenberg himself compiled the text) directly confronting the horrors of the Holocaust. In both, the unsung vocal part sets in even higher relief than might otherwise be the case a musical fabric whose twelve-toneness is shown to be open to striking dramatic allusions – in the *Ode*, to Beethoven (the third and fifth symphonies), and in *A Survivor* both militaristic fanfares (Ex. 7.3a) and a Hebrew hymn of exalted defiance sung by a male chorus (Ex. 7.3b).

Aspects of the 'dialectical opposition' that Schoenberg had begun to explore in his earliest twelve-tone instrumental works become very explicit in these highly dramatic contexts: as David Isadore Lieberman writes of *A Survivor*, the work 'draws meaning from processes of disjuncture and disruption, establishing frames of narrative, language, and musical style only to shatter them by the intrusion of radically

Ex. 7.3a   Schoenberg, *A Survivor from Warsaw*, bar 1

Ex. 7.3b   Schoenberg, *A Survivor from Warsaw*, from bar 80, beginning of male chorus (Hebrew text not shown)

dissimilar elements that refuse assimilation. The bifurcation of musical style in *A Survivor from Warsaw* is one of its most striking features; the music that accompanies the Survivor's narrative differs sharply from the setting of the Hebrew prayer', the latter overturning 'the quasi-expressionist musical style of the narrative, replacing it with an extended melodic line comprised of several statements of the serial row'.[15]

The use of serial technique to chart a healing progression from disorder to ordered, eloquent melody is also to be found in the work that immediately preceded *A Survivor from Warsaw*. In Schoenberg's String Trio (1946) – arguably the masterpiece of his American period – a sub-text to do with the composer's recovery from a near-fatal heart-attack inspired music of remarkable formal flexibility and expressive range, in which the role of the twelve-tone technique is to provide that balance between ordered pitch-class successions (as embodied in the constant unfolding of forms of the basic series) and the actual musical material which responds to the ordered series forms in ways which underline their potential for variety and renewal. More will be said about the Trio later in this chapter, but at this point it is important to stress the uncompromising inventiveness with which Schoenberg pursued the implications of his combinatorial twelve-tone processes to the very end of his composing life – an inventiveness that must have been underlined by his convictions concerning the relevance of serialism to his most fundamental spiritual and social convictions, even though the compositions could never be simple, direct analogies or equivalents to those convictions.

In connection with the brief vocal piece *Dreimal tausend Jahre* (1949), one commentator has suggested that 'through his handling of the row, his use of hexachords, and the integration of the voices in shared pitch and rhythmic material, we see a literal treatment of his serial technique that also metaphorically expresses the themes of renewal and resurgence; sentiments Schoenberg strongly felt for the newly created Israel'.[16] Nevertheless, such unambiguous integration was exceptional, and Schoenberg's more representative, and more productive, concern was to give opposition and tension stronger value, not out of the desire to celebrate chaos and despair, but from the impulse to try to do justice to the striving for order and coherence characteristic of modern life. Before the String Trio no work of his American years illustrates the positive musical results of this project more powerfully than the Fourth String Quartet (1936).

'Good old tradition!'?[17] The Fourth String Quartet

When Schoenberg wrote to the commissioner of the Fourth Quartet, Elizabeth Sprague Coolidge, to announce its completion, he declared that 'I am very content with the work and think it will be much more pleasant than the third'.[18] 'Pleasant' is hardly the first word to occur to most later commentators, even if they find no difficulty in suggesting close and productive relationships between the quartet and various models from the tonal past.

Schoenberg's own brief notes on the piece reveal his reluctance to over-simplify, or to identify specific models which it is difficult to recognise aurally. Quoting the opening idea of the first movement, he says that this 'can rightfully be called the main theme, because of its frequent recurrences, some of which one might be inclined to consider as recapitulations in the manner of the sonata form'.[19] But although he quotes other thematic statements from the movement he does not tie them down to sonata-form roles, saying rather that they 'function as landmarks, as guides in a complicated organization, where recognition is obstructed by continuous variations' (59).

Schoenberg is, however, less cautious about the remaining movements: the second, marked 'comodo', 'is closely related to the Intermezzo type. It is an A-B-A form' (60). With the 'Largo' he even uses a term familiar from tonal harmonic analysis: it 'is an A-B-A-B with a modulatory elaboration inserted before the recurrence of the B section. It begins with a recitative' (61); and although he begins his comments on the final Allegro by saying that 'it contains a great abundance of thematic material because every repetition is varied far-reachingly and gives birth to new formulations' (63), he makes clear that there is a main theme, and that a 'true repetition' of it, though with a different accompaniment, occurs towards the end (64).

It was in response to a query about how to analyse the serial content of his works that Schoenberg, citing the Third and Fourth Quartets in 1938 (hence his tentative English), claimed that he would have difficulty in providing such an analysis: 'it would mean that I myself had to work days to find out, how the twelve tones have been used and there are enough places where it will be almost impossible to find the solution. I myself consider this question as unimportant and have always told my pupils the same.'[20] Today it is tempting for musicologists to dismiss such remarks as mere defensiveness, the composer seeking to deflect all those claims that his music was mere mathematics. More significantly, perhaps, analysts after Schoenberg have come to realise that, while it is not such a demanding task to produce a list of all the forms of the twelve-tone series used in the quartet, it is rather more demanding to arrive at an interpretation of the music's style and personality, not simply in terms of thematic processes relating to traditional formal schemes, but by doing justice to an harmonic character that has evident associations with those varieties of tonality which he had once deemed 'extended' or 'suspended'. Just as theorists like Silvina Milstein, Timothy Jackson and Robert Pascall can plausibly propose different formal models from Beethoven's quartets for Schoenberg's designs in Op. 37, so others – most notably Richard Kurth – have felt justified in bringing tonal thought back into the harmonic frame.[21]

On the subject of form, J. Peter Burkholder has argued that analogies between Schoenberg's procedures and those of the first Viennese School (Haydn and Mozart, as well as Beethoven) are

> perfect. Schoenberg has created with his twelve-tone tools a plastic, living, newly grown form that shows the same organic relationship of form and material as in the music of those for whom the sonata principle was still a method or idea rather than a mold or pattern. Schoenberg's sonata does not follow a rigid pattern, but approaches the form in exactly the same way as his classical teachers and creates a unique expression of the sonata idea ... Schoenberg *chose* to use his twelve-tone method to create analogues to the tonal forms of the eighteenth and nineteenth centuries, and he made his analogues both as obvious and as deep and rich as possible.[22]

For some specialists, this goes too far in its transparent strategy of seeking to harmonise old and new. It fails to respond to the full intensity of what Robert Pascall has described as the sense of 'radical guardianship' which Schoenberg expressed with particular force in his famous comments about modelling. 'For if I saw something I did not leave it at that; I acquired it, in order to possess it; I worked on it and extended it, and it led me to something new.'[23] The complexity of that process of acquisition and extension explains why it is so difficult to determine a single, specific formal or stylistic model for any Schoenberg work. Moreover, if the interpretative emphasis shifts from form towards style and genre, the use of march-like figuration in the Quartet's first movement comes as close if not closer to Mahler than it does to Beethoven.[24]

Models for form and style

Martha Hyde's notion of 'dialectical opposition', and Michael Cherlin's discussion of Schoenberg's Heraclitan aura, are both particularly useful when it comes to contemplating the kind of multiple associations in Schoenberg's twelve-tone compositions being considered here. As Hyde argues, the concept of dialectical opposition captures the sense of struggle with tradition so crucial to Schoenberg's music, in which we 'recognise competition as well as continuity, dialogue as well as imitation'.[25] And such a sense of struggle becomes even more palpable when comparisons move from the sphere of form to the specifics of harmonic and tonal organisation. For example, Hyde considers the possible connections between Schoenberg's Third Quartet and Schubert's A minor Quartet, D.804. On the most basic level, Schubert's mediant modulations, dividing the octave evenly into minor or major thirds so that the main tonic can be thought of as forming the symmetrically placed centre of the harmonic structure, are matched by Schoenberg's use of twelve-tone areas delineated by axes of symmetry of which the fundamental P/I pairing provides the centre.

Nevertheless, the more precise and elaborate analogies that are drawn between Schoenberg's twelve-tone procedures and those of a classical or romantic predecessor become, the more difficult it is to claim that we can somehow hear the two types of music in exactly the same way. For example, Timothy Jackson's proposal that the Largo of Schoenberg's Fourth Quartet is modelled on the slow movement of Beethoven's first *Rasumovsky* depends on the thesis that 'Schoenberg discovered that it is possible to hear linear progressions, both small and large-scale, in a post-tonal context. He realized the possibility of creating leading tones, passing tones, and neighbour tones without relying upon traditional definitions of consonance and dissonance'.[26]

This could indeed be one way of understanding what Schoenberg meant by the claim that he 'extended' ideas taken from his revered tonal models, and made of them 'something new'. And Jackson is right to argue that we can learn to hear such linear progressions, recognising them as one of Schoenberg's ways of achieving relative stability and focus for his febrile twelve-tone counterpoint. This is especially so if we also come to understand these progressions not as ends in themselves but as functioning in support of broader generic and textural associations which, in the end, probably do more than the actual progressions to create a perceptible coherence. We can hear Schoenberg in the light of Beethoven, but not in exactly the same way as Beethoven.

Suspended tonality?

An interpretation of Schoenberg's twelve-tone practice that depends less on echoes of specific classical or romantic tonal compositions and more on matters of voice-leading and harmonic structuring is provided by Richard Kurth. In ways which are no less challenging for the listener than the ideas of Hyde and Jackson, Kurth argues for the role of **suspended tonality** and **pantonality** within twelve-tone composition. He suggests that, in Schoenberg's Fourth Quartet, tonality can be thought of as present, but suspended, 'because the tonal references are not explicit and because the logic and coherence of the music does not depend on them in any case. The twelve-tone method emancipates tonality from its role as a long-range and continuous form-building procedure.'[27]

At the end of the first movement (Ex. 7.4), according to Kurth, Schoenberg 'creates a remarkable mode of "closure" that is no longer final or static. He does so, nevertheless, by manipulating the relative gravitational power of several different

Ex. 7.4   Schoenberg, String Quartet No. 4, end of first movement

fundamentals, and by generating a sense of mobility and resolution with respect to them. The result, tonally fluctuant even after it has ceased sounding, is the simultaneous confirmation and suspension of B flat as a tonal centre ... The sensation of D minor ... is mitigated – and suspended – by equally powerful sensations of B flat tonality.'[28] And all this is possible by way of manipulating the particular forms of the work's twelve-tone series that Schoenberg chose as the vessel through which his suspended tonal harmony should pass. As Michael Cherlin argues, 'if Schoenberg's twelve-tone rows, and post-tonal compositions generally, evoke tonality, to that degree they are grounded in tonality. The relationship is circular and dialectical and cannot be reduced to tonal or atonal ... Schoenberg's music exemplifies the kind of art that gains density of meaning through conflicting forces.'[29]

Grammar or gibberish?

Different perspectives on the ending of the Fourth Quartet's first movement arise in a discussion by Roger Scruton. For him, this ending offers an example of 'gestures far removed from the orderly grammar of a tonal cadence'. The point

> is not to deny the reality of musical expectations in atonal music: it is to question whether these expectations can lead towards closure. When the first movement of Schoenberg's Fourth String Quartet comes to a conclusion, you hear the two hexachords of the basic series played alternately as tone-clusters. But if you know the movement will end on the hexachord containing C sharp, this is not because the harmony tends in this direction – rather than towards the rival hexachord – but only because the first violin has been insisting on C sharp for three bars, while the other instruments have studiously avoided it.[30]

There is no sense here of Kurth's subtle inferences concerning B flat major and D minor – rather a failed attempt to relate what is known of twelve-tone practice to aural 'reality'. But even within Scruton's terms it is possible to propose that there is a significant element of harmonic directedness built around Schoenberg's horizontal and vertical use of certain intervals, particularly D natural/C sharp. Of great importance here is the way the leading line (*Hauptstimme*) at the start of the coda's final period (first violin, bar 275) suggests the melodic superiority over D of the very C sharp which returns at the end. The movement contains many anticipations of and preparations for the coda's conclusive focusing of the musical argument around the intervallic invariant represented by D/C sharp as both a melodic and harmonic entity. For example, in the first two bars of the movement the initial melodic succession – D to C sharp, with D the stronger of the two – is complemented at the end of bar 2 by a vertical presentation which gives those same pitch classes an harmonic role. This initial focus on D yields, in the development section (from bar 94), to a much stronger emphasis on C sharp as a focal tone before the angrily ambivalent equilibrium achieved in the recapitulation (from bar 164) and coda, an equilibrium we can learn to accept – and hear – as closural.

Is this music 'outside tonality', as Hans Keller claimed,[31] or the outcome of subtle interfusions between twelve-toneness and suspended tonality, as Richard Kurth proposes? The issue remains the harder to judge when we recall that, despite Schoenberg's habitual tendency in his public pronouncements to downplay the technical and aesthetic consequences of using the twelve-tone method, he cannot, while composing the Fourth Quartet, have ceased to be conscious of the nature of his basic series and of the relationships it created within the twelve-tone group, or matrix, provided by its transpositions, inversions, retrogrades and combinatorial pairings.

Matters of quality

When analysts discuss ways of understanding the serial dispositions at the opening of Schoenberg's Fourth Quartet, the possible musical value of the result is not often dwelt on:[32] and so it is always possible to argue that aesthetic reservations about the consequences of using twelve-tone technique have been brushed aside rather than properly confronted. Such reservations are often, in practice if not in actuality, relatable to Adorno's arguments about the 'impression of meaninglessness' which is said to arise, as in the Fourth Quartet, when what Adorno calls the '"immanent flow" … of tonality, to an extent preserved in free atonality, has finally been "cut off"'.[33] From the way Ben Earle elaborates on these comments of Adorno's (complaining, along the way, that the great philosopher sadly failed to sustain the substance of his Schoenberg critique in his later years), this 'cutting off' of flow is equated with the kind of rejection of organicist continuities that were as much a product of the shift from classicism to modernism as of the specific adoption of twelve-tone serialism. Earle's principal complaint about the main focus on his discussion, Schoenberg's Violin Concerto (1935–6), is of a music that seems 'to drift in and out of sense, sporadically achieving melodic continuity only to throw it away a few moments later'. And 'the feeling of bewilderment' induced by this apparent wilfulness or incompetence on the composer's part 'was only exacerbated by the Concerto's often aggressive tone'.[34]

Earle makes it difficult for the reader to evaluate the status of his critique by refusing to generalise it in relation to post-tonal music in general, or to Schoenberg's twelve-tone music in general. How meaningful is it to judge Schoenberg's concerto by the criteria of those nineteenth-century formal models cited by Earle, to which the continuities of tonal classicism are fundamental? In any case, it could seem as if, after the Piano Concerto (1942), Schoenberg finally abandoned the attempt to achieve close conformities between his post-tonal thematic processes and formal outlines deriving from an earlier age. Does this suggest that he believed himself to have failed in the attempt to 'make something new' by way of such dialogues with tradition? That would have been a very serious admission of defeat, and there is no evidence that Schoenberg, in turning, or returning to new, more overtly modernistic modes of composition after 1942, at the same time renounced his twelve-tone works of the previous two decades as misguided and unsuccessful. Whether or not he thought of these works as embodying sustained dialogues between the positive discontinuities of post-tonal modernism and echoes of the traditional coherences of tonal classicism, it is possible that he saw his music after 1942 as working with those dialogues and confrontations in new ways, rather than as representing yet another completely new start.

Earle's dislike of 1930s Schoenberg seems to have as much to do with the music's alleged aura of aggressiveness as with the 'meaninglessness' of techniques that prevent the establishment of coherent continuities. But even in the Violin Concerto it is possible to hear tenderness and exuberance as well as more turbulent moods. And on the level of form (as suggested earlier), Schoenberg's understanding of twelve-tone properties by way of binary oppositions and combinations works through into structures where, even if local contrasts and conflicts are more disruptive, less continuity-promoting, than would have been the case under the aegis of tonal classicism, they do not result in incoherence. Rather they create a specifically modernistic kind of coherence – Cherlin's 'density of meaning through conflicting forces': that is, the symmetrical balance of opposites, rather than their total integration.

Ambiguous endings

Is it possible that Schoenberg, sensitive to the new challenges of his American environment, was concerned that the 'aggressive' confrontation between old and new in the Violin Concerto and Fourth Quartet was too demanding – as, for some, it still is? Did he concede, if only temporarily, that the explicit lack of organic continuity confused and disorientated listeners in ways which were neither desirable nor necessary? Was the Piano Concerto a conscious attempt to demonstrate a more connected, even organic, kind of twelve-tone composition, with lyrical themes and a more genial atmosphere, the composer's propensity for abrasive, dramatic writing kept subordinate?

If one wants to pursue the possibility of a Schoenbergian crisis of confidence in the early 1940s, one can point to several non-serial, neo-tonal compositions – the *Variations on a Recitative* for organ (1941), the *Theme and Variations* for Wind Band (1943) – in which an element of respect, perhaps even of nostalgia, for traditional compositional values cannot be denied. But the composer evidently decided not to continue down that path. Rather than producing further exercises in 'classicising' serialism, along the lines of the Piano Concerto, Schoenberg (perhaps sensing the new cultural climate after the end of the Second World War) moved to build bridges between post-Mahlerian late-romanticism and his own earlier expressionism, as well as his own very personal spiritual concerns. As the String Trio (1946) demonstrates, this did not mean that allusions to the musical world of, in particular, Beethoven, would no longer be possible. But they would take a very different form from that of the kind of 'serial sonata' to which Schoenberg had devoted so much time in the 1920s and 1930s.

Like its immediate twelve-tone predecessors, the *Ode to Napoleon* and the Piano Concerto, the Trio divides a single-movement into clearly defined sub-sections, but it achieves the kind of balanced oppositions just noted more intensely and flexibly than Schoenberg had managed before. No less radically, the Trio departs at the outset from twelve-tone orthodoxy in that the series used for the principal sections (Parts 1, 2 and 3) consist of eighteen tones: three hexachords, the third reordering the pitch classes of the first, while the twelve-tone series used for the Episodes maintains the order of the first hexachord of the series while reordering the pitch classes of the second (Ex. 7.5a, b). If nothing else, this shows how significant the principle of order was to Schoenberg: consistently treating the contents of each hexachord as, in effect, unordered, was not his primary concern. Instead, the eighteen-tone series balances the now-established twelve-tone principle of combinatorial complementation between hexachords 1 and 2 with the more long-standing compositional principle of permutational, variational pitch-class relations between hexachords 1 and 3 – a dualistic basis for melody which emerges into full focus at the very end of the Trio.

Elsewhere I have suggested that 'Schoenberg could not leave the tentative, yielding statement which ends the Trio – banishing the post-Mahlerian marching assertiveness of its Dionysian stratum – to stand as his most characteristic tone of

Ex. 7.5a Schoenberg String Trio, eighteen-tone series for Principal Sections

Ex. 7.5b Schoenberg, String Trio, twelve-tone series for Episodes

Ex. 7.6a Schoenberg, *Phantasy* Op. 47, ordered series forms, P-0/I-5

Ex. 7.6b Schoenberg, *Phantasy*, opening

voice', on the grounds that this was not the best way to fulfil his belief that 'music conveys a prophetic message revealing a higher form of life towards which mankind evolves'. I then stated that 'the assertive voice of prophecy and religious persuasion soon returns, however, and least ambiguously in *A Survivor from Warsaw* (1947)'.[35] It is this which Robert Pascall tellingly describes as 'perhaps his most Mahlerian work', continuing 'Mahler's line of setting texts of death in war, of combining song and symphony, of using a large orchestra in chamber-like ways, of drawing stylistic plurality into compelling unity, and of giving artistic expression to fundamental values of the human spirit'.[36] The Mahlerian – and Heraclitan – conjunction of violence and tenderness, aggression and submission, is less evident in Schoenberg's final (and ultimately incomplete) choral works, devoted as these *Modern Psalms* are to spirituality as an ideal state. But they are brought together with compelling energy and concentration in his last instrumental composition, the *Phantasy for Violin with Piano Accompaniment* Op. 47 (1949).

As the opening (Ex. 7.6b) shows, the complementary relationship between the violin part (which was written first) and the piano accompaniment is not just a balancing conjunction between violin melody and piano harmony, but a melodic presentation of P-0 placed against the complementary hexachords of I-5 (Ex. 7.6a).[37] This produces twelve-tone aggregates in each of the two full bars, and launches a composition whose vitality and resourcefulness completely belie the composer's age and frail state of health. With its systematic deployment of transpositions of the fundamental P-0/I-5 [A-0] pairing, the *Phantasy* is the apotheosis of the combinatorial, and of neo-expressionism, in a world where much younger composers were beginning to contemplate the possibility of relegating such allegedly compromising apotheoses to the dustbin of history.

Chapter 8

American counterpoints: I

From method to system

The American encounter with serialism has been a matter of extremes. It is almost as if frustration at the initial lack of concrete information, coupled with Schoenberg's refusal to teach twelve-tone composition during his years of residence in America after 1933, laid the foundations for the kind of prescriptive pedagogical initiatives and far-reaching explorations in both theory and composition initiated by (among others) Ernst Krenek and Milton Babbitt. These initiatives exceeded any that Schoenberg himself seemed to think necessary or desirable, but they were an important part of the evolution and dissemination of serialism as something which soon ceased to be the personal property of Schoenberg and his inner circle.

American serialism before the 1940s emerged tentatively from a musical climate in which broader post-tonal possibilities were being tried out. Even though the enormous significance of Schoenberg's contemporary Charles Ives (1874–1954) as a post-tonal pioneer was not widely appreciated during the decades between 1900 and 1940, progressive musical thinking was not confined to neo-classical disciples of Stravinsky. Although home-grown publication of the new twelve-tone music did not get under way until the end of the 1920s, and discussion in local journals before 1930 was tentative in the extreme, one German-speaking American, Adolph Weiss (1891–1971), travelled to Europe in 1925 to study with Schoenberg – first in Vienna, then in Berlin. We would not expect Weiss to have learned about serialism directly from Schoenberg himself, but Weiss' *Six Preludes for Piano* (1927), while no masterpiece, indicates that he was familiar with Schoenberg's Waltz, Op. 23 No. 5, and probably with the Suite Op. 25 as well.

After his return to America in 1927 Weiss became secretary of the Pan-American Association of Composers, a forum for progressive musical thinking in which Ives was involved, along with Edgard Varèse and Henry Cowell, among others. Weiss is believed to have passed on his understanding of twelve-tone technique to Wallingford Riegger (1885–1961), whose *Dichotomy* for chamber orchestra (1931–2) was the first work of his to reflect the new thinking. As a composer already experienced in post-tonal techniques, Riegger used inversion and retrogradation of his basic series, but that series was essentially one of pitches, not pitch classes, and freer, non-twelve-tone elements could be combined with it.

Varèse

The first significant post-tonal composer to emigrate from Europe to America – in 1915, eighteen years before Schoenberg – was Edgard Varèse (1883–1965). He was an outspoken enemy of anything he regarded as contrived or cerebral, and remarks like 'composition according to system is the admission of impotence'[1] appear to be a clear rejection of the serial initiative. Yet the music Varèse composed in America after 1920 is by no means divorced in all respects from serial thinking. It is always difficult in practice to draw a clear distinction between system and consistency, and I have been arguing throughout that – once the constraints of tonality have been loosened or abandoned altogether – degrees of ordering and regularity requiring definition by means other than those of traditional tonal theory make it possible and legitimate to invoke serialism as a guiding principle if not as a governing, all-determining law.

Such a view of Varèse emerges from Theo Hirsbrunner's study of *Octandre* (1923), in which 'various ordering principles can be detected. This music is far removed from chaotic noise.'[2] According to Hirsbrunner, the piece's invariant intervallic elements anticipate much more recent **spectralism** – another 'reaction' against serialism which proves to have elements in common with it. More strikingly still, Denise von Glahn points to sketches from the 1950s for *Déserts* (1950–4) which contain 'evidence of Varèse's attempts at serial composition', including 'over twenty pages of numbered row tables, each painstakingly laid out with the pitches in perfectly aligned columns. Varèse uses yellow colored pencil to identify patterns of reappearing pitches within each of the row transformations.'[3] And although the music found in these sketches does not appear in the final version of the work, the use of serialism as a stimulus – as system provoking its rejection or refinement – is notable. Comparable conclusions can be drawn from Jonathan Bernard's discussion of the same *Déserts* materials.[4]

Similarly, the 'hexachord diagram', apparently from as early as 1910, which Chou Wen-chung discovered in Varèse's papers after his death, indicates an interest in just the kind of ordered manipulation of the total chromatic which any thinking composer seeking to move beyond tonal functions and relationships is likely to have considered. Providing evidence for the relevance of such a formulation as late as *Déserts*, Chou says it is not meant to show 'that Varèse had a system (something he would have abhorred) but to reveal an intrinsic sense of growth and trajectory in his pitch organization, and of spatial and temporal symmetry in his formal structure'.[5] More comprehensive, systematic serialism was the product of comparable ways of thinking about intervallic patterning. If this confirms that at least part of Varèse's musical make-up had to do with what Kyle Gann defines as 'authoritarian modernism',[6] then the affinity between his non-systematic yet meticulously detailed musical processes and the serial techniques of Milton Babbitt and others is more comprehensible.

More pioneers

During the 1930s Ruth Crawford Seeger (1901–53) employed progressive methods which Joseph Straus has termed 'rotational serialism', and which demonstrate the kind of consistent working with pitch collections that could emerge independently of any contact with the Schoenberg school.[7]

Similar independence determined the approach of another member of the Pan-American Association of Composers, Carl Ruggles (1876–1971), whose *Evocations II* for piano (1941) is especially important in the early history of American serialism. On the one hand Ruggles is flexible, reordering the sub-sets of his series and using a subsidiary series in the piece. On the other, he recognises the possibility of a degree of systematic formal process, using the successive intervals of the main series to determine the transposition levels of successive series forms.

By the early 1940s, when Ruggles completed *Evocations II*, the influx of exiles from Europe had brought two composers to America who had already worked with serial techniques. Stefan Wolpe (1902–72) had moved to Vienna in 1933 'to study with Webern, and began using the twelve-note method ... Wolpe assimilated Webern's ideas to the concepts of Hauer and Schoenberg, with which he was already familiar. In *Vier Studien über Grundreihen* [Four Studies on Fundamental Rows] (1934–6) he worked with derived sets and combinatory hexachords, concepts he explored further in *Kleinere Canons* and *Suite im Hexachord*.' However, Wolpe also came under the influence of Jewish, Arabic and Middle Eastern musics, and never lost his commitment to the kind of more popular, practical projects that he had been involved with in 1920s Berlin and Weimar. He settled in America in 1938, and his works of the 1940s 'demonstrated that diatonicism and dodecaphony are not mutually exclusive modes of musical thought'. Although he continued to move with the times – 'the works of the 1960s achieve a synthesis between **Momentform** [pioneered by Stockhausen] and integral serialism' – these principles were applied 'with great latitude and spontaneity'.[8]

Krenek

Like Wolpe, Ernst Krenek (1900–91) was more directly influential and widely valued as a teacher than as a composer. He too reached America in 1938, having encountered Berg, Webern and Adorno in Vienna back in the 1920s, adopting the twelve-tone method, and rapidly becoming a fluent exponent: his *Karl V* (1932–3) was one of the first twelve-tone operas, coming hard on the heels of Schoenberg's *Von heute auf morgen* and *Moses und Aron*.

As a professor at Vassar College, Krenek produced what has a good claim to be the first textbook on the twelve-tone method in English, and its title – *Studies in Counterpoint: Based on the Twelve-Tone Technique* – shows that the author's principal objective was to legitimise serialism as a natural continuation of compositional, pedagogical principles established centuries before. As is clear from the examples of his own work which Krenek provides, he saw the twelve-tone technique as a way of reinvigorating aspects of earlier styles. He declared that 'the primary function of the series is that of a sort of "store of motifs" out of which all the individual elements of the composition are to be developed', and offered cheerfully dogmatic advice to students: 'do not use series with too many equal intervals, because the repetition of the same interval will make it difficult to avoid monotony in the melodic development'[9] – a claim spectacularly disproved by Berg in his Violin Concerto.

Krenek's short manual, with its Webern-derived perceptions about symmetry in serial construction, and one piece written at much the same time, *Lamentatio Jeremiae* (1941–2), were to be influential even on composers who disliked the style of his compositions – Stravinsky, Boulez and Stockhausen among them. And for the next generation of American theorists of post-tonality, including George Perle and Milton Babbitt, Krenek's status as a pioneer was never denied.

Sessions, Copland, Perle

Roger Sessions (1896–1985), Milton Babbitt's main composition teacher, became a committed twelve-tone composer some time after his pupil:

I used the twelve-tone principle for the first time in 1953, in my Sonata for Violin Solo, and have used it to various degrees and in various ways ever since – always, of course, in my own terms. My first use of it was, at the beginning, quite involuntary. I had at various times, for my own self-enlightenment, carried out quite small-scale exercises with the technique, but I still envisaged it as not applicable to my own musical ideas. It was therefore a surprise to me when I found the composition of the Sonata flowed easily and without constraint in its terms.[10]

Written in 1972, those comments describe what had become an increasingly common experience for composers in the 1950s, even if, like Sessions, they had felt rather differently about serialism in earlier years. In 1944, Sessions had declared that

'I believe that in his works written since 1936 Schoenberg has achieved a freedom and resourcefulness which carries them in this respect far beyond his earlier works, especially those in the twelve-tone technique. Regarding that technique itself ... I am in no sense a spokesman for it; I have never been attracted to it as a principle of composition' (260). That Sessions changed his mind probably had more to do with his admiration for Dallapiccola than with what he knew of Babbitt's work. Sessions' biographer, Frederik Prausnitz, believes that 'what Sessions had learned from his Italian friend was the way in which a twelve-tone melody might be combined with elements of apparently tonal reference, as in the case of the minor triads that underlie a deceptive message of hope at the beginning of Dallapiccola's opera *The Prisoner*. Conversely, a tonal idea could become an integral part of a twelve-tone environment, as Sessions found when he really set to work on [his opera] *Montezuma* in 1959' (266–7).

Another American composer, much more prominent and successful with the public by the 1950s than Sessions, had been thinking and working along similar lines. With his Piano Quartet (1950) Aaron Copland (1900–90) 'created a stir in musical circles by adopting Schoenberg's twelve-tone method of composition'.[11] According to Howard Pollack, it was 'after encountering the music of Pierre Boulez while in Europe in 1949' that Copland 'realized that the technique could be divorced from the "old Wagnerian" aesthetic, a lesson confirmed by a growing familiarity with late Webern as well as with the tonal twelve-tone pieces by the Swiss Frank Martin and the Italian Luigi Dallapiccola'. As Pollack makes clear, rejecting that ' "old Wagnerian" aesthetic' did not imply embracing new Boulezian austerities. Copland was convinced that 'in contrast to Schoenberg, Webern, and Berg, who often incorporated "classicalizing principles" derived from tonality or old forms, the new "serial" music threatened to collapse into "near-chaos" '.[12] As early as his *Piano Variations* (1930) Copland had been 'composing with the tones of a motive' in ways which had something in common with serial technique, and the abrasive economy of that work (which Copland orchestrated, belatedly, in 1957) remains a forceful presence in his most ambitious serial pieces, like the Nonet (1960), and the orchestral *Connotations* (1962) and *Inscape* (1967), though this can be effectively offset – as in the large-scale *Piano Fantasy* (1952–7) – by an equally personal lyricism.

Copland was just one of the American composers to attach great weight to possible analogies and accommodations between serialism and tonality. Another was George Perle (b. 1915), whose early fascination with the music of Berg led him to devise a system he called 'twelve-tone tonality'. As one authority has observed, this 'seems to combine two contradictory forces: the equality of the twelve distinct notes in twelve-tone music and the focus on tone centers characteristic of tonality. What the term envelops, however, is the hierarchical focus and priority on notes and note groups provided by symmetrical relationships within the larger symmetrical totality of the twelve notes. Perle has shown how symmetry emerged from within tonality as a "window of disorder", in this [twentieth] century.'[13]

Given this accolade, it might be thought surprising that Perle's actual compositions should be so little known. Perhaps the music is too orderly for its own good. It certainly has a strongly neo-classical stamp at times, the 'truly new' language not managing to reanimate those 'structural elements traditionally considered essential',[14] still less to replace them with viable alternatives. In general, composers since 1950 who have followed the rethinking of traditional formal and textural processes found in Schoenberg during the 1920s and 1930s, have had particular difficulty in achieving memorable and progressive methods of motivic invention and processing. Those who have more in common with the less classicistic phase of early serialism – whether pre-twelve-tone, or as found in Schoenberg's late expressionistic revival in the String Trio and *Violin Phantasy* – seem more successful. Paul Lansky concedes that

> Perle's work is deeply conservative in that his main effort has been to build a musical world whose logic and power is as consistent as that of traditional tonal practice. While this was also Schoenberg's aim in constructing the 12-note system, for Perle there was an intolerable contradiction in Schoenberg's concept of the 12-note series as 'invented to substitute for some of the unifying and formative advantages of scale and tonality' at the same time as it 'functions in the manner of a motive'. Perle's cyclic sets act solely as the basis of the harmonic and contrapuntal syntax of his music; they do not function as motifs.

Nevertheless, in seeking to eschew 'the veneer of the avant garde', and to use 'a few relatively simple musical ideas . . . in different ways and contexts so that the character and quality of these ideas become richer in the process', Perle set himself a formidable task, and the results often have less appeal – and no greater comprehensibility – than serially influenced works by other composers in which 'the veneer of the avant garde' is less strenuously resisted.[15]

Babbitt: words

Milton Babbitt (b. 1916) has written engagingly about his memories of Schoenberg in mid-1930s America, when the Violin Concerto and Fourth Quartet were being composed. 'He was crushed by the fact that these works were not widely performed. Schoenberg, you see, was rather naïve. That his works were not widely performed and widely celebrated changed him a great deal with regard to composing. It had a tremendous effect on him.' Yet Babbitt also refers to a letter from Schoenberg to the conductor Fritz Reiner pointing out that the *Variations* for Wind Band (1943) was 'not one of my main works because it is not a composition with twelve tones'[16]: and this reinforcement of the distinction between quite different ways of composing indicates the kind of *de facto* pluralism that might have been in Babbitt's mind when, during a speech made at the time of the Schoenberg centenary in 1974, he declared that 'Schoenberg could not have foreseen and probably was only peripherally aware of the wilderness into which his music led us'.[17]

The inference is clear: too many composers, unlike Babbitt himself, had spurned the promised land of twelve-tone composition, and those composers, as well as the audiences willing to listen to and admire their music, had failed to respond to the challenges and opportunities which serialism created. But was Schoenberg himself responsible for this failure, as Babbitt seems to imply? Quite understandably, Schoenberg made a distinction between his 'main' compositions and those subsidiary, tonal works which he occasionally produced alongside them – just as Babbitt in his earlier years of necessity distinguished between his serial works and his Broadway-style show songs. No less understandably, Schoenberg himself would probably have preferred an ideal world of exclusively twelve-tone composition to the real world of radically different compositional methods and styles. But he did not in practice deny the possibility of such differences coexisting, and such coexistence became the reality of music after Schoenberg. What Babbitt characterised as a wilderness seemed a rather more fertile and attractively diverse landscape to the vast majority of composers after 1950.

A very different perspective on this pluralism can be found in a brief essay on Schoenberg written by the leading musical minimalist Steve Reich in 1995. He accepts that 'Schoenberg's influence in America was quite pronounced during the 1950s and '60s', and 'anyone writing music that was not either serial or aleatoric [that is, with a certain freedom of choice allowed to the performer] was simply not worthy of the slightest consideration'. That this state of affairs did not persist is one result, according to Reich, of

> some fundamental problems in Schoenberg's musical thinking. The main problem is this: the reality of cadence to a key or modal center is basic in all the music of the world (Western *and* non-Western). This reality is also related to the primacy of the intervals of the fifth, fourth, and octave in all the world's music as well as in the physical acoustics of sound. Similarly for the regular rhythmic pulse. Any theory of music that eliminates these realities is doomed to a *marginal* role in the music of the world. The postman will *never* whistle Schoenberg. (It has been almost 100 years but even 200 more will bring no improvement in this respect.)

Reich is clear that 'this doesn't mean Schoenberg was not a great composer': but in Reich's view 'it is no accident that his (quite understandably) most popular works all predate his invention of the 12-tone system ... This is not due to a limitation in the intelligence of listeners, it is due to a limitation of Schoenberg's later music.'[18]

Such views are far from unusual: they are also given special weight in the quite different context of Roger Scruton's writings on aesthetics.[19] But Reich is seeking to maximise the differences between the serial music of Schoenberg, his pupils and followers, and the process or systems music written by himself, Terry Riley, Philip Glass and others. As a result, Reich doesn't pursue the possibility – as many composers have – that even if a 'theory of music' eliminates such 'realities' as the acoustic primacy of certain intervals, compositional practice can effectively recontextualise these realities in ways which remain true to some if not all of the principles of the twelve-tone method as Schoenberg formulated it. Reich's comments (his music will be considered briefly later) are more directly relevant to Babbitt and the younger generation of post-war European serialists centring around Boulez and Stockhausen than to the Schoenberg generation of twelve-tone composers, or to some other post-war serialists, especially Stravinsky and Dallapiccola, the effect of whose initiatives was to open up the possibility of a new progressive mainstream in composition, quite distinct from the bywaters of the strictest, anti-hierarchic serial technique. Nor can Reich's remarks be regarded as justifying the claim that his generation of minimalist composers had absolutely nothing in common with serial thinking.

In essence, the difference between Schoenberg and Babbitt is theoretical – to do with the way in which serialism is conceived. Bryan Simms has effectively summarised this as follows: 'when Babbitt first sketched his ideas in print in 1950, the theory of twelve-note music was in its infancy. Schoenberg's principal statement on the subject, the 1941 lecture "Composition with Twelve Tones", had just appeared. René Leibowitz's *Schönberg et son école* (1946: Eng. edn., 1949) continued pre-war conceptions of the twelve-note method by adopting the interpretation of it espoused by the Viennese composers, who stressed its congruity with traditional forms and compositional principles.'[20] This aspect of Leibowitz's work enraged his French pupil Pierre Boulez who, along with others of his generation, saw assertions about 'congruity with traditional forms and compositional principles' as a betrayal of what serialism should properly stand for.

'Babbitt's outlook on twelve-note music', Simms continues, 'was entirely different from that of any of these earlier writers. Twelve-note music, he says, is the product of a closely integrated and autonomous precompositional system': and Simms argues that Babbitt as a theorist is actually closer in principle to the ferociously anti-atonal Schenker, as well as to such very un-Schoenbergian composers as John Cage and – yes – Reich, for whom 'compositional freedom is an illusion that is readily abandoned to system and process'.[21]

The implication of Simms' comments – widely accepted at the present time – is that Babbitt's theories have been much more influential and significant than his compositions. Few writers who analyse serial music (including that of Schoenberg, Berg and Webern) would wish to avoid all contact with ideas stemming from Babbitt: yet, by the same token, few writers are inclined to look to Babbitt's compositions for definitive evidence of the aesthetic or even technical significance of those theoretical ideas.

Sometimes, contact with Babbitt's ideas about serialism takes the form of scornful dismissal, as in Roger Scruton's characterisation of 'a kind of elaborate pretence at musical discipline: a congeries of rules, canons, and theories, and a mock exactitude (manifest at its most comic in the scores of Stockhausen and the set-theoretic musicology of Babbitt and Forte) which strives in vain to overcome the listener's sense of the arbitrariness and senselessness of what he hears'.[22] Since Babbitt had previously described an article of Scruton's as containing not only 'outrageous preposterousness' but also a 'congeries [that word again] of absurdities',[23] it might be thought unprofitable to look further in either writer for any degree of constructive debate.

Scruton's diatribes amount, among other things, to a song in praise of that threatened if not completely destroyed bulwark of musical civilisation, the bourgeoisie, while Babbitt is even more despairing of 'the inapposite milieu of the public concert hall', where 'complex contemporary music' is concerned. Against Scruton's 'common musical culture', celebrating 'custom, habit, and tradition', Babbitt looks towards a situation in which music is best made available 'in recorded form, and is so available to anyone who is interested, to be played and replayed at the listener's convenience' (75). Babbitt made these remarks in 1960, well before those developments in digital technology which came too late for him to engage with, so that he 'returned to exclusively non-electronic media' (453). Yet he foreshadows the kind of thinking found in the British composer Richard Barrett (b. 1959), who in 1998 wrote that 'as far as I am concerned, the "modernist project" is still in its early stages': that project is 'crucially informed by what is becoming an "age of digital reproduction", beginning from the invention of electricity, in the same way as modal music has its roots in the human voice and tonal music in instruments. It is *far* too early to speculate meaningfully on what the implications of this may end up being. Nevertheless we ignore it at our peril.'[24]

Babbitt: music

If Barrett's prophecy proves accurate, it could also mean that Babbitt's compositions might yet be taken up as models by later generations more enthusiastic about the kind of possibilities for new technical developments they display than those of the later twentieth and early twenty-first centuries have been. Yet if, as Bryan Simms' summary implies, the kind of theory-based ideas about serialism that Babbitt carries over into his compositions render the details of his compositional practice even more difficult to hear in real time than those of Schoenberg or Webern, it is easy to conclude that intellectually conceived methods are even more likely to generate arid and non-communicative music. Babbitt's talk about the 'high degree of "determinacy"' that distinguishes his music from most other kinds – not just the popular songs he himself instances – prompts the pragmatic conclusion that it is the results of such determinacy, rather than its actual processes, that will be heard. Yet uppermost among those results are not so much the elements of thematic identity and process which many serialism-influenced composers have employed since 1950, but rather – and more challengingly to aural perception and contemplation – the particular textural consequences of a system of composition that brings the interaction between unity and diversity, the centripetal and the centrifugal, to new levels of intensity. The irony here – and it is surely a rich one – is that because the purest kind of serial music is, in effect, athematic, it becomes difficult not to hear the result as concerned with randomly rather than systematically ordered musical materials – pitches, rhythms, dynamics, modes of attack. The strictest serial music, lacking thematic identities and explicit generic associations, sounds and even looks unordered, at least as far as pitch content is concerned.

One of the simplest examples of such strictness and comprehensive control from his own music which Babbitt has discussed is the unaccompanied clarinet solo that begins his *Composition for Four Instruments* (1948). This comprises twelve different notes, but Babbitt intends to signal, by the strong contrast in register between notes 3 and 4, that a principle other than simple succession is involved. The most systematically ordered form of the series consists of the first trichord, as Prime, and transpositions of I, R and RI forms of the same trichord (Ex. 8.1a). But instead of these four trichords being presented in strict linear succession, they are stratified into four registral regions (which might be thought of as bass [I], tenor [P], alto [RI] and soprano [R]) and distributed irregularly, with a particularly complex intersection between the alto and soprano statements (Ex. 8.1b).[25]

Thus far, it might appear that Babbitt is using a fairly traditional kind of twelve-tone conjunction between fixed and free – the fixed order of the 'real' series and the actual, more freely conceived order of the melodic line. This is also an elementary instance of what, if the trichords were played by four different instruments, would be the kind of serial polyphony in which a single series form is divided up between different contrapuntal voices. Arrange the four trichords in a vertical format, as shown in the first column of Ex. 8.1c, and the result is an aggregate – a single twelve-tone sequence dispersed, in this case, into four registral regions. As the next three

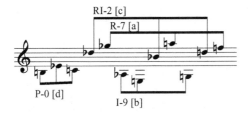

Ex. 8.1a Babbitt, *Composition for Four Instruments*, initial twelve-tone statement as four registrally distinct trichords

Ex. 8.1b Babbitt, *Composition for Four Instruments*, opening clarinet solo

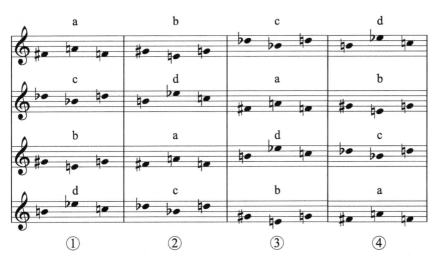

Ex. 8.1c Babbitt, *Composition for Four Instruments*, initial array of four aggregates

columns of the example show, however, Babbitt completes this initial four-aggregate array with complementary statements of the four ordered trichords from Aggregate 1, rather than building an array from four versions of the same ordered twelve-tone series.

Ex. 8.2a shows the array for the first seven aggregates of Babbitt's solo piano piece *Post-Partitions* (1966), with the particular notational refinement that the pitch classes with stems upwards are staccato notes, those with stems downward legato: this can be checked on Ex. 8.2b, which shows the first bar of the piece. Visually, and aurally, the relationship between the pitches of the score and the pitch classes of the twelve-tone aggregate are clear enough, with the six dyads well differentiated in register.

Babbitt's starting point for this work – hence his title – was the ordered hexachord type used in his earlier piano piece *Partitions* (1957). The nature of this can be deduced if the twelve horizontal lines from Ex. 8.2a are followed through. Not all of these present the full hexachord, but those that do derive from the same unordered hexachord [023457]. This could take the form F sharp, A flat, A, A sharp, B, D flat, and Babbitt's lowest line orders this as A, F sharp, A sharp, B, D flat, A flat. The next lowest line has a transposed inversion: E, G, E flat, D, C, F: the third and fourth lines up have the transposed retrograde and retrograde inversion of the same ordered hexachord. The ways in which these hexachordal lines are distributed across the array, sometimes with quite substantial gaps between constituent pitch classes, is a vivid indication that Babbitt is less concerned with the motivic potential of his series and more with the relative harmonic qualities achievable when different versions are combined in twelve-tone polyphony. In addition, it is much less important for Babbitt than for Schoenberg or Stravinsky

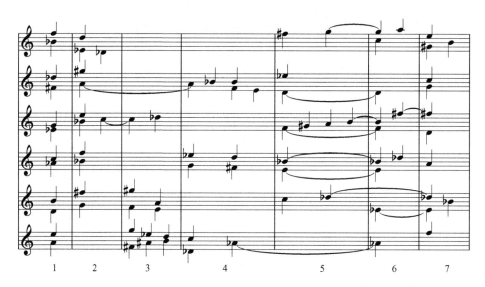

Ex. 8.2a   Babbitt, *Post-Partitions*, first array block of seven twelve-tone aggregates

Ex. 8.2b   Babbitt, *Post-Partitions*, bar 1 (first aggregate)

to determine which pitch class functions as the 'true' 0. Harmonic centring and hierarchy is less relevant to Babbitt than the relative relationships between all the twelve-tone materials.

Returning now to bar 1 of *Post-Partitions*, the music is notable for its extreme degrees of dynamic contrast, and for the many different rhythmic units present within the single 4/4 bar. This is a consequence of Babbitt's use of twelve-element series, not only for dynamic levels, but also to determine points of pitch onset, or attack. This is the **time-point series**: in Paul Griffiths' eminently straightforward explanation, 'the time point of a musical event is a measure of its position within the bar. Thus if the time signature is 3/4 and the unit of measurement is the semiquaver, a note attacked on the first beat is said to occur at time point zero, a note attacked a semiquaver later at time point one, and so on.'[26]

What ratchets up the serial complexity of *Post-Partitions* is Babbitt's elaboration of the principle of 'sixness' most immediately apparent in the six dyads of the pitch layout for the first aggregate. Rather than distribute these dyads throughout

Time points	0	1	2	3	4	5	6	7	8	9	10	11
Dynamics	*fffff*	*ppppp*	*pppp*	*ppp*	*pp*	*p*	*mp*	*mf*	*f*	*ff*	*fff*	*ffff*

Ex. 8.2c   Babbitt, *Post-Partitions*, series for Time Points and Dynamics

the bar by way of a single time-point series Babbitt presents each of the six by way of six different rhythmic grids which divide the crotchet in six different ways: by 8 demisemiquavers, 7 septuplet semiquavers, 6 sextuplet semiquavers, 5 quintuplet semiquavers, 4 semiquavers and 3 triplet quavers. The immediate consequence of this is that the six rhythmic grids run through twelve units (numbered 0 to 11 by Babbitt) at different rates within the bar. Ex. 8.2c shows the process for dyad 3 (E flat/G), where both statements of the dyad relate to the rhythmic grid which divides the beat by 8 demisemiquavers. The time-points in question are 5 (that is, after five demisemiquavers – 01234 – have elapsed) and 10, after a further four demisemiquavers have passed. Comparing these entries in the time-point series with those in the dynamics series shows that the comparable levels are 'p' and 'fff', and these are indeed the dynamic levels assigned to the two statements of dyad 3.

A similar operation for the other five dyads confirms the intricate connections between time-points and dynamics that represent Babbitt's version of integral serialism in *Post-Partitions*. One further example: the twin statements of the uppermost dyad, B flat/F – have the dynamic levels 'ff' and 'pppp', indicating time-points 9 and 2. These actually belong to two different rhythmic streams: the *ff* dyad is time-point 9 in the grid of quintuplet semiquavers, while the *pppp* dyad is time-point 2 in the grid of triplet semiquavers – 2 Mod. 12,[27] that is, since a full run of twelve triplet semiquavers have already passed before the second one begins.

This is just the briefest demonstration of the challenges which face analysts of this music – especially analysts attempting to provide an introductory explanation, rather than a discourse for specialists already well versed in such procedures. Possibly even more daunting are the challenges confronting the performer. Requiring a pianist to make the superfine rhythmic and dynamic distinctions shown in bar 1 of *Post-Partitions* renders Babbitt liable to the same kind of objections applied to the brief attempts of Boulez and others to employ twelve-level dynamic and duration series a decade earlier. The intended character of the music may well be conveyed adequately if basic ternary contrasts between very loud, moderate, and very soft dynamic values are achieved. To this extent, Ex. 8.2b represents the kind of extreme conjunction between system and sound whose intricacy is best justified as a stimulus to the composer to move towards less rigid ways of achieving similar musical effects, should these be deemed desirable.

Andrew Mead has plausibly stressed Babbitt's concern to distance his music as far as possible from entirely mechanistic routines:

> it is important to realize that Babbitt's musical thinking respects the profound perceptual differences between the various musical domains. His use of analogous abstract structures in perceptually different dimensions always takes advantage of the possibilities unique to each dimension. Thus, while his rhythmic and pitch structures may be based on the same abstract array, the ways details are composed out in each domain reflect the properties of that domain. The analogy between domains remains at the abstract level of similar distribution of material and patterns of recurrence.[28]

Hearing a wide range of Babbitt's compositions should reassure the listener that the result is far from an invariable emphasis on 'points' – on textures as fragmented and dispersed – to the exclusion of line, with all the connected, sustained qualities that go with that concept. Indeed, Mead's very fair conclusion is that 'nothing is unconnected . . . Compositional decisions at any level will ramify into every level, so that our sense of progression invokes not just our immediate sense of the moment but how that moment is echoed and reflected through the depths . . . Babbitt's music depends on the tension between levels, the interplay between the specifics of a moment, or a passage, or a piece, and their contexts within a passage, a piece, or his work as a whole, and ultimately within the chromatic world of the twelve-tone system' (263).

That is an eloquent summary of what one might regard as the essentially classical cast of Babbitt's musical thought, the interplay and tension subordinate to the unifying force of the grand design, the all-embracing system. Yet Mead's very last sentence – 'it is this inclusiveness that makes his work most deeply and affectingly human' – risks overkill. Why is inclusiveness more human and more affecting than working with the kind of less strenuously conceived tensions between freedom and flexibility that most other composers have found more productive? It is difficult to argue that Babbitt's music has as wide a range of expressive associations and concerns as that of such composers as Luigi Nono, Pierre Boulez, Elliott Carter and Peter Maxwell Davies, whose status as serialists is more ambiguous, even though their music is inconceivable without the example of serialism.

Babbitt: music, words and politics

On the relatively rare occasions when Babbitt sets a text it is possible to sense points of contact between verbal expression and musical character, even in the absence of thematic or motivic working of a traditional kind. In a detailed account of Babbitt's *A Solo Requiem* (1976–7), which includes settings of Hopkins, Meredith, Stramm

Ex. 8.3   Babbitt, *A Solo Requiem*, bars 83–85

and Dryden, and is dedicated to the memory of a friend of Babbitt's, the composer Godfrey Winham, Joseph Dubiel has much to say about the possible affiliations between textual and musical factors. But he sensibly creates the impression that vocal writing 'directly reflective of the text' is just one aspect of a rich and multivalent work whose interest for the serious commentator lies primarily in its aggregate technique.[29] Commenting more succinctly on the same work, *The New Grove* finds that it 'incorporates a wide range of vocal techniques and reveals the extraordinary range and sensitivity of Babbitt's response to a variety of dramatic and lyrical poetic texts'.[30] As one very short example suggests, the question asked in Gerard Manley Hopkins' sonnet – 'Comforter, where where is your comforting?' – is given extreme intensity by the contrast between fixed, repeated pitches on the one hand, and immense distances of register and dynamics on the other (Ex. 8.3). While the very precise musical values shown by the notation are evidence of Babbitt's characteristically convoluted serial manipulations, the raw feelings expressed by the text are in no way cauterised by the musical setting.

Richard Taruskin ascribes Babbitt's role as the earliest and truest pioneer of genuinely all-embracing serialism to a particular set of professional circumstances. He was 'trained in mathematics and formal logic as well as music'.[31] But his academic environment as a long-standing member of the Princeton University faculty did not mean that he was totally detached from the real world of politics and culture. While an optimist, to the extent that 'he sought in his own domain the joyous triumph of technology', his 'brand of post-war modernism' can be related to the 'overarching cold-war debate. Deeply concerned with the restraint that political tyranny can exercise on thought and expression, and aware that even in open societies majority opinion (or commercial interests) can marginalize – or even, without explicitly prohibiting, effectively exclude – unpopular or abstruse thought, Babbitt allied himself and his exceedingly rationalistic musical activities with the philosophy known as logical positivism, the toughest and most skeptical variety of "show-me" empiricism' (155). Similarly, as Martin Brody has described it, Babbitt acted from the conviction that 'scientific language is the medium of the responsible musical citizen', and that 'if the university is the fortress against cultural popularism, and cultural popularism threatens serious music, then scientific language safeguards serious music'.[32]

Taruskin does not regard the combination of politics and logical positivism as a good basis for musical composition. If 'the only definition of a work of art that truly matters … is not what its effect may be, but what skills its manufacture (or reception) may require',[33] this simply reinforces the modernist heresy. If 'Schoenberg saw the evolution of music as headed inexorably towards the triumph of literate practice (representing "culture" and "autonomy") over every aspect of oral practice (representing atavisms of the "primitive" and the "contingent")', then Babbitt can be seen as 'the ultimate protagonist of literacy over orality' (170). This is not to question Babbitt's integrity. 'The sacrifice of a listening (rather than a looking) audience was a price he was prepared to pay for purity', and 'it was only when some of Babbitt's colleagues and former pupils began claiming for academic serialism qualities (such as traditional emotional expressivity) that lay audiences complained of missing, that allegations of bad faith became common' (172). And the ironic outcome of academic serialism's concern with 'the sort of fixity and exactness in the domain of physical sound that it already possessed in the conceptual domain of notation' – computer-generated sound – involved those very electronic media that 'would subvert the triumph of literacy and give music a new future' (173). Babbitt's optimism, we infer, was as misguided as his fetishisation of readability, even though he might well be satisfied that, as an academic serialist, he has achieved as much by way of performance, publication and general exposure, against majority opinion and commercial interests, as could reasonably be expected.

Consequences and contingencies

Taruskin is right to follow the general historical line that the pure (in my terms, athematic) serialism explored in the early 1950s soon gave way to less abstruse forms of compositional thinking, in America and Europe alike. Just as there have so far been few reasonably prominent figures in American music who can be claimed as keepers of the Babbitt flame – or, for that matter, of the alternative, more explicitly hierarchic system ('twelve-tone tonality') proposed by George Perle – so in Europe the efforts of Boulez, Nono, Stockhausen and others to promote an integrated serial practice soon dissolved into more pragmatic adaptations and compromises, not necessarily rejecting all serial features but contextualising them differently. What this means in practice is that ultimately the influence of Schoenberg, Berg and Webern has proved to be rather more decisive than that of Babbitt. So, while it is richly ironic that the hothouse in which European integral serialism briefly flourished, centering on the Darmstadt summer schools of the early 1950s, and which owed much to American funding and logistical support, was not exposed to the Babbitt mode of thinking in any systematic way, that absence served to strengthen the role of earlier twelve-tone compositional practice as background to the new initiatives being tried out at that time.

Taruskin's characterisation of serial music in general as the acme of literacy against orality needs challenging, since it attaches primary significance to the perceptibility of a compositional method rather than to the use to which those methods are put. As I have indicated, the dictatorial optimism of post-1945 serialism is perhaps most fundamentally evident in the conviction that *twelve-tone* composition, eradicating motivic identities and processes, was superior to twelve-tone *composition* (to evoke the classic Schoenbergian distinction). Even though such music might not lack all aspects of harmonic rhythm and differentiation, it is only if texture as such, and the moods it creates, can be deemed 'thematic' that it can be profitably compared with more mainstream compositional methods.

Chapter 9

American counterpoints: II

Stravinsky: a balance of tensions

The greatest crisis in my life as a composer was the loss of Russia, and its language not only of music but of words. The second great crisis follows *The Rake's Progress* [1947–51], though I was not aware of it as such at the time, continuing as I did to move from work to work. The 'period of adjustment' was even longer, and looking back on it now [c. 1970] I am surprised myself at how long I continued to straddle two 'styles'. Was it because at seventy unlearning is as difficult as learning? In any case, I now see the *Movements* [1958–9] as the turn-of-the-corner in my later music.[1]

In these comments Stravinsky's American friend and collaborator, Robert Craft (b. 1923), assumes the persona of the composer in order to pin down certain crucial aspects of his later development. Igor Stravinsky (1882–1971), having settled in America in 1939, came to twelve-tone composition in the 1950s, working his way through that 'period of adjustment' before arriving at the fully fledged twelve-tone technique of *Threni* (1957–8). Perhaps it was Stravinsky's embrace of what seemed to be a genuinely non-tonal serialism, akin to his own, that encouraged Milton Babbitt to comment in a 1964 article on Stravinsky that 'the formal systems – of which the tonal system and the twelve-tone system are, respectively, instances – are, under no conceivable principle of correspondence, equivalent; they are so different in structure as to render the possibility of a work being an extended instance of both unthinkable'.[2] That is true, if the tonal system is interpreted in the way it was conceived by Heinrich Schenker (1868–1935), the theorist of harmony most admired by Babbitt.[3] But if tonality is regarded in the way Schoenberg conceived it, the situation is different[4]: and just as the concepts of extended and suspended tonality can be brought to bear on the analytical interpretation of Schoenberg's post-tonal, twelve-tone works, there seems no reason not to consider Stravinsky's in similar ways.

Here was a composer who, in the early 1940s, had already endorsed a concept of harmony involving 'poles of attraction' which 'are no longer within the closed system which was the diatonic system', and could be brought together 'without being compelled to conform to the exingencies of tonality'.[5] Add to that a long-standing modernist aesthetic which, in Richard Taruskin's words, makes Stravinsky 'the very stem' of a commitment to compositional designs founded in such qualities as 'stasis, discontinuity, block juxtaposition, moment, or structural simplification',[6] and it no longer seems quite so improbable that one reason why Stravinsky felt able to become a serialist was that he could continue to explore formal principles and harmonic procedures which were not totally opposed to those he had employed before.

> His music deploys strong centrifugal forces, with each of the formal units pulling away from the others by asserting its own independence and integrity. But the centripetal forces are equally strong, holding the sections together. The result in Stravinsky's music is not the gentle harmonic reconciliation of opposing tendencies, but rather a furious tension, at all levels, between the forces of integration and disintegration. Stravinsky's music gives no sense of spontaneous growth from a single seed, of a seamless fabric, a single improvisatory sweep. It is vigorously anti-organic and anti-developmental; its jagged edges are everywhere apparent. The forces of abruption, however, are everywhere balanced by equally strong ties that bind the music together.[7]

In themselves, none of these technical considerations serve to guarantee that any of Stravinsky's serial compositions are artistic achievements on the same level as such late-romantic or neo-classical works of his as *The Firebird*, *The Rite of Spring*, the *Symphony of Psalms* or *The Rake's Progress*. The story is still told of a tired, depressed Stravinsky, approaching his seventieth birthday, and convinced that his largest neo-classical score, *The Rake's Progress*, was probably a failure which had worn him out, coming under the influence of the bright young American musician Robert Craft, whose enthusiasm for the work of Schoenberg and Webern, and experience in conducting it, was rare in America at that time.[8] Even if Craft was primarily responsible for ensuring Stravinsky another fifteen years of active creative life, the story continues – and Craft himself has declared that 'I do not believe Stravinsky would ever have taken the direction he did without me'[9] – those years amounted to little more than an addendum to the period which really mattered. One can be moved by the pathos of an ageing composer desperately attempting to keep up with those young Turks like Boulez and Stockhausen whose praises he sang in the pages of the conversations put together by Craft, and concerned in his final works to leave behind memorials in sound to a range of his most illustrious contemporaries, including Dylan Thomas, T.S. Eliot, Aldous Huxley and J.F. Kennedy. But Stravinsky's embrace of serialism demonstrates that he had not lost his awareness of the strengths which had been so important in the earlier part of his career, and on which his remarkable success between 1910 and 1940 had been founded.

Stravinsky could well have believed that *Movements for piano and orchestra* was the work in which he had 'turned the corner' into full mastery of serial technique along the non-tonal, athematic lines preferred by Babbitt and the new European twelve-tone composers. But he quickly returned to more familiar territory, with the use of something akin to tonal centres, and with echoes of his earlier modal practices, in such later serial compositions as *Abraham and Isaac* (1962–3) and *Requiem Canticles* (1965–6). For this reason alone it is far from futile to explore an unambiguously non-twelve-tone composition like *The Rite of Spring* in terms of pitch-class sets, as Allen Forte has done, arguing that it was here that 'Stravinsky employed extensively for the first time the new harmonies that first emerged in the works of Schoenberg and Webern around 1907–8'. Forte also asserts that 'the *Rite of Spring* is unified ... by the unordered pc sets, considered quite apart from the attributes of specific occurrences. In this respect, *The Rite of Spring* resembles the extraordinary early atonal works of Schoenberg and his students, and, indeed from our contemporary vantage point it has more in common with those works than with the later works of its composer – in particular, with the so-called neoclassical works, at least as we understand them now.'[10]

Forte wrote this before the publication of extensive analytical studies of Stravinsky by Pieter van den Toorn and Richard Taruskin, which rejected the claims that *The Rite* had little in common, technically, with the neo-classical works, and that the work's most important 'harmonic units' benefited from alignment with contemporary Schoenberg and Webern rather than with other, more tonally orientated uses of modality – primarily the octatonic (eight-tone) scale, with its regular tone/semitone, or semitone/tone alternations – by Rimsky-Korsakov and Skryabin.[11] Forte's own later writings have given due emphasis to octatonicism as one of the most significant post-tonal initiatives, even for Webern[12]: and study of Stravinsky's serial pieces reinforces those elements of continuity between modal symmetries and serial pitch structuring which are by no means completely alien to his earlier procedures.

Stravinsky: series and centres

Evidence of the kind of hierarchic harmonic thinking, amounting to a degree of tonal centricity in most if not all of Stravinsky's serial works, aligns them with the serial 'mainstream', extending from Schoenberg, Berg and Dallapiccola to, among others, Peter Maxwell Davies and even to a degree, the later Boulez. As Joseph Straus notes, 'Stravinsky accepted from the outset the Schoenbergian idea that four members of the series class, bound together by some musical relationships, might function as a referential norm, somewhat in the manner of a tonic region in a tonal composition'.[13] And even if, as Straus goes on to suggest, Stravinsky's practice amounts more to a critique of Schoenberg than an endorsement, it underlines the point that Stravinsky's twelve-tone compositions are by no means in abject thrall to Craft-promoted Webern. They profit from Stravinsky's magpie-like fascination with that composer's economy and contrapuntal dexterity, as well as with the fervent spirituality of such texted pieces as *Das Augenlicht* and the two cantatas. Yet the result was a very different kind of harmonic character, deriving from a different way of exploiting symmetry, and a quite different religious perspective, the Russian Orthodox Stravinsky coming rather closer to Catholic liturgy and biblical texts than the Roman Catholic Webern ever did. As Stephen Walsh memorably describes Stravinsky at work on *Threni*: 'from the start, Stravinsky does things differently from Schoenberg, or even Webern, "weighing" the intervals in his row like an assayer, tossing them from hand to hand, turning them over, subtracting one element and adding another, until the whole makeup of the music seems almost cruelly clear and peremptory. The famous opacity of Schoenberg is completely absent. This is *par excellence* an objectified music, take it or leave it.'[14]

The vital technical difference between Webernian and Stravinskian serialism can be seen by comparing a typical Webernian matrix (see Ex. 6.3 above) with the material given in Ex. 9.1. This reproduces Joseph Straus' representation of the serial charts for *Movements*,[15] and shows that, rather than relying on transposition (as well as inversion and reversion) of the ordered series to generate new versions, Stravinsky adopts Krenek's method, using multiple rotations of the various series forms: hence Straus' preferred designation of Stravinsky's technique as 'twelve-tone serialism based

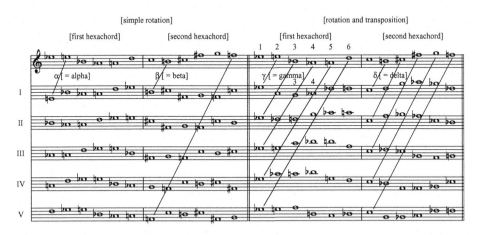

Ex. 9.1   Stravinsky, *Movements*, matrices of rotation for P-0; see Straus, *Stravinsky's Late Music*, p. 66

on rotational arrays'. First, simple rotation, as in the left-hand matrix: Stravinsky treats each hexachord as a loop of interval classes (including the interval class between the sixth and first notes) and rotates each hexachord to generate six different orderings of the six pitch and interval classes. Second, in the right-hand matrix, rotation and transposition: Stravinsky repeats the interval-class rotational process, but this time retains the first pitch class of the first ordering for each of the subsequent rotations. Clearly, it is this second technique that most obviously suggests the possibility of centring the music in some way on that privileged, emphasised initial pitch class.

Another special feature of Stravinskian serialism is his preference for the **inverted retrograde**, rather than the retrograde inversion, for one of the four basic series forms. What this means can be shown with respect to one of the series used in *Requiem Canticles*, whose prime form starts on F and ends on A sharp. R-0 reverses this, moving between A sharp and F, and the four basic forms would normally be completed with I-0 (F to C) and RI-0 (C to F). What Stravinsky does instead is to replace RI-0 with IR-0. This means starting with the first note of R-0 – A sharp, and then moving back through the interval classes of the reversed inversion: ascending major second, descending minor second and so on. The results are shown in Ex. 9.2.

An even more basic technical difference between Stravinsky and the Second Viennese School is that, like many other serialists of the post-war era, Stravinsky saw no reason not to regard the vertical columns of his matrices as sources of material – even when, as with the first left-hand column of the right-hand matrix in Ex. 9.1, the result is just one pitch, E flat. Later serial composers – Peter Maxwell Davies, in particular – have happily taken diagonal, zig-zag and more convoluted linear routes through their matrices, in addition to the purely horizontal and

Ex. 9.2 Stravinsky, *Requiem Canticles*, basic group of series forms, with IR instead of RI

vertical lines used by Stravinsky. Later composers would also use sets of fewer or more than twelve tones: but in Stravinsky's case only his earliest attempts at serial composition used shorter collections.

Straus has rightly rejected any tendency to see Stravinsky's serial compositions as closely related to each other in all necessary respects: 'Stravinsky's late works are not only radically different from the earlier ones, but are highly individuated from each other as well.'[16] Yet, as he also points out, Stravinsky 'had always composed with ostinatos and repeated groups of notes, and the series represented a kind of apotheosis of the ostinato' (152). Against this background, Straus traces an evolutionary path from the use of a 'six-note series drawn from the notes of an A major or A minor scale … elaborated amid non-serial lines' (Septet, 1952–3), by way of 'diatonic serialism' (deriving a series from an E flat minor scale in the third of the *Three Shakespeare Songs* (1953)) to 'non-diatonic serialism'. *In memoriam Dylan Thomas* (1954) is entirely based on a five-tone series which orders a chromatic scale segment (E, E flat, C, C sharp, D: Ex. 9.3a), and the sense of economy is intensified when adjacent series forms are made to overlap. In the cello part (Ex. 9.3b) D flat, the last note of I-7, functions simultaneously as the first note of P-9, while in the voice part the last three notes of I-6 are also the first three of R-0. Even if the serialism here counts as 'non-diatonic', at least compared to what preceded it, Straus notes that 'a desire to maintain a clear sense of pitch focus … remains intact in this chromatic serial work, as throughout Stravinsky's last compositional

Ex. 9.3a   Stravinsky, *In memoriam Dylan Thomas*, five-tone series

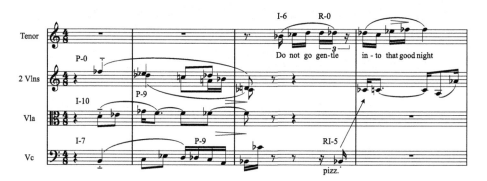

Ex. 9.3b   Stravinsky, *In memoriam Dylan Thomas*, opening of 'Song'

period' (163). That focus is clearest in the work's C-based cadence points. In other words, 'non-diatonic twelve-tone serialism' is not by definition atonal, and it is possible to trace the influence of Stravinsky's favourite symmetrical mode, the octatonic scale – a structuring element in many works throughout his 'nationalist' and neo-classical periods – in the serial works too. That is certainly not to claim that tonal centricity is apparent throughout these pieces: as with Richard Kurth's interpretation of suspended tonality in Schoenberg's serial compositions,[17] the point is rather that moments of tonal quality, especially at cadences, enter into dialogue with serial processes that can equally well tend away from single-pitch centricity and focus.

Cage and Nancarrow

It has often been argued that the so-called 'experimental' music from the second half of the twentieth century was prompted in large part by a reaction against serialism; against calculation and premeditation in favour of spontaneity and essential simplicity.[18] Nevertheless, the serial principle has some genuine points of contact with most music in which repetition or ostinato plays a prominent part, and even works which sound totally different from what twelve-tone compositions are normally held to sound like – for example, those of Varèse, considered in chapter 8 – might turn out to possess significant affinities with serial thinking. A composition can be concerned with number and proportion without being serial, still less twelve-tone. But it is more difficult to detach ordered thinking from serial thinking after Schoenberg and Webern than it is before. For example, John Cage (1912–92) studied with Schoenberg for a time during 1935–6 (and possibly through to 1938). Cage later declared: 'I worshipped him. It sounds foolish to say that I thought he was extraordinary, but I mean that in every sense. I thought of him as superior to other people.'[19] So it makes sense to argue, as Brenda Ravenscroft does, that Cage's *First Construction* (in Metal) of 1939 'is a fascinating example of the effect of Schoenberg's teaching on Cage's compositional practice, both conscious and otherwise. Not only is *First Construction* an intentional attempt to experiment with his teacher's method of serial composition, but it is also an example of Cage's integration of Schoenberg's approach to motivic design.' As Ravenscroft notes, 'a single numerical series – 4, 3, 2, 3, 4 – controls both the small and large-scale structures', and she concludes that 'the serial aspects of the work are ... clearly attributable to Schoenberg, although the elements subjected to Cage's serial manipulations are fixed rhythmic patterns, rather than pitch classes'. However, Ravenscroft concedes that 'despite Cage's reference to these elements as "motives", it is misleading to consider them in terms of the Schoenbergian idea of motive with its inherent concept of development. Such thinking can only find Cage falling short of Schoenberg's ideals.'[20]

As Virgil Thomson said of Cage, 'he liked a mathematical approach and knew all about square roots as the basis of the musical form of his pieces – also the whole theory and practice of the accidental approach to composition which was also systematically based, usually on the *I Ching*. It was a kind of planned accident.'[21] It is indeed plausible to think of Cage as using elements of Schoenbergian thinking to pursue quite unSchoenbergian – even anti-Schoenbergian – ends, to a degree where it seems possible that any associations with Schoenberg and serialism have arisen accidentally. Similarly, Kyle Gann's claim that the *Study No. 25* (written before 1960) for player piano by Conlon Nancarrow (1912–97) 'is the only one to make even slightly conventional use of a twelve-tone row – that is, in transposition, retrograde, and inversion' only becomes significant given the parallel claim that 'for Nancarrow to use a tone row is not unusual, but most of his rows are longer than twelve notes: twenty-eight in Study No. 48, for example, thirty in No. 1, fifty-one in No. 4, fifty-four in No. 21.' And Gann continues: 'as one might expect, his use of the twelve-tone row is a far cry from Schoenbergian practice. Study No. 25 is by no means twelve-tone in a global sense, and the row is limited sometimes to melody, other times to harmonic control: often it serves as a basis for triadic harmony, with pitches rotated (in the manner Stravinsky was developing at about the same time.' Moreover, 'Nancarrow professes little interest in dodecaphony, and he had forgotten that No. 25 contained a row'. So, having made his claims about the presence of a twelve-tone element, Gann concludes that 'the piece gets its distinctive and exciting sound . . . not from any inner system, but from Nancarrow's realization at this point that the player piano is more than just a rhythmically adept substitute for conventional instruments . . . This is the piece in which Nancarrow discovered what is *idiomatic* about the player piano, and in the studies that followed he made excellent use of his findings.'[22]

The Minimalists

It might be assumed that any attempt to connect such composers as Steve Reich (b. 1936) and Philip Glass (b. 1937) with serial thinking is futile. Keith Potter observes that, like Cageian indeterminacy, 'the early phases of American musical minimalism . . . represent an American reaction to the serial models of modernism offered by European composers such as Pierre Boulez and Karlheinz Stockhausen, and by American serialists such as Milton Babbitt'. Nevertheless, certain minimalist compositions are not called 'systems music' for nothing, and Potter proceeds to argue that 'just as Boulez and Cage found common ground in the late 1940s and early 1950s in their use of procedures the details of which were generated by forces outside their conscious control, so it is possible to make connections between integral serialism and minimalism: a commitment to the consequences of rigorous application of processes independent, to a significant degree, of the composer's note-to-note control is evidently the key here.'[23]

In the case of La Monte Young (b. 1935), Potter notes that an early attraction to serialism was the result of his teachers' interest in Schoenberg and Webern: 'Webern's integration of serial technique and motivic materials interested Young more than the sorts of integral procedures being developed "out of Webern" by the Europeans; so did the extent to which Webern's serial processes were audible. But it was the apparent contradiction between an aesthetic still rooted in the dynamism of classical forms and a resulting music that was often essentially static that probably fascinated him most.' Indeed, 'Webern and, more selectively, Schoenberg turned out to offer models as potent for the development of a "static" music as did jazz and non-Western musics' (28–9). So, 'while Young's compositions of 1956–8 adopt the basic principles of the twelve-note method, they soon depart quite radically from any of the styles to which the method had previously given rise', and Potter's analytical discussion of Young's Trio for Strings (1958) demonstrates these differences and similarities very clearly (34–41).

Whereas the Schoenberg pupil Leonard Stein was a significant influence on Young's early development, the powerful combination of Darius Milhaud and Luciano Berio helped to form Steve Reich's early compositional thinking. Reich has described 'his attempt to simplify – or subvert – serialism' while at Mills College, California, 'by composing twelve-note music' – like the *Music for String Orchestra* (1961) – 'which entirely avoided inversions, retrogrades and transpositions' (157). As with Young, it was the static effect of the Webernian approach which was the strongest attraction: 'I would just repeat the row over and over. By doing this you can create a kind of static harmony not entirely dissimilar to the Webern orchestral Variations, which are very static and intervallically constant and which suggest this kind of world.' As Potter adds, 'the interest displayed' in *Music for String Orchestra* 'in static harmony and repetition is the earliest indication in his pre-minimalist output of the direction Reich's mature music would take' (157). Once again, therefore, serialism was not incompatible, in principle, with quite different stylistic qualities from those embraced by 'mainstream' twelve-tone composers, and by the time of Reich's *Pitch Charts* (1963), 'while the tendency to unfold the complete chromatic gamut remains, pitches are now repeated in small units, rather than in twelve-note cycles' (160). No less pertinent is Robert Schwarz's assessment of Reich: 'although he appreciated the systematic approach to composition that serialism offered, he quickly discovered that he disliked atonal music of any kind', and his sardonic comment about working with Berio – 'it was like being at the scene of the crime with one of the major criminals' – indicates a not entirely lighthearted conviction that techniques 'portraying in very honest terms what it was like to pick up the pieces of a bombed-out continent after World War II' were less relevant to Americans of his generation than 'the sounds that surrounded America from 1950 through 1980 – jazz and rock-and-roll', which 'can be refined, filtered, rejected, or accepted in part, but they can't be ignored, or you're an ostrich, you're ill-informed'.[24]

The serial inheritance

The distinctiveness of American thinking about serialism is difficult to assess when opportunities to hear the compositional results are so limited. Stephen Peles has sought to underline what he regards as a deep divide between American and European perceptions after 1945. Juxtaposing statements by Boulez (1952) and Babbitt (1955), he claims that 'these radically different orientations toward history in general and the twelve-tone system in particular were symptoms of a cultural divide as deep as that which separated Schoenberg from Americans of his gener-ation, and was exaggerated by the participants' different experiences of the war. Americans, by and large, emerged from World War II convinced that their values and institutions had been vindicated by the conflict, while Europeans, even the victors, were apt to see the war as a failure of theirs.'[25]

Peles therefore implies that Boulez's (negative?) ambition to 'purge ... music of anything associated with the immediately pre-war past' was quite different from Babbitt's evolutionary concern to study, if not celebrate, the music of the past 'for what it is'.[26] Whether the compositional consequences of this distinction were quite as clear-cut as Peles seems to imply is a matter of opinion. However, it is certainly useful to be reminded that serial composition in the United States since 1955 has not been uniformly arid and obsessed with theory. Even the concentration of serial and other kinds of post-tonal music in universities has provided the composers 'with a livelihood, an audience (if a small one) and some semblance of a community of shared interest and expertise'.[27] Perhaps this is as much as could be expected in a culture with little government-derived subsidy.

Another factor contributing to the range of American serial composition was the example of Stravinsky, whose incorporation of elements of tonal centricity into a twelve-tone context was a particular stimulus to Charles Wuorinen (b. 1938). Described by Peles as 'an important presence on the New York scene, and an outspoken advocate of the twelve-tone composers in their disputes with the Euro-serialists and others', Wuorinen the composer was notable for 'combining ... Babbitt's time-point system [of rhythmic organisation] with pitch orderings fre-quently derived from Stravinsky's rotational procedures' (513). The lists of names provided by Peles and other commentators sketch out the diversity and persistence of serial thinking in the United States. It is another good sign that, in addition to Babbitt and Wuorinen, several others – notably Donald Martino and Robert Morris – have managed to combine important contributions to twelve-tone theory with worthwhile compositional demonstrations of theory in practice.

Carter

One of the most interesting comments on the state of music in America in the late 1950s comes from Elliott Carter (b. 1908), whose own contribution to compositional developments was only just beginning to make itself felt at that time. 'When listening to the recent works of Stravinsky, such as *Agon* or the *Canticum Sacrum*, or Copland's new *Piano Fantasy*, there can be no doubt in the mind of the listener accustomed to the new music that these works make a kind of impression that more immediately accessible music never can': and Carter cites the contribution of twelve-tone thinking to the 'mixture of digested techniques'[28] for which such works are especially notable. Polemically, Carter was even prepared to argue, at least by 1958, that there was an American tendency, as with Babbitt in particular, to 'use the twelve-tone system emphasizing coordinative possibilities rather than its disintegrative ones as the Europeans do' (11). For Carter, neither the 'retrogressive' dodecaphony of the Second Viennese School (though he made an exception for Schoenberg's String Trio) nor the 'mechanical, musically arbitrary routines' of the new European serialists were the answer to the post-war musical crisis: 'they have dealt with tiny musical microstructures, the basic material of music, but very little with the potential of their interconnections for musical thought and expression' (18).

Whether this is a fair judgement or not, it is enormously significant in respect of Carter's own determination to develop post-tonal techniques that owed something to serial thinking without confining themselves to twelve-tone principles of the sort that Babbitt and Boulez were deriving from Schoenberg and Webern. Writing at much the same time about his efforts 'to extend the scope of my musical flow', Carter contended that the important features of 'Second Viennese' music were not twelve-tone routines, but those that had already been established in the earlier, expressionist compositions: the

high degree of condensation, lending itself to rapid change and the quick, intense making of points. The use of equally intense melodic shapes, often broken up into short, dramatic fragments, joins with a very varied rubato rhythmic technique to produce a new kind of what might be called instrumental recitative. The rapid increases and decreases of harmonic tension, quick changes of register, and fragmented, non-imitative counterpoint are also worthy of note. This all adds up to a style of remarkable fluidity which seems to have been derived from the late works of Debussy but seen through the expressive extremes that characterize late Romantic German music, particularly Mahler and Richard Strauss. (207)

Asked straight out in 1960, 'do you use the twelve-tone system?', Carter replied: 'some critics have said that I do, but since I have never analyzed my works from this point of view I cannot say. I assume that if I am not conscious of it, I do not.' He then added: 'naturally, out of interest and out of professional responsibility, I have studied the important works of this type and admire many of them a great deal. I have found that it is apparently inapplicable to what I am trying to do … Perhaps another more useful and not so arbitrary kind of serialization could be devised' (219–20). Whether or not it can be shown that Carter himself has devised just such a less 'arbitrary' kind of serialism, the wealth of analytical work on his music since 1960 has supported the verdict that, while his techniques are not identical to those of composers who use ordered twelve-tone collections and matrices, unordered collections, such as **all-interval tetrachords** and **all-trichord hexachords**, as well as all-interval twelve-tone chords, and even twelve-tone 'tonic' chords, are fundamental tools of his trade. That Carter prefers to talk about 'chords' rather than 'sets' does not mean that his music cannot be fruitfully considered in relation to the kind of extensions and elaborations of serial principles that are under examination here.

Carter's practice

For a simple example from his later years, there is Carter's response to the musical stimulus of Paul Sacher's name, treating the hexachord E flat ('Es' in German), A, C, B (H flat in German), E and D ('Re') as an invariant generator of pitch materials. In 1996, to mark Sacher's ninetieth birthday – he himself was a mere eighty-seven at the time – Elliott Carter wrote *A 6-Letter Letter* for Heinz Holliger to play on the English Horn. This is a short monody which limits itself to the six Sacher pitch classes (Ex. 9.4) but makes music out of the freedom which arises when phrases project different numbers of pitches in varied registers, treating the hexachord as an unordered reservoir of material, whose elements can be permuted, repeated and even omitted, as the creative spirit moves the composer.

By these criteria, Carter is undeniably aware of serial principles, though he has continued to distance himself from those aspects of twelve-tone tradition he finds alien. It is perfectly reasonable to connect some of his most fundamental and far-reaching compositional procedures with Schoenberg and Babbitt, as Andrew Mead

Ex. 9.4   Carter, *A 6-Letter Letter* for English Horn, opening

does.[29] But Carter's inherent pragmatism – his *Harmony Book* 'does not present or even imply a compositional system', nor does it 'claim to set forth a general theory of atonal practice whether for purposes of analysis or composition' – helps to make his personal response to the organisation of total chromaticism the more distinctive. Above all, as David Schiff underlines, 'Carter's music is at once arcanely constructivist in some of its methods and yet traditional in others'.[30]

Attempting to explain Carter's distinctive practice in technical detail can have the familiar effect of generating a mass of arid, knotty prose about music of great expressive presence. Andrew Mead starts from the claim that Carter's 'solutions to writing music using the total chromatic collection are strikingly original, yet deeply related to developments of other major twentieth century composers'. This means that the theoretical arsenal developed for Schoenberg, Webern and Babbitt can have some relevance to music which 'suggests a wealth of extensions to existing twelve-tone theory'.[31] Carter's structures can indeed be generated from the kind of total-chromatic background found in the orchestral piece *Remembrance* (1988), 'based on twenty-nine registrally ordered all-interval twelve-tone rows that succeed one another at a steady pace'.[32] Yet Carter's gradual, increasing engagement with ways of composing post-tonally without at the same time rejecting all aspects of his early, Boulanger-inspired concern with voice-leading by way of common tones, has had a profound effect on his technical development. In particular, the transformation of his language from tonal and neo-classical to post-tonal did not require him to abandon his resistance to the mechanistic in theoretical or compositional systems.

An especially important feature of Carter's technique is his use of the all-interval collections of pitch classes. This means that the collections in question yield all six interval classes between any pair of their members: so, with the tetrachord [0146] we can find [0,1] between order numbers 1 and 2, [0,2] between order numbers 3 and 4, [0,3] between numbers 2 and 3, [0,4] between numbers 1 and 3, [0,5] between order numbers 2 and 4, and [0,6] between order numbers 1 and 4. As Schiff writes, 'Carter had ... begun to co-opt, or at least establish a dialogue with the mechanistic approach in the late 1940s. In the opening of the Cello Sonata [1948],

Carter turned his ambivalence into a new kind of counterpoint by opposing the expressive cello and the mechanical piano.'[33] Elsewhere, Schiff has described the sonata's opening (the first movement was actually the last to be written) as 'containing a six-note set (0,1,2,5,7,8) that is immediately repeated in transposed form'. This set 'is not given consistent serial treatment', but it lays down a principle for hexachordal structuring that Carter would find unfailingly fruitful in the years ahead.[34] Carter's set-class thinking soon came to rely as much on three- or, in particular, four-note collections as on larger ones: for example, in the String Quartet No. 1 (1951) Carter 'employed one of two all-interval tetrachords (18: B, C, E flat, F) as a defining harmony', and 'non-serial twelve-tone thinking' was also present in the Variations for Orchestra (1953–5). Then, 'for the Second Quartet and Double Concerto, composed in the late 1950s, Carter developed a chart of various combinations of the two all-interval tetrachords, [0137 and 0146]. In the 1960s Carter composed two large orchestral works, the Piano Concerto and Concerto for Orchestra, that required a richer harmonic vocabulary. For these he developed catalogues of the three-note and five-note chords respectively.' He also 'used twelve-note chords as defining sonorities in the concertos of the 1960s, and, characteristically, expanded their use systematically later on, particularly in *Night Fantasies* (1980), which employs 88 such chords'.[35]

Schiff's summary is at the opposite extreme from the laborious intricacy of Mead-style analysis, and no doubt reflects the composer's own impatience with responses to his work that appear to deal entirely in arcane and complex technical data. Mead and others have been useful in indicating where the teeming masses of notes in a typical Carter piece come from. But analysts seeking more than the definition of theory-based source materials find themselves constantly forced away from reductive generalisations by the protean variety and inventiveness of Carter's surface multiplicities.

Gra: playing with sets

As already chronicled in detail in this book, serial composers have always delighted in the dialogue between the ordered pitches as displayed in a set group or matrix and the deployment of these ordered elements in lines which will preserve the original order only if there are as many set sequences as there are lines of texture, or – as, classically, with Babbitt – if an array sequence is devised to preserve fixed orders within a polyphonic texture. Composers who give priority to ordered series will acknowledge those particular properties which can be identified in terms of the unordered source set of that series: but it is understandable that such composers will resist the suggestion that they compose with unordered collections rather than with ordered series.

It is perhaps part of Elliott's Carter's Ivesian heritage that he seems to regard the drama of interactions between different orderings of a source set as a more appealing compositional strategy – offering a better balance between fixity and freedom – than the more traditional sense of working with a set which has a primary order, however much that order is disrupted by compositional necessities. Carter is probably also motivated by a wish to avoid too close an analogy to traditional thematic or motivic working with its goal-directed, organicist connotations. Unordered collections as reservoirs of certain types of material are therefore primary, and *Gra* for solo clarinet (1993), while atypical in that, as a monody, it obviously has no vertical, chordal content (its climactic multiphonic dyads apart), it is nevertheless representative in its use of two of Carter's favoured sources – the all-interval tetrachord [0146] and the all-trichord hexachord [012478].

Gra begins (Ex. 9.5) capriciously – 'Ghiribizzoso' – with a distinctly improvisatory fantasy on the registrally fixed close-position pitches of the [0146] tetrachord E, F, A flat, B flat: a tribute, perhaps, to the controlled spontaneity of dedicatee Lutosławski's 'aleatory counterpoint'.[36] Between bars 5 and 8 the tetrachord is expanded into the source hexachord C, B, B flat, A flat, F, E [012478]; in other words, the expansion is also a basic transformation which includes the retrograde of

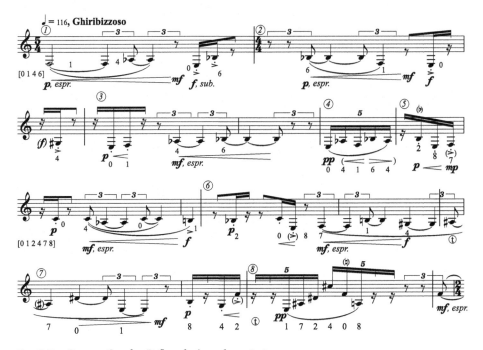

Ex. 9.5 Carter, *Gra* for B flat clarinet, bars 1–9

the original all-interval tetrachord. This initial hexachord statement continues the dialogue between 'doux' and 'rude' characteristics with which the piece began,[37] and the next pair of statements develops these characteristics more expansively: between bars 5 and 8, C, B, B flat, A flat, F, E: then in bars 8–9, D sharp, E, F, G, A sharp, B: then (bar 9's quintuplets) F, E, D sharp, C sharp, A sharp, A.

Why does Carter choose to follow two statements of the same version of his source hexachord, descending from C to E, with one ascending from D sharp to B? It's clear that the ordered forms of the second and third hexachord statements – B flat, C, E, F, B, G sharp and A sharp, D sharp E, B, G, F – are run together to underline a transition from smoother to more volatile material, and also to begin the process of opening up the higher register of the instrument. The two begin with the same pitch (B flat/A sharp) but the second tends to present the intervals of the first in inverted form or to include different intervals (the perfect fourth and fifth, for example). But the last thing Carter wants is to align musical phrases with complete series statements, and such surface intricacies strongly suggest that he is not interested in a series matrix that is the systematic and sole source of the sequence of surface events. Rather, he seeks out ways of pursuing a dialogue between difference and similarity. Hexachord 1 is used twice to establish an element of invariance: but although Hexachord 2 in its unordered form has two dyads in common with Hexachord 1 (E/F, B/B flat) the ordered versions make nothing of the similarity beyond preserving the register of all the notes except the F. Webernian motivic invariance is shunned in favour of a more natural, flowing line.

Carter's use of serial thinking in works spanning more than half a century has helped to ensure not just the survival but the continued vitality of serial thought. While at the present time it is difficult to ascribe the adoption by other composers of comparable methods to Carter's direct influence – there is little significant music that sounds strikingly similar to his – the increasing prominence of his work in Europe during the years after 1970 helped to create an atmosphere in which younger composers could still regard some aspects of serialism as viable, even if the character of serial music had long since lost contact with the more traditional textural and formal features that were so important to the composers of Schoenberg's generation. The evolution of contemporary music in Europe after 1950 was closely bound up with reactions to the different phases of serial composition as they were perceived in a musical world that, while growing increasingly heterodox, proved capable of adapting to an enormous variety of technical and stylistic precedents.

Chapter 10

European repercussions: I

Facing both ways

With Webern dead, Schoenberg distant in America and, as always, unwilling to teach twelve-tone technique, the dissemination of serialism in Europe after 1945 was nevertheless a more rooted and ramified phenomenon than it was in the United States. Europe immediately after the end of the Second World War was mired in austerity and uncertainty, as the devastating economic aftermath of the conflict persisted alongside the emerging anxieties of the 'Cold War' against the Soviet Union and its Eastern bloc satellites. As it re-emerged, European cultural life was not totally resistant to the radical, the experimental, the avant-garde. Yet, by definition, those pursuits had a limited appeal. For listeners willing to show an interest in contemporary music, there was a range of living composers, from Richard Strauss and Vaughan Williams to Britten and Shostakovich, who could be approached in much the same way as the great masters of classic and romantic tradition – even if, as with Britten and Shostakovich, twelve-tone elements came to play a part in their work.

There was never much chance that serialism would be permanently identified with one compositional style, one neatly packaged set of technical principles and aesthetic criteria. Even if, from time to time, small groups of composers appeared to achieve the utopian ideal of such collective commitment to principle, their distinctive stylistic predispositions would soon erode that unity. As one of the few named techniques of composition to emerge in the post-tonal era, serialism has evolved and survived precisely because it brings with it few if any stylistic imperatives to restrict the composer's imagination. One result of this essential neutrality is that it has been possible for composers to introduce twelve-tone successions incidentally, sometimes as conscious gestures towards an exotic, forbidden world, a glimpse of otherness functioning as an expressive intensifier in music which otherwise makes little or no attempt to use the structural principles of serialism. Bartók had shown the way, not only in the intensive motivicism of the String Quartet No. 4 (1928), but also with the twelve-tone second subjects – in an extended-tonal context – of the outer movements of his Second Violin Concerto

Ex. 10.1   Bartók, Violin Concerto No. 2, twelve-tone themes from first and third movements

(1937–8) (Ex. 10.1).[1] Of those who followed Bartók's example, none was more striking than Benjamin Britten (1913–76).

Britten and the British

In 1963, Britten said that twelve-tone composition 'has simply never attracted me as a method, though I respect many composers who have worked in it, and love some of their works. It is beyond me to say why, except that I cannot feel that tonality is outworn, and find many serial "rules" arbitrary. "Socially" I am seriously disturbed by its limitations. I can see it taking no part in the music-lover's music-making. Its method makes writing *gratefully* for voices and instruments an impossibility, which inhibits amateurs and children.'[2] Many composers have proved that last judgement exaggerated: but at the time it was all the more telling, appearing as it did within a statement that was far from roundly dismissive.

Britten's respect for twelve-tone composers was rooted in his admiration for Alban Berg, and in memories of his desire to study in Vienna in the early 1930s. Also, his British friends after 1945 included the Schoenberg pupil Erwin Stein (his editor at Boosey & Hawkes, music publishers), as well as the Schoenberg advocate Hans Keller. Indeed, well before the comments just quoted were made, Britten had given a twelve-tone theme a large-scale, central role, in his opera *The Turn of the Screw* (1954), where it provides the basis for the instrumental variations that link the opera's scenes (Ex. 10.2a): and he had also alluded to serial technique in making the sequence of tonal centres used in Act 2 a transposed inversion of those found in Act 1 (Ex. 10.2b). Most commentators see this as a recognition of the symbolic force of a totally chromatic theme in this particular dramatic context, and although

Ex. 10.2a   Britten, *The Turn of the Screw*, twelve-tone theme

Ex. 10.2b   Britten, *The Turn of the Screw*, scheme of tonal centres

Britten often used melodic lines and chord progressions that exhausted the total chromatic in later works – a hauntingly beautiful example occurs in the *Sechs Hölderlin-Fragmente* of 1958 (Ex. 10.3) – he did so from the conviction that tonality could be enriched and extended by such means. Recurring twelve-tone successions became even more important in Britten's works after 1960, when his harmony shifted its emphasis from the triadic to the centric, an increased emancipation of the dissonance reflecting Britten's awareness of new compositional tendencies and the growing prominence of younger, more radical composers like Peter Maxwell Davies.[3]

Up to that time, serial composition had not made much headway in Britain, though several significant composers had committed themselves to it. One of the earliest was Elisabeth Lutyens (1906–83), who had met the Schoenberg pupil and BBC producer Edward Clark in 1938. She began to compose serially around that time, probably (in part at least) as a response to hearing Webern's *Das Augenlicht* performed in London, also in 1938. This occasion also inspired the Italian Luigi Dallapiccola, who (as will be discussed later) would have such an important influence on many younger contemporaries after 1945.[4]

Edward Clark was Schoenberg's only English-born pupil, though two other pupils, Roberto Gerhard and Walter Goehr, became long-term British residents. Webern's only English-born student was Humphrey Searle (1915–82), who succeeded where Britten failed in the sense that he was able to travel to Vienna (1937–8) to continue composition studies begun in the rather different atmosphere of the Royal College of Music under R. O. Morris and John Ireland. As Searle's work-list suggests, however – it includes five symphonies, two piano concertos, three operas and a substantial piano sonata – his preferred approach to form and

Ex. 10.3 Britten, *Hölderlin-Fragmente*, No. 3, progression of twelve different major triads

texture was not particularly Webernian. Rather, it was the late-romantic rhetoric of Liszt which Searle sought to recreate in a post-tonal, twelve-tone context. Despite this orientation, however, his works did little more than hover around the fringes of a British musical scene dominated between 1950 and 1970 by Britten and between 1970 and 1995 by Tippett.

That serial composition achieved a certain prominence in Britain, especially during the 1960s and 1970s, was due mainly to successive controllers of BBC

Radio 3, William Glock and Robert Ponsonby, who worked with Pierre Boulez and other conductors willing to promote the music of Schoenberg, Webern and certain of their – mainly European – disciples.[5] Harrison Birtwistle apart, Boulez himself was not an enthusiast for British composers, whether serial or not. Yet both Lutyens and Gerhard received a degree of belated attention (mainly by way of smaller-scale pieces) under the aegis of the BBC, and of various performance groups specialising in new and recent music which had sprung up during the 1960s: for example, the Pierrot Players (later The Fires of London) and the London Sinfonietta. It was from within this core of specialised activity that composers of the next generation using or influenced by serial techniques – Alexander Goehr, Hugh Wood and Peter Maxwell Davies among them – began to emerge in the late 1950s and early 1960s.

Shostakovich and the Soviets

Britten's prominence in the United Kingdom between 1950 and 1970 was matched by that of Dmitri Shostakovich (1906–75) in the Soviet Union. Much has been made of the Russian composer's not-dissimilar embrace of twelve-tone thematic elements in works from 1967 onwards – the time when relations between East and West were becoming easier, and performers such as Sviatoslav Richter and Mstislav Rostropovich were acting as vital links between composers in different countries. In his invaluable survey of this topic, Peter Schmelz quotes various condemnatory remarks about serialism attributed to Shostakovich from the early post-Stalin years: for example, 'dodecaphony not only has no future, it doesn't even have a present. It is just a "fad" that is already passing' (1959).[6] Schmelz points out that the severity of these comments is the more significant, since serial compositions had already begun to appear in Soviet Russia.

Andrei Volkonsky (b. 1933) had been the first of the 'young composers', as they were labelled in official publications, to apply twelve-tone techniques, doing so in a 1956 piano composition with the loaded title of *Musica Stricta*. Volkonsky was also the first to be rebuked for doing so. Yet several young Soviets, including the Estonian Arvo Pärt, Alfred Schnittke, Edison Denisov and Nikolai Karetnikov among others, were not far behind. They consistently explored serialism well into the 1960s. Many applied twelve-tone techniques strictly, and several serialised multiple parameters within their compositions, as Schnittke did in both his *Music for Piano and Chamber Orchestra* and his other 1964 composition, *Music for Chamber Orchestra* (304).

For Schnittke, as for many young composers in the 1960s, Boulez and the post-war Western European radicals were more challenging and stimulating than serialism's

Ex. 10.4a   Shostakovich, String Quartet No. 12, opening of first movement

Ex. 10.4b   Shostakovich, String Quartet No. 12, from first movement

founding fathers. 'By the mid-1960s, [twelve-tone music] had filtered to nearly all levels of Soviet musical life, official and non-official alike. Shostakovich's very personal adoption of the technique in the late 1960s was but the tip of the iceberg' (305). Schmelz claims that, by the time of the Twelfth String Quartet (1968) 'twelve-tone rows had become a more integral aspect of Shostakovich's vocabulary, both as a clear, condensed opposition to tonal writing and, in an expanded sense, as a means of fleshing out lengthier, highly chromatic sections' (311). This is clear from Ex. 10.4a, b, showing the relation between twelve-tone unfoldings and tonal centredness (complete with key signature) in the Quartet No. 12. Even though there are 'extended passages of atonality' (320) in these works, Shostakovich only rarely dispenses with the closural return to tonal cadence. Twelve-tone passages are more in opposition to tonality than a permanent and preferred alternative to tonality, and Schmelz notes that 'the more official composers, like Salmanov and Karaev, would actually go further than Shostakovich in their application of twelve-tone devices' (323). This could have been because they were less strongly rooted in the Musorgskyan–Mahlerian traditions so crucial to Shostakovich himself. But, in any case, the outcome seems close to the more academic, neo-classical kinds of serial composition that had become all too common in both Europe and America after 1950. Adopting serial procedures did not automatically confer either modernity or greatness on the compositional result.

Lutosławski and the Poles

Parallels between Russia and other Eastern bloc countries can easily be established. For example, in both Hungary and Poland, there were composers who moved permanently abroad during the 1950s – György Ligeti (1923–2006), Andrzej Panufnik (1914–91) – and composers who stayed behind: György Kurtág (b. 1926) in Hungary, Witold Lutosławski (1913–94) in Poland. Staying behind did not mean complete lack of contact with Western developments, however, and the effects of these in Hungary will be considered later. As far as Poland was concerned, Adrian Thomas has sketched a history of response to serialism dating, at least, from a work of Panufnik's, the *Tragic Overture* (1943), whose fundamental four-note motive 'is clearly derived from the twelve-note manipulations he observed when analysing Webern's scores in Vienna in 1937'. Panufnik was no Webernian, however: he later asserted that 'I threw my dodecaphonic sketches into my waste-paper basket'.[7] Such distancing from the twelve-tone pioneers of the Schoenberg generation was equally strong in Lutosławski: 'what is alien to me in Schoenberg is the pre-eminence of the system over ear control. The latter is of course also present in his music, after all Schoenberg was an outstanding musician. However, the system in his art assumes universal significance and determines the composition of not just one work but a whole series of works. That never occurs in my case. I always work out new elements of a system for every new work which serves my musical imagination.'[8]

Such assertions do not mean that twelve-toneness, and with it certain serial practices, were entirely absent from Lutosławski's music – even if he was never as committed to mainstream twelve-tone techniques as Tadeusz Baird (1928–81) and Kazimierz Serocki (1922–81). Perhaps the volatile cultural atmosphere in mid-1950s Poland created the situation in which 'he did not want, under any circumstances, to be associated with the ethos of the Second Viennese School'.[9] So, with respect to his *Funeral Music* for strings (1958), he wrote of developing 'a set of means which allow me to move in a certain sense within the confines of twelve tones, naturally outside the tonal system and dodecaphony' (96): in other words, a use of total chromaticism that avoided both the intensified yet still ultimately functional tonality of Britten or (later) Shostakovich, and also the particular technical routines of Schoenberg or Webern.

The pointer in *Funeral Music* to what is distinctive in Lutosławski's later compositions is not so much the twelve-tone melody built entirely from semitones and tritones, but rather the climactic 'procession of twelve-note chords which concertina inwards onto the single note which initiates the recapitulation of the initial twelve-note theme [Ex. 10.5 shows the early stages of this 'procession']. It is in

Apogeum - Apogée

Ex. 10.5   Lutosławski, *Funeral Music*, 'Apogeum,' initial twelve-tone chords

chords such as these, which verticalise all the twelve pitch classes, that Lutosławski found the key to his future development' (97), and which he described in this statement from 1961:

The fundamental unity of which I make use in my latest pieces is the vertical aggregation of all the notes in the scale – a phenomenon of harmonic nature. Practically, there exists, as we know, an infinite possibility of creating twelve-tone chords which are unceasingly new. However, my technique preoccupies itself primarily with harmonies which for me possess an expressive physiognomy, a special and characteristic colour and, consequently, a peculiar structure. There are often striking [contrasts] between the different chords of twelve notes. The interplay of these constitutes, among other things, one of the fundamental principles of my technique. As you can see, this has nothing in common with either twelve-note technique or with serial music. The only common trait is the 'chromatic whole'.[10]

As usual, Lutosławski rather overdoes the 'nothing in common' line of argument. By 'twelve-note technique' he meant, in the style of Schoenberg, Webern, Berg and (probably) Dallapiccola: by 'serial music' he meant, as understood by Boulez, Stockhausen and all those composers associated in the 1950s and 1960s with the Darmstadt courses and the European practice of integral serialism. In fact, surviving sketches for his later works and other materials have shown 'how indebted he was at times to basic twelve-note techniques, including hexachordal complementarity'.[11] As one account of his 'studies in twelve-tone rows' concludes, 'there is more "twelve-tone logic" and more consistency in Lutosławski's *oeuvre* than its surface may suggest'.[12] Even more importantly, the quality of that *oeuvre* helps to strengthen the argument that music conceived against a background of ordering principles linked to total chromaticism could make a major contribution within the highly pluralistic compositional world after 1960. At its best, Lutosławski's personal blend of pitch materials deriving from twelve-tone chords and lines articulated in part through the processes of '**aleatory** counterpoint' created as distinctive and memorable a sound world as any at that time. And a crucial aspect of that memorability is the carefully controlled interplay between centred, focused harmony and more freely diffused and active textural processes. The stature of Lutosławski's later works stems from the fact that their idiom arose by way of a dialogue with the principles of serialism and aleatoricism, rather than through dialogue with the stylistic characteristics of any particular composers.

This is distinctive music which could hardly have taken the form it did without long and penetrating thoughts about serialism, or without the positive attempt to engage with those aspects of serialism which had permanently changed modern music. Writing of Henryk Górecki (b. 1933), Adrian Thomas notes that his 'move through serialism towards new horizons'[13] was a characteristic of Polish music during the second half of the twentieth century. Naturally enough, on the wider horizon, not all composers undertook that 'move through serialism', and not all the 'new horizons' continued to engage with aspects of that serial heritage. But the impact and influence of serialism remained strong, long after the original stylistic and technical concerns of Schoenberg and his contemporaries had been either digested, or set aside.

Cold War and style wars: Dallapiccola

That impact and influence was most intensively questioned in the years around 1950, when the conflict between tradition-embracing and tradition-rejecting serialism became fully apparent. Twelve-tone music was more likely to win approval if it made itself accessible by underlining affinities with earlier styles and structures, as had been the case in 1935 with Berg's Violin Concerto. And accessibility might be further enhanced if twelve-tone music were aligned with a text or a dramatic subject of immediate relevance to contemporary society.

As noted earlier, Schoenberg's *A Survivor from Warsaw* (1947) was just such a work, though its brevity and abrasive sound-world made it hard to categorise in terms of the well-established genres of concert music. What better, as a more viable alternative, than an opera, *Il prigioniero* (1944–8) by Luigi Dallapiccola (1904–75), in which a lyric intensity matching that of Puccini at his best was allied with a subject that, in painting a compassionate portrait of a social outsider under supreme, even self-destructive, stress, invited comparisons with Berg's post-tonal but pre-twelve-tone *Wozzeck*?

For some years after its first staged performance (Florence 1950) *Il prigioniero* was held up as the acceptable face of serialism to a still sceptical public. The rather sadistic story of a religious prisoner in sixteenth-century Spain whose cruelly aroused hopes for freedom are ultimately dashed as he is led away to death by the Grand Inquisitor had immense allegorical significance at a time when the full horror of the Holocaust was becoming known, and it was a direct result of the composer's own wartime experiences. Dallapiccola's wife was Jewish, and 'in World War II he was forced into hiding. The opera was conceived in an atmosphere of anonymous denunciation, when petty Fascist officials would "stare meaningfully when they met you in the street."'[14]

Dallapiccola devised his own libretto from a pair of nineteenth-century texts, and although the musical idiom is more concentratedly post-Bergian than expansively post-Puccinian (in one act, the opera lasts barely an hour) commentators – especially those keen to promote the virtues of serial technique – seized on its uncerebral, rather melodramatic qualities as evidence of the new technique's vitality and adaptability. Reginald Smith Brindle, a British pupil of Dallapiccola, and long-term advocate and exponent of post-tonal composition, wrote that 'the incredibly poignant atmosphere and expressive beauty of this work, together with its great humaneness, seem to me the greatest proof we possess that atonal music can serve mankind in the future as effectively as tonal music has in the past'.[15] Yet Smith Brindle's use of 'atonal' rather than 'serial' was probably the result of his awareness that Dallapiccola, like Berg before him, had aspired to approachability by way of heterogeneity, using twelve-tone elements alongside others. Peter Evans, writing several years after Smith Brindle, at a time (the 1960s) when 'serialism' still connoted the strictness and exclusivity of the Boulez generation, observed that 'Dallapiccola's variety of rows and motives, his evocative use of traditional chord structure, his mingled echoes of Verdi, Debussy and Berg, all offended against *a priori* conceptions of serialism; but his right to profit as he chooses from serial discipline is vindicated by the powerful impact the work has continued to make'.[16]

What these commentators praised as the music's flexibility and humanity was seen very differently by T. W. Adorno, for whom the 'musical substance' was 'so simplistic and straightforward that it does not need twelve-tone technique at all for its organization ... Twelve-tone technique is superfluous, and at the same time, so primitive – under the constraints, partly of the theatre, partly of the underlying musical material – that meaning is lost.'[17] Dallapiccola's avoidance of 'strictness' in *Il prigioniero* is evident in many ways, including his use of three different rows to symbolise freedom, prayer and hope respectively. But this was not the result of ignorance or inexperience where the history of twelve-note practice was concerned: Dallapiccola made a 'slow and gradual approach to serialism ... in the period after his first acquaintance with Berg's and Webern's music in 1935, gradually importing more and more significant serial elements into his music'.[18]

Il prigioniero includes passages from an earlier work, *Canti di Prigionia* (1938–41), an example of what Raymond Fearn identifies as the composer's characteristic 'musical dualism', combining 'the timeless lines of modal plainsong taken from the opening of the *Dies Irae* with the greater tensions and modernity of the twelve-tone row' (60). For Fearn, the outcome is 'a truly remarkable degree of unity within diversity. The musical language hovers between modality and twelve-tone writing, and between structures of the utmost rigor and a free, rhapsodic lyricism, and these diversities in the musical language create an intense drama within each movement of the work' (62). This might be thought to offer a paradigm for the essential nature and also the future of twelve-tone composition, which according to this model comes into its own not in isolation from but in conjunction with quite different approaches – even though the question of whether that conjunction can result in synthesis or only in juxtaposition remains open.

Another question concerns how 'natural' the outcome of such conjunctions might be. In 1950 Dallapiccola described the twelve-tone method as 'a natural development of music' which 'I have adopted ... because it allows me to express what I feel I must express'.[19] That 'natural' use of the method is heard at its most refined and convincing in the series of relatively small-scale, mainly vocal works which Dallapiccola wrote between 1942 and 1953, and in which the contrapuntal sophistication and subtlety of tone colour he admired so intensely on first hearing Webern's *Das Augenlicht* in 1938 are more prominent than the expressionistic turbulence of those compositions which have a story to tell, a sermon to preach. It was in the *Cinque frammenti di Saffo* (1942) that Dallapiccola used twelve-tone techniques consistently for the first time, though even here he refused to confine himself to a single row for all five lyrics, or even, in Song 4, to a single row within a single lyric. The aim here is presumably to balance the post-Bergian triadic emphasis of Series 1 against the less tonally-allusive Series 2 (Ex. 10.6). However, Dallapiccola is at his most subtle when post-Webernian lyricism, deployed with Webernian economy and rhythmic flexibility, doesn't prevent the allusion to tonal centres. The second of the *Goethe-Lieder* (1953) is a fine example, both in the delicate motivic links between voice and clarinet in the concluding superimposition of R and I series forms, and in the play with echoes of E major and/or minor (Ex. 10.7).

Dallapiccola continued to use serial techniques, and to align them with other, freer elements, for the rest of his life, and several substantial works were completed, including a final opera *Ulisse*, on which he worked for eight years (1960–8). Most of these works have been very rarely heard, and it certainly cannot be claimed that the kind of mainstream, serially aware compositional style adopted by Dallapiccola guarantees survival in a market where only the highly traditional (not precluding originality!) seems assured of 'immortality'. In the early twenty-first century, the signs are that, the more complex and allusive a composer's style, the less likely their music is to retain a marked presence in live performance, once the flow of new works has dried up and the often charismatic presence of the ageing composer on the public stage is no longer possible. Such composers are therefore remembered more through recordings, and the attention devoted to them by music historians and critics, than they are as the result of regular live performance. Of course, in a cultural context where modes of listening tend increasingly to favour the more solitary convenience of recording and downloading to concert attendance this is not in itself a drawback for the progressive composer.

Ex. 10.6 Dallapiccola, *Cinque frammenti di Saffo*, No. 4, two different twelve-tone series

Ex. 10.7   Dallapiccola, *Goethe-Lieder*, No. 2

Nono: commitment to progress

Dallapiccola was important, historically, as an example to younger composers, especially in Italy, who admired the conjunction between 'humanitarian and libertarian concerns' and progressive forms of musical expression. While the Cold War was at its height, such a conjunction was easy to compare with the repressive aesthetic climate within which Soviet composers – whether truly sympathetic to the brand of communism then dominant in the Soviet Union or not – were forced to function.

Luigi Nono (1924–90) built far more radically on the conjunction of serial techniques and social principles than Dallapiccola did. This underlines the contrast between a composer of avant-garde predispositions coming to maturity after the Second World War and a composer – Dallapiccola – whose cultural context was religious as much as political, and who shrank from the kind of extreme positions that avant-garde affiliation then involved. Nono is also very different from the pioneering American radical, Milton Babbitt, whose embrace of abstraction, and view of technical processes as autonomous, fits with his avoidance of explicit social and political content. Babbitt has written no *Moses und Aron*, no *Ode to Napoleon*, no *A Survivor from Warsaw* and although, like Babbitt, Nono built on Schoenbergian technical foundations, he worked much more directly with the kind of non-abstract subject-matter deemed appropriate by Schoenberg for serial works.

Nono's awareness of the *Ode to Napoleon* and *A Survivor from Warsaw* in the late 1940s fitted with his knowledge of Dallapiccola's anti-fascist twelve-tone songs of liberation, and with the thinking of another important influence, the conductor Hermann Scherchen (1891–1966). 'Scherchen, socialist, anti-fascist and pioneer of committed music, became a model also as a political artist for Nono', and 'that he [Scherchen] always stood up for the music of Schoenberg and Webern only served to confirm Nono's blossoming conviction that politically committed music had to be of the most technically advanced nature'.[20] Nono might also have found things to identify with in Jean-Paul Sartre's existentialist views on commitment in art, as well as the more specifically musical writings of René Leibowitz.[21] But there was another more directly musical association, with Bruno Maderna (1920–73), an uneven composer yet of huge importance to Boulez as well as Nono on account of his abilities as a conductor and his sensitivity to the issues involved in serial thinking. It might even be that Maderna was a 'post-avant-garde' composer before his time, in that 'for him ... contradiction was a necessary and productive part of a composer's make up'. This 'dialectic of rigour and fancy set him apart from his avant-garde colleagues; yet, in retrospect, it is what constitutes his essential modernity'.[22]

By the time Nono engaged with the Darmstadt summer school in 1950, his contacts with Maderna and Scherchen meant that he was already predisposed to resist the advocacy of music's autonomy – its possible detachment from pressing social or political concerns – that emerged there. As Christopher Fox has written, although today 'it is Boulez and Stockhausen whose names are most immediately associated with Darmstadt ... it was the controversial première of Luigi Nono's *Variazioni canoniche* during the 1950 Darmstadt courses which symbolised the advent of a new musical direction'. This work has the subtitle 'on the series of Schoenberg's Op. 41' – the *Ode to Napoleon* – and Fox sees Nono's 'evocation of Schoenberg' as 'a declaration of alliance with serialism and, at the same time, a rejection of the other musical directions being considered in the post-war years, principally neo-classicism and free atonality'.[23] Nono treats the basic series and its inversion as a sequence of six dyads, and derives further series forms by rotating this sequence (Ex. 10.8a). The shift of priority from twelve to six embodied in this procedure, which other post-war European serialists observed, is one result of the

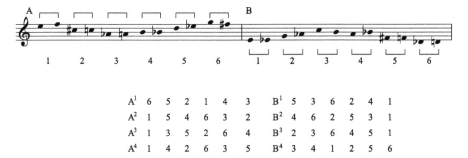

Ex. 10.8a   Nono, *Variazioni canoniche*, 'Allegro violento', series and derivations

Ex. 10.8b   Nono, *Variazioni canoniche*, series of six rhythmic values

close associations between pitch and rhythm, as the six-element duration series used in *Variazioni canoniche* shows (Ex. 10.8b).

Despite these radical features, Fox hears echoes in the music which reinforce Nono's individual response to diverse traditions: 'the percussion writing may suggest the influence of Varèse but generally the orchestral writing has a limpid clarity which reminds one more strongly of Mahler than of any of his Viennese disciples; the use of octave doublings is especially Mahlerian and of course flies in the face of Second Viennese serial orthodoxy' (117). These features also counted as impurities by the standards of Boulez and Stockhausen who, in the early 1950s, were seeking to free serialism from all associations with past styles.

In practice, of course, such absolute eradication was only very rarely achieved, as in Boulez's *Structures Ia* (1951–2), to be discussed in chapter 11. By contrast, Nono's *Polifonica-monodia-ritmica* (1951) 'demonstrates that "Darmstadt" was also capable of assimilating many different facets of musical language and regenerating them in new and exciting ways'. The work's serial processes follow on from those deployed in *Variazioni canoniche*. Nevertheless, 'the music's heart is revealed to be a Brazilian rhythm from a song to the sea goddess, Jemanja' (119).

While 'Nono's music is striking for its commitment to contemporary social issues and for the clarity with which it constructs a network of meaningful cultural and historical relationships' (113), that initial pair of works failed to resolve 'the central problem of serial composition after Webern – how can the series have an explicit role in the music's formation of meaning if it is not to have a thematic function? ' (119). As already stated, a kind of 'mainstream' compromise between serialism and thematicism was to prove the most fruitful way forward for the many serialism-influenced composers in later years. But in the mid-1950s it still seemed important to regard the issue as a problem, not an opportunity, and to try to solve the problem as rigorously as possible.

Nono: *Il canto sospeso*

The 'solution' for Nono came in *Il canto sospeso* (1955–6), immediately preceded by the *Canti per 13* (1955), his first consistently serial work. This was written for Boulez to conduct in Paris, and uses full twelve-tone series forms for pitch as well as serial organisation of durations and dynamics. The generative pitch series in both these works, and most of Nono's later pieces up to 1959, is the wedge-shaped all-interval succession whose basic form spans A and E flat, those Schoenbergian initials which could also serve as the focus of pitch processes. In *Il canto sospeso*, Christopher Fox argues, Nono chooses 'a series whose interval structure can be both a neutral pitch-source *and* an integral part of the music's expressive imagery' (119). The hope represented by the words of members of wartime resistance movements is reflected in the gradually expanding form of the series as an abstract succession of pitch classes and intervals.

In Part 4 of *Il canto sospeso*, where Nono's music is at its least complex, the first six bars (Ex. 10.9) begin to deploy this ordering of pitches in a texture divided into sustaining solo strings and more fragmented wind and percussion. Following the sequence in the wind/percussion layer shows that after the first six pitches have been stated – A, B flat, A flat, B, G, C – Nono does not simply continue with the single note F sharp (xylophone), but restates another A (flute) at the same time. This is the example of a kind of serial technique that has certain things in common with the derivational procedures found in earlier composers, especially Berg, as noted in chapter 5 with respect to *Lulu*. This is the ' "technica degli spostamenti" (literally "technique of displacements", but better understood, perhaps, as "technique of mutation")'.[24]

In simple terms, what Nono does is to restate the A after each intervening presentation of five elements of the basic pitch series, and this leads to the establishment of a quite different series in which the distance between each statement of A is shown as a sequence of fives (mod. 12) – thus, 5, 10, 3 (15 minus 12), 8 (20 minus 12, etc.), 1, 6, 11, 4, 9, 2, 7, 12. Nono then follows this up with rows for each of the other pitch classes which use different numerical values between 1 and 12 (Ex. 10.10).

Ex. 10.9 Nono, *Il canto sospeso*, No. 4, bars 1–6

A	5	10	3	8	1	6	11	4	9	2	7	12
B♭	10	8	6	4	2	12	5	3	1	11	9	7
A♭	8	4	12	3	11	7	10	6	2	5	1	9
B	4	3	7	6	5	9	8	12	11	10	2	1
G	3	6	9	12	10	1	4	7	5	8	11	2
C	6	12	1	7	8	2	3	9	10	4	5	11
F♯	12	7	2	9	4	11	6	1	8	3	10	5
C♯	7	9	11	1	3	5	12	2	4	6	8	10
F	9	1	5	2	6	10	7	11	3	12	4	8
D	1	2	10	11	12	8	9	5	6	7	3	4
E	2	11	8	5	7	4	1	10	12	9	6	3
E♭	11	5	4	10	9	3	2	8	7	1	12	6

Ex. 10.10 Nono, *Il canto sospeso*, No. 4, 'distance square'; see Nielinger, " 'The Song Unsung' ", table 1, p. 100

These distance values are not to be confused with durational values. As Carola Nielinger explains, Nono assigns one duration value to each system of the distance series, and one durational factor to each pitch element within the series. For the first six bars of this movement, the durational value which underpins the rhythmic succession of the individual pitches is three, meaning that the basic crotchet pulse is sub-divided into triplets. But the durational factors, the lengths of the individual pitch events in triplet quavers, are determined by taking the first *vertical* column of the distance square and reading it from bottom to top. Thus, 11 (vibraphone), 2 (flute), 1 (trumpet 3), 9 (clarinet), 7 (marimba), 12 (trumpet 5), 6 (flute/xylophone), 3 (horn), 4 (clarinet, marimba, trumpet 5), 8 (bells), 10 (trombone 1), 5 (trombone 3, trumpet 2, clarinet). The remaining eight sections of the movement use other columns from the distance square in the same way. In addition, each has its own distinctive dynamic profile or 'envelope': in the case of Section 1, *ppp–p*.

Nielinger's detailed demonstration of how Nono's various serial techniques work in practice needs to be studied in full, since all attempts at summary explanations can easily do more harm than good. But the most significant general point about those techniques is that they reinforce the tendency in serial music of this period to distance itself from the 'simple' successions found in Schoenberg, Berg, Webern, Dallapiccola and other earlier serial composers – even if, within the same work, as is the case in *Il canto sospeso*, such simple successions can also be found. By systematically transforming an elementary twelve-tone entity like the **all-interval series**, Nono was increasing the tension between pre-compositional, calculative processes and the use of surface successions exposing the series in unmodified form in ways which – he firmly believed – were not inappropriate to the aesthetic, even political purposes of his composition. In addition, elements can be found in *Il canto sospeso* which work 'against the grain of the underlying serial principles. As so often in Nono's work, compositional freedom of this kind is symbolically linked to content.'

In the composer's own words, 'it was a lot of fun for me to try out how systematic elements could be totally muddled up' (106, 110).

By aligning the overall form of *Il canto sospeso* with that of 'a Baroque cantata or mass setting', and its character with the kind of neo-classicist aesthetics that brought notions of order into the centre of compositional practice, Christopher Fox reinforces Nono's independence of what seemed to him the Boulez–Stockhausen line: 'the tendency for the explanation of techniques always to take precedence over thinking about content'.[25] This led to the contemptuous dismissal of Nono's work by one hard-line Darmstadt figure, Heinz-Klaus Metzger, as 'serial Pfitzner'.[26] So it is not surprising that Nono's strict serial phase was relatively brief, and that his importance and achievement as a serialist should often be seen as less significant or substantial than is in fact the case.

Chapter 11

European repercussions: II

From Messiaen to Boulez

It is possible to draw parallels between the Dallapiccola–Nono connection in Italy and the Messiaen–Boulez connection in France, though the differences are no less palpable. Despite his willingness to conduct Messiaen's more progressive works, Pierre Boulez (b. 1925) never had much sympathy with his teacher's compositional style, or with his intensely orthodox Roman Catholicism: and he was still less tolerant of Messiaen's failure – as Boulez saw it – to follow through on those elements of rapprochement with twelve-tone technique which had emerged in his music during the early post-war years. Olivier Messiaen (1908–92) was always more a modal than a serial composer, consistently favouring unordered collections to ordered series, and devoting much attention to those 'modes of limited transposition' that had been an early obsession of his.[1] Although Messiaen sometimes made use of twelve-tone successions and series of durations, his harmonic thinking was too deeply rooted in an enriched, extended tonality, stemming from Debussy and his French contemporaries, for any more consistently serial structuring of pitch to attract him. Nor did his melodic thinking, and its idiosyncratic associations with chant and birdsong, encourage him to develop serial strategies.

For Boulez, all such qualities were useless, though perhaps not as seriously useless as the misguided efforts (in Boulez's eyes) of another teacher he encountered in Paris in the late 1940s. René Leibowitz preached the gospel of a twelve-tone method rooted in strong links with traditional forms and textures: a Schoenberg-imitating rather than a Schoenberg-rejecting serialism.[2] The young avant-garde despised what they saw as the lack of intellectual rigour and musical imagination in Leibowitz-style academicism: in this respect, at least, it was not academic enough. Hence the willingness of Boulez and those who thought like him to teach the new techniques – if only indirectly, by way of urging on their students the complex general principles from which true serialism, as distinct from the antiquated twelve-tone method, could germinate.

As Alexander Goehr, a Messiaen pupil in the mid-1950s, has commented, 'Messiaen did not really appear to me to have much in common with the composers of the post-Schoenbergian, or post-Webernian avant-garde'.[3] In his brief piano piece *Mode de valeurs et d'intensités* (1949), Messiaen had begun with the three series forms shown in Ex. 11.1a. But, as the opening of the actual piece shows (Ex. 11.1b) these are treated as unordered collections, with repetitions like the middle line's G, C, B flat much more evident than proper serial technique allowed. Boulez – the pupil intending to teach the master a lesson – took Messiaen's upper-line ordering of the same collection as the basis of his *Structures Ia* for two pianos (1951–2). Ex. 11.1c shows the initial presentation in *Structures Ia* of P-0 in Piano 1 with I-0 in Piano 2, making clear that Boulez was more interested in using this exposition as a means of traversing large areas of musical space than for connected linear statements.

Ex. 11.1a   Messiaen, *Mode de valeurs et d'intensités*, three series for pitch, duration, dynamics and articulation

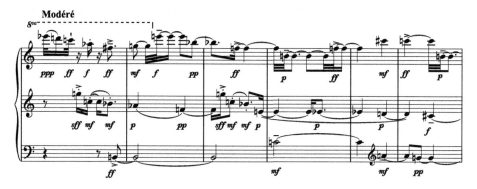

Ex. 11.1b   Messiaen, *Mode de valeurs et d'intensités*, bars 1–6

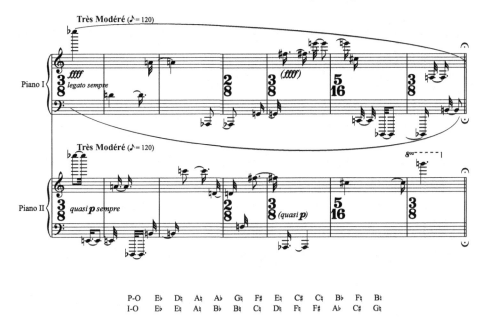

Ex. 11.1c Boulez, *Structures Ia*, bars 1–7

As Goehr comments

inevitably and systematically Boulez takes something that in Messiaen stands on its own in free association or in counterpoint with musical ideas drawn from quite other sources, and gives it a functional significance as a matrix ... In the fifties and sixties, the concept of matrix-structure was so firmly implanted in our minds that really it was assumed that it, and only it, constituted the interest and ultimately the value of music. It was this that drove Messiaen away from the Darmstadt avant-garde.[4]

Boulez had actually begun his engagement with serial principles at least six years before *Structures*, in a relatively straightforward, even Schoenbergian fashion, with the set of piano miniatures, *Douze Notations*, composed and published in 1945. Boulez's first substantial work soon followed – the *Sonatine* for flute and piano (February–March 1946): and here too there is a Schoenbergian dimension, the form acknowledging the four-movements-in-one principle of the Chamber Symphony No. 1, Op. 9, and the twelve-tone working starting out from a pairing of P-0 and I-5: non-combinatorial, but linked in a linear chain by shared pitches (Ex. 11.2a, b).

As the 1940s progressed, it could have been a degree of embarrassment with the stylistic conservatism and relative technical naïvety of his own earliest efforts that

Ex. 11.2a Boulez, *Sonatine* for flute and piano, first three series forms; the D and A of I–11 are reversed in the music (bar 5)

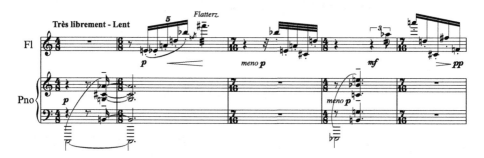

Ex. 11.2b Boulez, *Sonatine* for flute and piano, bars 1–5

fuelled Boulez's embrace of an intransigent rhetoric in critical writings that in turn stimulated the search for an equally intransigent serial technique. By 1949, in strong contrast to Babbitt and Nono, who were both able to respect Schoenberg's technical and aesthetic achievements without imitating his style, Boulez was witheringly contemptuous of what he rather simplistically described as that Schoenbergian aspiration 'to reconstitute tonal language within the dodecaphonic system. Witness the *Ode to Napoleon*, whose feebleness of thought and poverty of execution are completely typical.'[5] And in the notorious essay 'Schoenberg is Dead' (1952) Boulez claimed that Schoenberg's serial compositions demonstrate the 'yawning chasm' that had opened up 'between the infrastructures of tonality and a language whose organisational principles are as yet dimly perceived'.[6]

Testing extremes

Between 1945 and 1951, Boulez showed how it was possible to build on Second Viennese school formal and technical foundations without lapsing into limp neo-classicism. The *Sonatine* for flute and piano (1946), Piano Sonatas Nos 1 and 2 (1946, 1947–8), *Livre pour quatuor* (1948–9), *Le soleil des eaux* (1950), *Polyphonie X* (1950–1), which survives only in a recording of its sole performance, and *Le visage nuptial* (1951–2) were all impressively ambitious, accomplished and – especially in the case of the second sonata and *Le visage nuptial* – expansive achievements. But Boulez became increasingly involved with ideological debates about the true path that music should take in the post-war, Cold War years, both at Darmstadt after 1949, and also through his contacts with John Cage (their correspondence being at its most intense during 1949–50).[7] The more impatient Boulez became with the tradition-boosting ideas of Schoenbergians like Leibowitz, the more he felt driven to pursue the logical conclusion of an all-embracing rather than partial, and therefore primitive, serialism.

Structures

Boulez's *Structures Ia* (1951–2), though very rarely performed, is the most-frequently cited manifestation of European integral serialism, and its attempt to weld series for durations, dynamics and modes of articulation onto a series of pitch classes has been pored over in countless surveys of twentieth-century music. Boulez was soon persuaded that this particular Everest was not a comfortable place to live: that an on-going, socially engaged musical life demanded a less rarefied atmosphere. Yet even if one takes the view that such ideology-driven experiments were dead ends which have no lasting influence even on the work of Boulez himself, it has become clear that they were very significant in terms of a radical cultural practice responding to the particular tensions and opportunities provided by the Cold War.

As Ben Parsons has argued, in *Structures Ia* Boulez 'did not hold up a mirror to his first audience to reflect their own ravaged world back at them, as Schoenberg and Leibowitz had done, but . . . was intent on smashing the codes and hierarchies of their world – the world whose values so immanently threatened world peace once again – to clear space for a new and brave vision of what it could be like'. What Boulez himself later acknowledged to have been a Utopian 'glimpse of the ideal' therefore shares common ground with Babbitt and his role in the cultural practice of the Cold War: and Parsons has plausibly suggested that *Structures Ia* 'was heard as a rallying cry not only for musical revolution, but also for socio-political change'.[8] Linking serialism and political radicalism in the early 1950s, the critic Guy Demur claimed that Boulez was using strictly serial music directly to subvert the pre-war values that the American-backed Congress for Cultural Freedom was seeking to reaffirm.[9]

True to form, Richard Taruskin has interpreted the intransigence and intolerance he finds not only in Boulez's writings but in those by Leibowitz which Boulez himself despised, as virtual if not actual evidence of fascism. Ultimately, the fault was Schoenberg's, 'the greatest apostle of teleological history, who saw the evolution of music as headed inexorably toward the triumph of literate practice over every aspect of oral practice'.[10] This fails to distinguish between serial music that is thematic and serial music that is not. Yet even if it is true that, with *Structures Ia* 'the real work ... was all "precompositional"' (30), and involved a set of twelve dynamic levels [see Ex. 1.2, p. 4] that 'is entirely utopian, both in its assumption that the twelve levels can be manipulated as discrete entities on a par with pitches and durations, and also in the way levels are assigned to pitches regardless of register' (36), the exercise of creating the piece helped Boulez to define how far true strictness, pre-compositionally determined, could go, and how degrees of strictness and freedom might, in future, interact more productively.

Hearing techniques

According to Taruskin, 'the paradox created by "total serialism" is this: once the algorhythms governing a composition are known (or have been determined) it is possible to demonstrate the correctness of the score (that is, of its component notes) more decisively and objectively than is possible for any other kind of music; but in the act of listening to the composition, one has no way of knowing ... that the notes one is hearing are the right notes, or (more precisely) that they are not wrong notes' (36). Taruskin's fixation on audibility as it functioned in the tonal and modal past leads to the conclusion that emancipated dissonance should itself be proscribed, because right and wrong notes become indistinguishable as soon as the rules of functional harmony and counterpoint are set aside. Yet it could well be that those rules are themselves as much to do with musical literacy as with musical experience through the ear. So it is rather more constructive to ask what listeners do actually hear, in a work where Boulez's thinking about serial principles reached its most sophisticated form – *Le Marteau sans maître* (1953–5). This was as much a reaction against the relative primitivism of *Structures Ia* as a fulfilment of its implications for serial composition – a reaction that involved elements of a reversal to the 'expressive territory' that Boulez had worked with in his pre-*Structures* compositions.[11]

In tonal music, the distinction between 'right' and 'wrong' notes can usually be mapped onto the functional distinction in which dissonance is subordinate to consonance. This creates a basic hierarchy of functions which means that a tonal composition concluding with a dissonance would be generally thought of as ending on a 'wrong' note. This aural reaction to hierarchic stucturing principles is by no means the sole preserve of expert listeners capable of formulating precise technical descriptions of the phenomenon. In any case, when tonality is enriched or abandoned, and dissonance is 'emancipated', as in most serial compositions, that particular hierarchical factor no longer obtains. And so, as Boulez's discussion of his own techniques shows, there was a recognition, at its strongest during the first half of the 1950s, that the extreme and rather mechanistic 'democracy' of the all-parameters-are-truly-equal kind of serialism found in *Structures Ia* was less effective as the basis for musical expression than an idea of the series that made the creation of new hierarchies possible. In his essay ' . . . Near and Far' (1954) Boulez wrote that 'the series is not an order of events but a hierarchy – which can be independent of that order'.[12] This is to suggest (in ways which come close to Nono's thinking at much the same time) that instead of being inscribed directly onto the fractured surface of the music, as was the case in *Structures Ia*, the ordered twelve-tone series of pitch classes and interval classes (with its associated durational and dynamic structures) should provide the background and basis for a range of musical materials that creates the aural impression of a dialogue between the extremes of stability and instability, fixity and freedom.

Behind *Le Marteau sans maître*

Le Marteau remains faithful to the intransigence of *Structures* in one basic respect. Boulez was still resisting what to him was the greatest weakness of Schoenbergian serialism: 'the appearance of the series in Schoenberg is . . . linked to a thematic phenomenon; the series, for him, is an "ultra-theme"; to the end of his life he thought of the series as something which had to take on the role of the theme in tonal music'. Webern, by contrast, showed that 'it is more helpful to imagine the series as a hierarchical function which begets permutations in the form of a distribution of intervals, independent of any horizontal or vertical function' (235).

After 1970, Boulez would be less resistant to allowing for some kind of perceptible thematic or quasi-thematic process in his music. But before 1970 he was reluctant to concede that a motivic process can often if not always be perceived in Webern's twelve-tone compositions. Boulez's impulse was to see Webern as the bridge between Schoenbergian thematicism and his own conviction that 'it was necessary . . . to generalize the principle for all the elements of the sound phenomenon, that is to unify and universalize the theoretical principle of the series. The series has become a polyvalent mode of thought', and 'a complete reaction against classical thought . . . Classical tonal thought is based on a universe defined by gravity and attraction; serial thought on a universe in continuous expansion' (236).

Half a century later, it is possible to interpret Boulez's theoretical and practical initiatives as an intensification rather than rejection of classical thinking, at least in the sense of the ambition to unify as well as universalise compositional principles. There was more to classicism than 'gravity and attraction', and any concept of hierarchy has the potential for linking the most fundamental elements within the hierarchy with gravitational attraction, a move to the centre. Such factors would indeed become significant in Boulez's music from the mid-1970s onwards. Nevertheless, in *Le Marteau* the principal dialogue which takes place against the background of the piece's serial materials is one that, in Boulez's own terms, is between 'delirium' and 'organisation'. At the same time, a degree of violence, like that which pervades the fractured surfaces of *Structures Ia*, is set against a more seductive lyricism, in which we can sense not so much the promise of a return to melodic thematicism as a hint of a willingness to refer back to generic prototypes in ways which the intransigent athematic serialist had aimed to reject.

Serialism in *Le Marteau sans maître*

Le Marteau's serial background projects surface interactions between fixity and freedom, its proliferating materials demanding choices of the composer at every stage of the creative process. This fits with Boulez's choice of poems by René Char in which a surreal rejection of conventional meanings is set against relatively straightforward poetic forms. And although *Le Marteau* offers less rich an inter-action between words and music, voice and instruments, than the Mallarmé-based *Pli selon pli* (begun in 1957), the fierce concentration of Char's verse makes the composer's unWebernian expansiveness the more remarkable. There is even, as the alto flute solo at the beginning of the third movement shows (Ex. 11.3a), a sense of the not-so-distant presence of one of Boulez's most admired precursors, Debussy.

This flute line is not only supple in rhythm: it also bears no obvious relation to the pitch sequences of twelve-tone serialism. After the seven notes of bar 1, bar 2 begins as a retrograde, diverging to present a total of nine notes, two of which – after the initial B flat and A flat – repeat pitches from bar 1 (B and A) in the same register. It seems that Boulez is rejecting, not only the motivic explicitness of Schoenberg and Webern, but also the linear unfolding of twelve-tone sequences from which that thematicism derived. The question inevitably arises: is this music serial at all?

Ex. 11.3a   Boulez, *Le Marteau sans maître*, third movement, opening

Boulez himself provided clues at quite an early stage to indicate that serialism was indeed fundamental to *Le Marteau*. His clues were nevertheless cryptic enough to keep musicologists busy trying to establish exactly what the relationship could be between music like Ex. 11.3a and 'classic' twelve-tone procedures. The following summary barely scratches the surface of their conclusions, and only hints at the complexities which attend attempts to analyse the work as a whole.[13]

At its simplest the technique works like this. Boulez generates a twelve-by-twelve matrix in which both the horizontal and vertical lines show prime forms of the series. From this, it will be clear that the six horizontal series forms shown, which I have labelled from P-1 to P-9, also appear in the series forms shown in the vertical axis, reading from top to bottom. Ex. 11.3b shows only the top half of the twelve-by-twelve matrix, with both pitch-class names and integers relating to C as '0'.

For Schoenberg and Webern, the linear successions – horizontal and vertical – of the series forms shown in the matrix were what mattered: and when linear unfoldings of more than one form of the series were superimposed, they were chosen on the basis of the kind of complementary or invariant properties illustrated earlier. Boulez is different: he wants to move deeper into the design of the matrix, replacing focus on the linear with emphasis on the content of particular segments which range across several different series forms.

One of his fundamental decisions concerning the *Le Marteau* series was to segment it into five different groups (A, B, C, D and E), which operate for both horizontal and vertical axes. The complete sequence, A, B, C, D, E for the horizontal axis, is shown on Ex. 11.3b, together with the A and B Groups for the vertical axis, reading downwards. (The same sequence of letters is used for both axes to underline the interaction of the two dimensions.) In the following Group designations, the letter referring to the horizontal axis always comes first, that referring to the vertical axis comes second.

		A		B				C		D	E		
A	[P-1]	1	3	0	11	8	9	7	10	6	2	5	4
		C♯	E♭	C	B	A♭	A	G	B♭	F♯	D	F	E
	[P-3]	3	5	2	1	10	11	9	0	8	4	7	6
		E♭	F	D	C♯	B♭	B	A	C	A♭	E	G	F♯
B	[P-0]	0	2	11	10	7	8	6	9	5	1	4	3
		C	D	B	B♭	G	A♭	F♯	A	F	C♯	E	E♭
	[P-11]	11	1	10	9	6	7	5	8	4	0	3	2
		B	C♯	B♭	A	F♯	G	F	A♭	E	C	E♭	D
	[P-8]	8	10	7	6	3	4	2	5	1	9	0	11
		A♭	B♭	G	F♯	E♭	E	D	F	C♯	A	C	B
	[P-9]	9	11	8	7	4	5	3	6	2	10	1	0
		A	B	A♭	G	E	F	E♭	F♯	D	B♭	C♯	C

Ex. 11.3b Boulez, *Le Marteau sans maître*, third movement, partial matrix of series forms

So, AA identifies the four pitch classes which result from the conjunction of vertical and horizontal A segments – C sharp, E flat, E flat, F (1, 3, 3, 5). BA identifies the eight pitch classes which result from the conjunction of Segment B in the horizontal axis and Segment A in the vertical axis (0, 11, 8, 9, 2, 1, 10, 11).

All this means that Boulez has groups of fewer than twelve pitch classes which provide material quite different from that found in the original, linear P-0. Analysts have detected that the flute line which begins the work's third movement uses the pitches made available when the four series forms labelled B in the vertical axis (P-0, P-11, P-8, P-9) are combined, and segmented into five collections (or 'objets sonores') according to the basic 2 (A) +4 (B) +2 (C) +1 (D) +2 (E) division of the matrix. The collection formed from the four notes of the two group A series forms – P-1 and P-3 on Ex. 11.3b – which belong in Group B has eight notes, with one (B natural) duplicated: and since the composer's rule is not to include duplications the final total is the seven pitches used in bar 1. Group BB has sixteen notes, but duplications abound: G appears four times, E, F sharp, A flat and B flat twice each: that leaves nine different notes, the ones used in bar 2. The same principles determine the pitch content of bars 3 to 5.

The specialist literature on *Le Marteau* has provided much information about the theoretical and practical considerations which helped to determine Boulez's choices. For example, the matrix shown in Ex. 11.3b turns out to have been generated arithmetically by adding the pitch-class integers of a prime form beginning with 3 to those of another prime beginning with 10 (Ex. 11.3c). If we take the four integers from the B group of P-3 (2, 1, 10, 11) and add them in turn to the four integers of the P-10 B group (9, 8, 5, 6) the results are as given in Ex. 11.3d. To summarise, this means that the pitch-class numbers of the first, P-1 line of the matrix (Ex. 11.b) are the result of adding 10 to each of the integers of P-3 in turn. Then the second, P-3

	A		B			C	D	E		
P-3	3 5	2	1	10	11	9	0	8	4	7 6
P-10	10 0	9	8	5	6	4	7	3	11	2 1

Ex. 11.3c   Boulez, *Le Marteau sans maître*, P-3 and P-10 series forms

Group B:	2	1	10	11	2	1	10	11	2	1	10	11	2	1	10	11
	+9	9	9	9	+8	8	8	8	+5	5	5	5	+6	6	6	6

result:	11	10	7	8	10	9	6	7	7	6	3	4	8	7	4	5
	B	B♭	G	A♭	B♭	A	F♯	G	G	F♯	E♭	E	A♭	G	E	F

Ex. 11.3d   Boulez, *Le Marteau sans maître*, each element of the B group from P-3 added to the equivalent (Group B) elements from P-10

line adds 0 to each of its integers – which means that P-3 appears unchanged. The third line, P-0, is the result of adding 9 to each of the P-3 integers – and so on.

Boulez's serial technique throughout *Le Marteau* has been termed 'pitch-class set multiplication', or alternatively – and perhaps more usefully – 'transpositional combination': that is, a group of transpositions, like Group BB, is treated as a complex of pitches within which the composer can move freely. How did Boulez settle on the various orderings present in the melody shown in Ex. 11.3a? The shape of the line seems to involve giving priority to certain intervals, such as the major seventh and major ninth. There is also a clear distinction between pitches which are part of rapidly moving flourishes and those which are more sustained. But at this stage of melodic invention it would appear that serial processes have been left to one side: 'organisation' has given way to 'delirium'. Also, as can be inferred from the character of the music, Boulez is no longer using durational and dynamic-level collections that map directly onto all twelve pitches of the initial series. Rather, according to Lev Koblyakov's analysis,[14] he works with durational proportions in the rhythmic sphere, governed by the prime number eleven (semiquavers) and with a basic collection of five levels in the dynamic sphere – a looser procedure than in *Structures Ia*, and an indication of the ways in which Boulez's work would evolve in the years ahead, attaching less importance to fragmentation and wide registral distribution and more to a new kind of connected, melodic writing that would bring thematicism back into his music.

Stockhausen: Cologne, Paris, Darmstadt

Karlheinz Stockhausen (1928–2007) was three years younger than Boulez, and the work which best represents his early serial achievements – *Gruppen* for three orchestras with three conductors (1955–7) – followed *Le Marteau* by three years. 1957 was just eight years after the pair of events at the Musikhochschule in Cologne which, according to Robin Maconie, 'brought Stockhausen into contact with twelve-tone composition'. The first was a hearing of Schoenberg's piano music at a recital in December 1949. The second was 'a formal presentation on the twelve-note method ... by a former student ... of Josef Matthias Hauer'.[15]

Thirty years before, one of Stockhausen's mentors, Herbert Eimert, had shown particular interest in Hauer in his *Atonale Musiklehre* (1924). Maconie sees this as helping 'to explain why, after the Schoenbergian twelve-tone thematicism of the 1951 *Sonatine* for violin and piano, Stockhausen's serial style changes so drastically', to reflect certain features of Hauer's aesthetic: 'his hatred of the dynamic and the emotional, and his flight into a world of abstract, oriental mysticism lent his work a coolness, as his adherents would have it, or a monotony to the uninitiated.' It follows that Hauer's 'approach to twelve-tone composition chimes with what we now know of Stockhausen's musical aspirations, extending to the point-fields and note-showers of some of the early piano and electronic compositions' (23, 24). In such early pieces as *Kreuzspiel* and *Formel* (both 1951), Stockhausen used a Hauer-inspired 'distributive serial process': 'the music advances in unit sections within which a pre-ordained set of pitches is repeatedly reconfigured. In *Kreuzspiel* structural time-units or modules are of fixed duration, and in *Formel* they are variable in duration by a process of serial addition' (56).

Stockhausen began to advance beyond his relatively strait-laced early serial pieces when he encountered the Belgian composer Karel Goeyvaerts (1923–93) at Darmstadt in 1951, and his intransigent view of Schoenbergian initiatives at that time is summed up by his dismissal of the 'Dance round the golden calf' from *Moses und Aron* as 'serial Verdi' (51). Stockhausen also spent several months studying with Messiaen in Paris (1952–3), and adopted the Boulezian anti-Leibowitz line, arguing that 'radical twelve-tone music of the first half of the twentieth-century ... was effectively "impure", since it used existing materials in a non-functional way'. In his *Konkrete Etüde* (1952), a tape piece completed in Paris, Stockhausen made 'a first attempt at totally integrated serial music', creating 'artificial tones whose inner structures were microcosms or scale models of the form of the entire work' (106). Also in 1952, in *Punkte*, he made 'a conscious attempt ... to devise an orchestra exhibiting serial properties' (113). The speed and intensity of Stockhausen's advance is confirmed by the composition of *Gruppen*, begun only three years later, and introducing 'a new grandeur of scale to the serial music of the fifties' (148).

Stockhausen and the piano

A telling illustration of the multivalent richness of Stockhausen's serial technique in these early years can be found in Richard Toop's detailed analysis of a work that came just before *Gruppen*, *Klavierstück VIII* (1954). (Another similar discussion, too elaborate to be summarised here, will be found in Stephen Truelove's study of serial processes in *Klavierstück XI*, 1956.)[16] As Toop indicates, he has aimed 'to portray in as lucid a manner as possible all those aspects of Stockhausen's *Klavierstück VIII* which stem from a predetermined organisation scheme; in particular, I have tried to show how most local and formal details of the piece are derived from a single 6×6 serial square and its permutations, and to account logically for all deviations from the fundamental scheme'.[17]

The more detailed and comprehensive such demonstrations, the more they resist summary, but a few indications of what is involved can be attempted here. Serial rigour is represented by the fact that the pitch series shown in Ex. 11.4a 'is used throughout ... without recourse either to permutation or to the classic

Ex. 11.4a   Stockhausen, *Klavierstück VIII*, twelve-tone series

Ex. 11.4b   Stockhausen, *Klavierstück VIII*, opening

dodecaphonic techniques of inversion, retrograde, and retrograde inversion. It is transposed, however: the initial degrees of each transposition are determined by the series itself', and 'the pitches for the grace notes derive from the same series and the same transposition procedure' (100). What might be thought of as the first chink in the armour of total serial control is revealed in the omission of one of the six interval classes (ic 6 – the tritone) – at least as an immediate, ordered pairing – from each half of the pitch series: to this extent, the pitch series is less faithful to the 6 × 6 principle than the matrices used for form, tempo and dynamics which Toop illustrates. So it comes as no surprise to find him pointing out that 'the score of *Klavierstück VIII* reveals a very substantial number of cases where serial definitions have been modified, interchanged, or simply disregarded' (101). Such tensions between surface and substructure seems only appropriate, given the highly fragmented nature of the keyboard writing: the beginning is shown in Ex. 11.4b. Stockhausen shared the avant-garde reluctance of the time about displaying the basic series straightforwardly: not only are the grace notes (though using the same series) formed independently of the main text, but the composer used 'a sort of filtering system: in each of the five main sections, one pitch is consistently omitted' (101). So, at the very beginning, the first main pitch is the second from the series, C, not E. Nevertheless, such 'deviations' are best thought of as compositionally positive modifications, not weaknesses: as exceptions which, if not literally proving the rule, enable the analyst to respond to the composer's judgements about when potentially all-determining rules can be enforced, and when they cannot. As such, this kind of music has the potential to dramatise the dialogue between conflict and continuum in specially sophisticated and satisfying ways.

As M. J. Grant argues, implying an essentially modern-classic aesthetic principle:

serial music is integrative, in the sense that it deals with differences in such a way that the individual characters are maintained while at the same time a unity is achieved. The defining difference of serial from thematic music derives from the relationship of the elements; in thematic music, the elements do battle; here [Grant has been discussing Stockhausen's sixth and seventh piano pieces] they are elements in a continuum . . . Serial music strives for equilibrium, and attains almost perfect balance – 'almost' since as Klee pointed out, it is the process that is more important than the attainment of form, the way that is more important than the goal.[18]

Grant offers a well-nigh lyrical appraisal of the ideals that can be discerned in the serial project at its least compromising, its most visionary. She is even able to claim, of Stockhausen's *Klavierstück VII* (1954–5), that one of its most striking features, 'the consistent repetition of certain pitches', to the extent that the note C sharp sounds as a kind of 'centre', is not an indication of the composer sliding back into the comfortable embrace of traditional hierarchic thinking. 'The remarkable aspect of the piece is that it employs such simple elements without distorting its serial character. By this point, serial music has come of age, to the extent of working with openly "dangerous" material such as repeated, middle-register notes, without damaging the equilibrium.'[19] To 'damage' the equilibrium is presumably to reject, or attempt to reject, that 'abiding feeling of tension', of 'a balance which is extremely precarious', that Grant also associates with Stockhausen's composition. If it is felt that this is exactly what happens in later, more substantial serially influenced compositions, where hierarchical, centripetal potential is more explicitly admitted, and thematicism again begins to contend with serial disposition, then the damage wrought would seem to be severe. But there can be few today who either hear or think of those later 'compromises' as betrayals of serialism. Rather, they are, in some cases at least, a realisation of its true potential.

Gruppen

Such a realisation comes rapidly closer in *Gruppen* for three orchestras (1955–7), which is, for Maconie

a monumental achievement, an ingenious hybrid of theory and fantasy. Its musical imagery is turbulent and dynamic, its texture of unprecedented sharpness of detail; as one might expect, the role of the conductors as movers and shapers is correspondingly vital. When the three orchestras come together in the same tempo, the music has tremendous *élan*; at other times, when structures in different tempi are superimposed, the effect can be robustly impressionistic, and comparisons with Debussy's statistical forms, of which Stockhausen has written approvingly, are not far away.[20]

Appropriately, then, Stockhausen's serial technique also has a 'French' dimension, as if in acknowledgement of close contacts with Messiaen and Boulez, who was one of the conductors at *Gruppen*'s first performance.

Playing for about twenty-five minutes, the work consists of 174 groups, 'each one lasting on average a few seconds, and being distributed around one orchestra or another or, more occasionally, two or three at once. Also, for much of the time different groups will overlap, one starting in one orchestra before the previous group has finished in another orchestra. Because nearly every group has a different tempo marking one frequently gets three tempi occurring simultaneously.'[21] This surface heterogeneity is underpinned by strong, unifying serial principles, and Stockhausen embraced the avant-garde tendency of the time to deprive the generative twelve-tone series of any surface, thematic role by choosing one which was quite devoid of characteristic personal to Stockhausen himself. The series in question is of the fundamental all-interval kind (with the tritone linking the two halves) whose two hexachords order discrete segments of the chromatic scale, D sharp to G sharp, A to D (Ex. 11.5). Stockhausen also devised a chromatic scale of tempi with '0' as crotchet 60, '1' as 63.5, '2' as 67 and so on, reaching crotchet 120 with '12' – the '0' an octave above the original one. Nevertheless, as Jonathan Harvey says, 'the tempo plan ... remains something of a background prop whose main function is to give variety-within-limits rather than a real experience of form in the macrocosm' (62).

Harvey's remains the most lucid narrative of how serialism works in detail as well as on a larger scale in *Gruppen*. He agrees with Maconie that *Gruppen* is 'a paradoxical work; it is possibly the most involved of European total serial works, and yet there is an enormous amount of freedom in the details': and for all the elaboration of its theoretical and technical basics, 'the parts in which Stockhausen is being most himself and at his best are those in which the theory has least influence' (76). The idea that creativity might be stimulated by the instinct to react to system

Ex. 11.5 Stockhausen, *Gruppen*, twelve-tone series

spontaneously, sometimes conforming, sometimes not, provides a hint as to the value most composers since the 1950s have placed on serial thinking. Where *Gruppen* remains most strongly linked to the rigours and radicalism of the compositions that preceded it and made it possible is in what Harvey calls a 'deficiency of motivic purposefulness' (57): that is, the conviction that music should be not only serial but athematic and generically innovative.

In Stockhausen's case, the struggle to rethink thematicism eventually led to what Richard Toop has called 'the return to melody' in his music.[22] It also promoted the serially inspired use of generative thematic formulae, first in *Mantra* (1970) and ultimately in *LICHT* (1977–2003); but this process did not immediately sweep away the kind of fraught and flexible equilibrium so majestically displayed in *Gruppen*. In particular, Maconie regards *Zyklus, Refrain* (both 1959) and *Kontakte* (1960) as three works 'of unequivocal genius and perfection: formally, musically, and philosophically'. They 'reconcile so elegantly and explicitly those critical polarities of freedom and determinism, of open and closed form, and of objective and subjective experience, that define serialism in the fifties and its relationship with the sciences of communication'[23]: and they are 'perfect' in that 'they are compelling musical statements, and also . . . perfectly imagined, both serially and also philosophically' (201). The more willingly we go along with this concept of perfection, the happier we may be to accept that music could not continue for long in exactly the same way. In order to progress, it had also in some respects to retreat, to work positively with imperfections once again.

Chapter 12

European repercussions: III

Xenakis

Iannis Xenakis (1922–2001) told the story of how, having won first prize in a competition with his orchestral work *Metastaseis* (1953–4), he was encouraged by Hermann Scherchen to sign a publication contract with Schott. Nevertheless, Schott 'didn't undertake to publish my scores within a certain period of time. After two or three years I wrote to them and asked how much longer I had to wait. They replied that my music was outside the mainstream of the avant-garde and couldn't receive the same treatment as Luigi Nono, who was the central figure of the new music. Of course, he was a serial composer, a member of the Darmstadt group. You see how those people were thinking? I left them and went over to Boosey & Hawkes.'[1]

It might be thought that such comments could only have been made by a composer whose primary aim was to uphold at least some of the harmonic and formal values of pre-modernist traditions, as Britten and Shostakovich, among many others, were doing in the 1950s. Yet Xenakis, like all the composers considered in this chapter, was more a transformer than a rejector of serialism. *Metastaseis*, the last of a trilogy of orchestral works, was preceded by *Le Sacrifice*, which James Harley deems

> an edifice worthy of the European avant-garde of the 1950s. In the manner of Messiaen's 'modal' serialism as exemplified by the *Mode de valeurs et d'intensités* (1949), Xenakis bases his composition on a series of eight registrally-fixed pitches, each linked to a duration derived from the **Fibonacci series** ... These pitches are elaborated by neighboring notes and glissandi in between, characteristic features of later pieces, along with the exclusion of vibrato. The deployment and repetition of the associated durations follows a mathematical process, its completion signalling the music's conclusion.[2]

Harley's view is that, immediately after *Le Sacrifice*, *Metastaseis* carried Xenakis 'past the strictures of serialism, and most other compositional conventions of sonority and form ... The title, *Meta* ("after", "beyond") – *staseis* ("immobility"), refers to the contrast – or dialectic relationship – between movement, or change, and nondirectionality or standstill. There is also a sense in which the title refers to the composer's own evolution, moving on from the arid formalization of *Le Sacrifice* (and serialism in general) and the constraints of the classical tradition' (10). Yet Xenakis' note in the score that 'the *Metastaseis* are a hinge between classical music (which includes serial music) and "formalized" music', reinforces the sense in which elements of calculation and structuring, derived from serial thinking, mattered to him at that relatively early stage: and they continued to matter throughout his life.

Harley himself acknowledges that *Metastaseis* by no means abandons all contact with serialism: the second section contains

> an angular, Webernian passage that, after *Le Sacrifice*, is the most serial music Xenakis ever wrote. A ten-note set (or series) is partitioned between the violins (four notes) and cellos (six notes). All twelve transpositions of the set are displayed in succession, though in the fifth and twelfth the cellos are absent. Xenakis developed his own method of permutating the intervals within each presentation of the set, a precursor of methods he would implement in the 1960s based on group theory ... The result is that, in spite of the strict organization of the music, there is a certain 'statistical' quality that nudges the contrapuntal nature of the music toward a more textural character. (11)

'The crisis of serial music', as Xenakis referred to it in an article written around this time, was less the result of any reluctance to bring mathematical models to bear on compositional practice than of what he saw as a failure on the part of the Darmstadt generation to develop appropriate statistical, 'stochastic' models for musical structures.[3]

Xenakis' continued commitment to system and rigour is well demonstrated by the piano piece *Herma* (1962), 'in which the form is built from successions and combinations of large pitch sets' (26). But it was only after a period of research (1963–5) built around the theories of Pythagoras and Aristoxenos, and studies in Byzantine music, that Xenakis evolved his own fully realised compositional technique. Central to this was a process in some ways analogous to sieving – the systematic creation of derived series, as used by Berg and Maxwell Davies, among others. However, Xenakis' sieves 'explore asymmetrical scales which reject octave equivalence and generate seemingly chaotic structures'.[4] This reinforces the point that, even if Xenakis' reliance on mathematics is not so different in principle from that of Milton Babbitt and his American disciples, the dialectic between order and disorder, system and stochastics, was of much greater interest to Xenakis than it was to them.

In Harley's formulation, what Xenakis achieves 'is a method by which ordered structures (pitches, durations, etc.) of any degree of regularity or irregularity can be

Ex. 12.1 Xenakis, *Jonchaies*, pitch sieve for opening passage

constructed and then subjected to a regulated sequence of permutations'[5]: and the potential for sieves to constrain musical materials, thereby enhancing the aural perceptibility of musical identities, gradually becomes more prominent. In the orchestral work *Jonchaies* (1977) one sieve takes the form of a Pelog-like[6] tempered scale, exemplifying Xenakis' highly productive interest in musics from beyond Western cultivated traditions. As Ex. 12.1 shows, this scale involves three cycles of a descending eight-interval pattern, each cycle beginning an octave and a perfect fourth below its predecessor. Just as intervals recur within the basic pattern, so do pitch classes. By the end of the quoted sequence of twenty-seven notes, the 'missing' twelfth pitch class – F natural – is still awaited.

As often with the radical music of the time, the distance between the simple, systematic outline of the series or scale which underpins the first part of *Jonchaies* and the turbulent, dense surface of the actual music is immense. However, James Harley argues that 'the intervallic structure of the sieve, which often remains fixed throughout a section or piece, creates a certain identity of "timbre" . . . With six rhythmically independent lines carrying on together, the string sound is certainly complex, but the strong identity of the intervallic structure of the underlying sieve produces a clarity that would otherwise be missing' (109). In later works, Xenakis would often exploit the contrast between passages constrained by sieve construction and those which modify or abandon such construction. This process is not so different in principle from that which contrasts consistent modality with more general chromaticism: a quality found in many post-twelve-tone composers of the twentieth century's later decades.

Ligeti

Xenakis' scepticism about serialism as a compositional method – or 'classical', Schoenbergian serialism, at least – was by no means unusual, even in the 1950s. It was shared by György Ligeti (1923–2006) who, having been welcomed by Stockhausen on his escape from Hungary at the time of the anti-Communist uprising in 1956, was soon in close contact with the latest Western European developments. Yet, as Richard Toop reports, 'while fascinated by the revolutionary new world of sound' that Stockhausen's *Gruppen* opened up, 'he was less convinced about the methods Stockhausen had used to produce it',[7] and this scepticism found early expression in Ligeti's technical and critical analysis of Boulez's *Structures Ia*.[8]

Richard Steinitz has noted that Ligeti had arrived at a kind of 'quasi-dodecaphonic writing' during his Budapest years simply through working with chromaticism in a relatively systematic way – as Bartók had before him.[9] (Although Ligeti had a copy of Leibowitz's *Introduction à la musique de douze sons*, 'he had scarcely opened it'.) Before leaving Hungary, Ligeti 'had composed his entirely serial *Chromatic Fantasy* for piano, and started a twelve-note oratorio and Requiem and another serial piano piece, to be called *Chromatic Variations*'. Nevertheless, he was hostile to what he saw as the anti-hierarchical nature of recent extensions of serialism. In an essay on Bartók from 1955 'he rails against serialism's elimination of differences between "attraction and resolution, consonance and dissonance" … and applauds Bartók's refined chromatic architecture, his "twelve-tonalism" being a higher synthesis of two contradictory systems, functional tonality and what [Ligeti] calls the "distance principle" of symmetrical divisions laid out between opposite harmonic poles, as defined by [the theorist] Ernö Lendvai' (85).

In 1971, Ligeti made his most detailed comments about serialism in a 'conversation' with himself: and although the historical accuracy of such constructions can always be questioned, too many details ring true for their overall validity to be seriously doubted. Ligeti approached the topic by way of remarks about the 'musical situation' as he found it in the second half of the 1950s, when 'harmony was in dire danger of toppling over into intervallically neutral and a-harmonic sound structures; rhythmic articulation was in the no-less dire danger of toppling over into undifferentiated continuous progressions'.[10] In a later interview, he made an even starker comparison between 'a generally accepted musical language, such as tonality used to be', and within which different 'dialects' could be tolerated, and 'twelve-note music and serial music', which 'are synthetic constructions, incapable of organic change' (32). Whether this distinction between tonality as 'natural' and serialism as 'unnatural' is valid or not, Ligeti's development (like that of many of his most important contemporaries and successors) was driven by the possibility of working in ways which he could regard as extensions or modifications, rather than rejections, of the serial idea. In this respect, his discussion of the orchestral work *Apparitions* is particularly significant.

My first version of the music that later became the first movement of this work was sketched in 1956 in Budapest, at which time I knew nothing about serial practices, by then fully developed in Western Europe [but see Steinitz's comments on Ligeti's early twelve-tone works, quoted above]. When at the beginning of 1957 I went to Cologne and soon got to know the music of Webern as well as that of the post-war generation, I came to realise that the technical and structural standards of my Budapest version [of *Apparitions*] were unsatisfactory, measured by Cologne standards. Leaving the initial inspiration untouched, I composed in 1957 a second version, in the working out of which my experiences with serial music were absorbed – I emphasize, my experiences with, not the serial technique itself: I reacted to serial music just as I reacted to my own earlier compositional methods, rejecting it and at the same time building on it, modifying it. Equally dissatisfied with this 1957 version, I composed in 1958 a third version of the movement, this time the definitive one. It was only then that I achieved inner consistency and a sufficiently tight network of structural links. My knowledge of serial music put at my disposal a whole new compositional apparatus, but I was content to regard that just as a *possibility* and made no actual use of it. What I owe to serial music is to a much greater extent an insight into structural relationships and refinements of thought in regard to the subtlest of musical ramifications. A fruitful exchange of ideas with Stockhausen and [Gottfried-Michael] Koenig proved a decisive factor in my development as a composer, together with a study and analysis of several works by Boulez. It was clear to me from the start that my development would not be along the path of serialism: I was already steeped in compositional assumptions and previous experiences of a totally different kind. The modifications to which my own music was subjected after contact with serialism then exerted their influence, feedback fashion, on serial music itself producing yet further modifications in its ideas and techniques. (127–8)

Ligeti's techniques

Ligeti went on to explain that 'there were two aspects of serial composition that struck me as problematical. Firstly, the equal status accorded to all musical areas such as pitch, duration, timbre, degree of intensity' led to 'the erosion of intervallic relationships, that is to say, of harmony of any kind'. Even more drastically, Ligeti could not accept the serial principle of 'the organization of all the musical elements within a unified plan ... Uniformity of organization was the fundamental tenet of serial music: a quantifiable basic order, a modulus, had to be laid down, and every single part of the composition had to be derivable from the chosen modulus', whereas 'I did not see any necessity for this kind of unified treatment of all the elements' (128–9).

Ligeti is here characterising serialism in the most abstract, extreme and 'integral' fashion, the more easily to dismiss it. Yet he was also questioning all compositional thinking dominated by serial principles, even in less than totally 'pure' form, since 'the discrepancy in the serial outlook lies above all in the unmotivated equation of the physical and mental levels of approach': and this brought with it the failure to develop a properly hierarchical mode of procedure which 'can make its effect directly on the sensory level of musical perception' (130). Ligeti nevertheless claimed that he was 'talking about modifications, not total abandonment', and that his working methods at this time 'could be regarded in a very general sense as serial' (131). In the first movement of *Apparitions*, in its final form, 'there are predetermined formulae in the areas of rhythm, dynamic, timbre, pitch, compass, note density, character of motion, formal articulation. There is no single order governing all these areas together ... but a relative unity is achieved through the manner in which the various areas are linked together ... In the area of rhythm, for example, there is a quasi-serial repertory of duration elements' but its purpose its to establish 'a hierarchy that is contrary to the a-hierarchical principle of serial music' (131–2).

Other composers, even Boulez, would come to accept that music needed some sense of hierarchy in order to be properly meaningful: and that such a sense could be achieved by way of techniques founded on serial thinking. As Steinitz sees it, 'what mattered more' to Ligeti 'was the dramatic character one could achieve without the nullifying constraints of serialism. He preferred to listen with his inner ear and trust where it led: the stranger and more rarefied, the more in tune with his deeper vision.'[11] Yet this did not mean that Ligeti's later music was never 'influenced by serialism' (183). His systematic control of number, especially rigorous in the two-piano piece *Monument* (1976), is further evidence of serialism's constructive legacy, as are the various cellular 'mechanisms' for pitch and rhythm that contribute structurally to many of his later works. In one of the most spectacularly virtuosic of his *Études* for piano, 'L'escalier du diable', No. 14, in Book 2 (1988–94), everything stems from a 'pitch module' consisting simply of an ascending chromatic scale with trichordal segments of a whole-tone scale superimposed (Ex. 12.2a). Ex. 12.2b shows the piece's first two cycles of the pitch module, in counterpoint with a rhythmic module, as indicated above the staves. The two pitch modules each have a total duration of twenty-seven quavers, but the rhythmic module's alternation of groups of seven and nine quavers creates a lack of fit between pitch and rhythm which fuels the piece's phenomenal energy.

'Rhythmic and melodic patterns combine differently on each occasion ... But the process is never rigid. Typically, it is tempered by Ligeti's instinctive sense of development and by what the hands can physically play. Entries soon overlap, come more frequently, begin on different pitch classes and are doubled in a variety of parallel thirds, fourths, fifths and sixths' (309–10). What is, initially, fixed or predetermined in well-nigh mechanistic fashion is more a foil to subsequent freedom and fantasy than a constraint on inspiration and invention. Does it have anything to do with serialism, as distinct from total chromaticism? Perhaps music like this makes the question

Ex. 12.2a Ligeti, 'L'escalier du diable,' initial pitch module

Ex. 12.2b Ligeti, 'L'escalier du diable', opening

irrelevant. Since serialism exists, and despite Ligeti's criticisms of it, it seems pointless to exclude its principles of dialogue between ordering and reordering from a work like 'L'escalier du diable': and there are plenty of examples in Ligeti's music from all periods where the presence of total chromaticism as a basis for the interplay of ordered twelve-tone statements within more freely ordered contexts can be detected.

Berio

Like Ligeti, Luciano Berio (1925–2003) is a composer whose materials and methods were far too diverse to ensure that a single, constraining technical process would have over-riding significance for him. Yet even though Berio's explicit compositional engagement with serialism was confined to a few years during the 1950s, the serial experience remained with him and did much to determine his later development. A general indication of how he saw this himself can be found in his Harvard lectures (1993–4), where he comments on the degree to which 'post-Webern serialists extracted from Webern's poetics those elements that would give concrete and conceptual drive to the break with the past': the result was that 'the excess of estranged formal order generated disorder – just as the hyper-thematization of Webern's music obliterated themes as such'.[12]

The cure for such 'disorder' was not a simple reversal of that 'break with the past': nor was it a root and branch rejection of the 'fixation on homogeneity' that 1950s music displayed. Berio, who described himself as a 'pragmatic egoist',[13] had encountered little if any contemporary music in his early years. As David Osmond-Smith explains, it was not until the end of the war, when the twenty-year-old Berio entered the Conservatorio in Milan, that 'he was suddenly able to explore the music of his own century'.[14] 'In 1946 he heard the first Milan performance of Schoenberg's *Pierrot lunaire*. At the time the experience left him baffled, but within a few years he was beginning to explore the scores of Schoenberg, Berg and Webern with increasing interest' (4). In this environment, encounters with the music of Dallapiccola were as important for Berio as they were for Nono:

> Dallapiccola was a point of reference that was not just musical, but also spiritual, moral and cultural in the broadest sense of the word. It was perhaps he, more than anyone else, who deliberately and unremittingly forged relationships with European musical culture. As often happens to me with important encounters, I reacted to Dallapiccola with four works [composed between 1951–4]: *Due pezzi*, for violin and piano, *Cinque variazioni*, for piano (based upon the three-note melodic cell – 'fratello' – from *Il prigioniero*), *Chamber Music* (setting poems by Joyce) and *Variazioni*, for chamber orchestra. With these pieces I entered into Dallapiccola's 'melodic' world, but they also allowed me to escape from it.[15]

Even this early, however, Berio shunned the more Webernian, contrapuntal aspects of Dallapiccola's twelve-tone style, while his resistance to Dallapiccola's lyricism was a predictable consequence of visits to Darmstadt – the first in 1953 – and of close contact with composers whose view of serialism was very different from Dallapiccola's. 'In 1953 Stockhausen was the theoretical pivot of the *Ferienkurse*, Pousseur provided the speculative machinery, Boulez the analytical spirit and Maderna was a benign father-figure' (61).

In 1953, Darmstadt was already beginning to move beyond the 'Year Zero' obsessions of the years since 1949. 'Boulez was turning his back on the combinatorial extremes which he had inherited from Messiaen and Cage, and which had acted as a catalyst within being either formative or, I would say, creative (the most notable and least satisfying results being Messiaen's *Mode de valeurs et d'intensités* and the first volume of Boulez's *Structures*).' While declaring Stockhausen's *Kontrapunkte* 'an indisputable masterpiece', Berio was most appreciative of Maderna, who

> with both feet firmly on the ground and an innate sense of history (he was never a disciplinarian or a visionary in his musical activities) gave an unself-conscious lesson in Humanism. It is mainly thanks to him that I approached serialist procedures (that is, the possibility of quantifying musical perception on the basis of proportions invented *ad hoc*) as a means of rediscovering and reorganizing things that were already familiar. It was Bruno, for example, who used overtly isorhythmic and therefore neutral criteria to experiment with taking conventional rhythmic modules, some of them with popular (especially Spanish) origins, and developing them so that sound and silence, rhythms and durations, formed an organic and inseparable unity whose relationship to the original popular models was indecipherable. (61–2)

This narrative confirms David Osmond-Smith's claim that, as early as 1953, Berio's life-long 'ambivalence towards highly restrictive "pre-compositional" systems' was already in place, and was 'only temporarily eclipsed by his encounters with Darmstadt radicalism'.[16] 'The extension of serial thought to cover all aspects of sound ... was a phenomenon that Berio approached with a characteristic mixture of curiosity and caution. But such was his flair for rapid assimilation that by 1954 he was already putting these techniques to use in planning his first major orchestral work, *Nones*' (16).

Nones is based on a seven-tone succession which, intersecting with its transposed RI form, comprises a thirteen-tone series – the repeated note being D, in two different registers (Ex. 12.3). Crucially, however, Berio makes 'relatively free use of these resources', which were 'to be used as flexibly as the composer's imagination dictates ... Rather than impose serial orderings upon rhythm, dynamics, etc. and leave these to interact, Berio assigned to each of the four factors – position in the pitch series, duration, intensity, and mode of attack – a numerical value ... Although

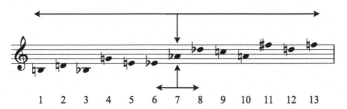

Ex. 12.3   Berio, *Nones*, thirteen-tone series

much of the score shares with totally serialized pieces note by note changes of dynamics, attack, etc., it is in fact the result of choice within a more malleable matrix of possibilities' (18). In his next orchestral composition, *Allelujah I* (1955), Berio retained a strict serial organisation for pitch and rhythm, but assigned dynamics and modes of attack more freely, even though the music remains close in style to the pointillist textural conventions of the time.

Allelujah I was soon withdrawn and reworked as *Allelujah II* (1957–8) – considered by Osmond-Smith to be 'a remarkable step forward' (20). Berio's own later discussion of *Allelujah II* reflects his concern to reinforce what amounts to a classicising tendency to hierarchisation. The instrumental groups involved 'are in a hierarchical order. The most important instrument in *Allelujah II* is the flute and the most prominent note is B flat. It is round that pitch centre that related harmonic fields, constellations and structures rotate. The piece starts with that note and ends with it – it is sounded by the flute in the second instrumental group. The B flat is present practically throughout and serves as a kind of focal point amidst the complex and rather centrifugal musical processes.'[17]

In this way, Berio was composing-out his Maderna-inspired conviction that

> as far as I was concerned, the serial experience never represented the utopia of a language, and so it could never be reduced to a norm or to a restricted combination of materials. What it meant to me above all was an objective enlargement of musical means, the chance to control a larger musical terrain (such as the ethnic materials that I have often worked with) while respecting, even admiring, its premises . . . This interest in exploring the continuity of musical processes . . . explains why the pieces that affected me most during those years, and about which I was most enthusiastic, constituted a fairly heterogeneous group: Stockhausen's *Gesang der Jünglinge*, Maderna's *Serenata*, and later on, Pousseur's *Rimes*, and *Agon* by Stravinsky.

The inclusion of *Agon* in this list is particularly noteworthy, given Berio's concern to counter the prevailingly centrifugal qualities of *Allelujah II* with that focal flute B flat. '*Agon* is a triumph not only of invention and, in its own way, of awareness and of courage, but also of the transformation of materials. Onto a subcutaneous tissue (as Schoenberg would have called it) that is, a harmonic structure that glides from G major to a Webernian series (and back again) through various stages of chromatic corruption, there unfolds in remorseless, exemplary and naïve fashion, the hyper-intelligent parable of a "short history of music" that performs a lucid, but tragic autopsy on itself under the pretext of a game' (64–5).

Many of Berio's own aims and achievements can be deduced from this powerful accolade, and particularly the modern-classic impulse to balance stark heterogeneity with centripetal tendencies and possibilities. In *Two Interviews*, Berio discusses Beethoven in almost mystical fashion in order to illustrate his conviction that 'there can be no *tabula rasa* in music' (66), and to claim that

> with Beethoven, the great gesture, the great process, the great musical event ... seems to emerge every time, dripping with precedents, from a totality that contained that great process, and from which Beethoven, like Michelangelo, has hacked it out ... We thus have a totality that 'speaks' the piece, and to which the piece continually alludes through innumerable, and disconcerting ways. And here we are naturally at the opposite pole from the general principles of Webernian serialist practice. Principles that were, essentially, of an additive and conventional nature: an embryo, a three-note cell that is projected, as if within a transparent prism, into all the interstices of the piece. (67–8)

What Berio termed 'the final offshoots of serialism' foundered through an 'indifference between material and form' that 'finally broke down into a total absence of relationship between the conceptual and the physical, between project and result' (69). The solution was not to reject every concrete element of serial thinking, but to bring those elements into the great debate which, in Berio's case, became focused around dialogues between control and flexibility, or, more specifically, between serial order and modal 'unorder'. Asserting that composition is about 'the ability to transform' is, in essence, asserting a serial principle: 'we're always dealing with models, even those that we make for ourselves, and our work consists in widening the field of transformational paths until we manage to transform one thing into another as in a fairy tale' (102).

Berio's transformations

Berio was at his most passionate when discussing transformation and transcription, and when (as Boulez also does in his later interviews and writings) he declares his conviction that a memorable thematic or quasi-thematic surface to complement 'the deeper structure' is vital. 'One of the reasons for the objective difficulties involved in coming to grips with the neo-classical Schoenberg of say, the Wind Quintet is – quite apart from the general incompatibility and indifference between rhythm and harmony – the frankly repulsive character of the dodecaphonic "themes" which disfigure the discourse, and whose useless recurrence I find utterly depressing' (103). Behind such an extreme reaction, and such a questionable analysis, one senses the frustrations of a composer who had the greatest difficulty in framing a surface sufficiently memorable melodically, motivically and thematically, to do justice to the music's deeper structure. He was even, perhaps, a little fearful that the much-derided Schoenbergian precedent was more successful in this respect than most later composers, so resistant to 'neo-classicism', even when it was also twelve-tone, could bear to acknowledge.

Berio's preference for a built-in degree of flexibility, while recognising the continued need to maintain 'harmonic control within complex textures',[18] led him to use pitch fields (also known as harmonic fields) – 'temporarily fixed pitch groupings characteristically dominated by one or two intervals, and the notes chromatically adjacent to them' (24). The capacity of such fields to provide distinctive motivic, melodic and harmonic materials indicates the strength of their appeal to composers whose practice veered away from serial ordering towards modality. As Osmond-Smith was aware, such frameworks were ideal for the enactment of forms built from tensions between centripetal and centrifugal impulses, and the possibility of tension turning into dialogues in which constantly shifting degrees of synthesis and opposition were perceptible (27). And although 'from *O King* [1967] onwards, the articulation of a large-scale melodic/harmonic process by a central line which throws off a constantly evolving cloud of harmonic formations around it became a dominant feature of his work' (36), it was perfectly possible for a line to be built up from the gradual assemblage of 'the notes of a fixed dodecaphonic field', as in *Sequenza V* for trombone of 1966 (34).

In this respect Berio shared with many of his contemporaries and successors the tendency to organise a post-tonal language, which involved a continuum between centred and non-centred processes, in ways which occasionally acknowledged the systematic core fundamental to serial thinking. In what Osmond-Smith characterises as 'the most incisive' of Berio's 'studies in harmony and texture', '*Points on the Curve to Find . . .*' (1974), 'the basic pitch process at work in the piano line is of disarming simplicity', involving as it does a twelve-tone succession used to generate 'a sort of developing variation form, allowing Berio to display an almost Brahmsian delight in creating variety out of an underlying unity' (59). Ex. 12.4 shows the initial assembly of a ten-tone collection as the piano is gradually joined by other instruments, the 'missing' two notes – B flat and G – soon asserting their independence in the Double Bass. This is characteristic of Berio's later, unfussy allusion to aspects of serial thinking: as Osmond-Smith demonstrates, even a large-scale work, the opera *La vera storia* (1977–81), can derive all its 'major materials . . . more or less directly' from an eight-note group, or pitch-field (Ex. 12.5: 104).

Kagel

With Mauricio Kagel (b. 1931), the late-modernist problematisation and celebration of a musical work's ambiguous identity is all-pervasive. The core of this

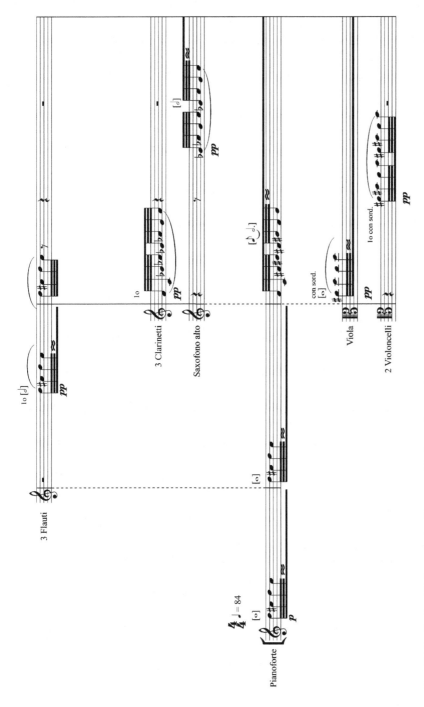

Ex. 12.4 Berio, '*Points on the Curve to Find . . .* ', opening

199

Ex. 12.5   Berio, *La vera storia*, eight-tone pitch framework; see Osmond-Smith, *Berio*, p.104

ambiguity is the range of degrees of dependency – on other compositions, or other things altogether – that any particular work can suggest. In Björn Heile's words,

> what is so specific about Kagel's art is that it is always *about something or reflects on something*. It is an art of commentary and of conceptual thinking, and these principles can be realized in a variety of art forms. This amounts to a radical re-conception of the notion of composition: for Kagel, composition is not necessarily connected with sound, since it is characterized by procedures rather than product – a way of doing something. Likewise, the focus lies more on the referential character of a composition – on how it relates to the world – than on how it is constituted in and of itself.[19]

Given Kagel's date of birth, it is not surprising that his early compositions reveal an awareness of twelve-tone techniques. However, 'these often sound as if he was mocking the technique he used himself, thus combining the exploration of integral serialism with its parody' (4). This in turn raises the complex question of how one can distinguish parody from the direct, if not especially inspired, use of a method with certain stylistic consequences. With Kagel's first twelve-tone composition, *Variations* for flute, clarinet, violin and cello (1952), it is not so much the desire to be parodic as 'the lack of technical experience' that 'can be felt in the somewhat didactic exposition of the series as an unaccompanied solo line at the beginning and the predominating horizontal unfolding of the series in mostly polyphonic textures ... Nevertheless, the wide variety of textures and expressive characters as well as the flexible rhythmic structures belie the age [21] of the composer' (13), and promise well for a future career in which variety is of the essence.

Kagel has consistently continued to refer to serial principles in his music, and just as 'his early works often ... appear to mimic the typical sound world of integrally serial works of the late '50s even when they are not actually serially constructed' (17), so he has in common with most of his contemporaries (however strict, comprehensive and exclusive their serial procedures were in the 1950s) the fact that his later compositions would tend to derive from such procedures, and include serial manipulations in their preliminary workings, but not necessarily carry these through rigorously into the finished piece. Kagel was never concerned with that ' "serial organicism" whereby the generation of a whole composition from a single serial germ is supposed to guarantee some kind of pseudo-metaphysical unity or wholeness' (21). So, in his *Anagrama* for speaking chorus, soloists and chamber ensemble (1958), 'his transformations do not centripetally refer back to any basic series, but lead centrifugally further and further into the open, protruding and proliferating uncontrollably into all directions' (24).

In acknowledging the potential of serial discipline to provoke conflicting, even parodic qualities of both form and style, Kagel was only following up – and greatly intensifying – the cues given by Schoenberg as early as the variation movement in the Suite Op. 29.[20] Kagel's implicit critique of monolithic rigour was aimed more at his own Darmstadt contemporaries than at his predecessors, and the power of that critique was fuelled by his increasing interest in Cageian experimentalism, as emerges in *Transición II* for pianist, percussionist and two tape recorders (also 1958). 'With its bold and idiosyncratic combination of serialism, graphic notation, aleatory technique, open form, live electronics, Cageian piano preparation, cluster composition *à la* Cowell and theatrical action, the piece appears to be summing up all current developments and then surpassing them by adding even more novelty.'[21] But the result is problematic, since 'much of the piece sounds really like the cliché of serial piano music, making the elaborate techniques for notation and performance appear somewhat pointless', especially as 'only a small part of the structure is actually controlled serially' (28).

During the course of his narrative, Heile stresses the continuing role of serialism within Kagel's heterogeneous style. Yet comments like 'as in *Kantrimiusik* (1975), the bizarre mixture of tonal chords, serial techniques and chromatic lines [in *Die Erschöpfung der Welt*, completed in 1978] always goes slightly awry' (124) risks suggesting that a unified, 'unbizarre' style should still be regarded as some kind of norm: that is, a classical rather than a modernist aesthetic, which is surely inappropriate for the 1970s. This makes Heile's evaluation of *Intermezzo* (1983) – 'together with the colourful mixture of materials used – triads and chromatic agglomerations, diatonic lines and twelve-note rows, waltzes and serial rhythms – these recurring elements and patterns of similarity seem to aim for a classical dialectics between unity and diversity' (136) – particularly questionable, since in normal circumstances classicism suggests synthesis, not unresolved dialectics.

At other points, Heile avoids these problems, as when he comments simply that *Vox humana?* (1979) uses tonal material such as triads and pulse rhythms, but combines them using avant-garde techniques, often involving serial methods. In this way, the expressiveness of the tonal era is evoked, but instead of uncritically exploiting our habitual reactions to certain tonal tropes, these means are de-familiarized, thus adding an element of self-reflective critique' (128). Heile is also clear about how the persistence of serial thinking makes it possible for Kagel to give greater emphasis to this aspect when he feels it appropriate. Thus, the 'Lieder Opera'

Aus Deutschland (1981) 'shows some of Kagel's most consistent serial writing, accounting for large parts of the rhythmic and metrical structure, but also for harmonic development and melodic writing (which is often dodecaphonic)' (132).

In Kagel's hands – at least from the 1980s onwards – modernist heterogeneity does indeed tend to dissolve into degrees of modern-classic integration. Following on from his comments about *Intermezzo*, Heile observes, in connection with the Third String Quartet (1988) and other pieces of this period, that 'what is unique about Kagel's use of such diverse materials is that they are not juxtaposed in heterogeneous collages but fused together – if in idiosyncratic and deliberately incongruous ways ... Kagel seems to have transcended both the idea of the organic artwork and that of the surrealist collage as a juxtaposition of heterogeneous elements' (140). Even so, it is indicative of the problems Heile has in sustaining this more synthetic line that, in referring to the Third String Quartet (1986–7), he says that 'passages ... with diatonic tunes, pseudo accompaniments, dodecaphonic lines and serial rhythms all [raise] conflicting associations' (151). It is entirely appropriate that Kagel should keep his critical interpreters suspended – even conflicted – between apprehensions of unity and diversity: and also that, for this acme of late-modernist methodology, serialism and all it has stood for during its different stages of evolution, should have such a central, yet far from exclusive, function.

Chapter 13

European repercussions: IV

The later Boulez

During the last quarter of the twentieth century there were far-reaching technological advances in electronics and computer science. But the musical applications of these evolved in parallel with degrees of retrenchment from the avant-garde ideals of the earlier post-war decades, bringing new perspectives to the issues of compositional control and comprehension that were already being confronted. As Pierre Boulez commented in an interview from 1997: 'in my youth, I thought that music could be *a*thematic. In the end, however, I am now convinced that music must be based on recognizable musical objects. These are not "themes" in the classical sense, but rather entities which, even though they constantly change their form, have certain characteristics which are so identifiable that they cannot be confused with any other entity.'[1]

One can argue that Boulez is over-simplifying to some extent here. Nevertheless, as seen in chapter 11, the degree of motivic differentiation detectable in a very early Boulez work, the *Sonatine* for flute and piano (1946), was not sustained in more mature and characteristic compositions like *Le Marteau sans maître* and *Pli selon pli* (begun in the later 1950s and still being revised during the 1990s). It seems to have been at the time that *IRCAM (Institut de Recherche et Coordination Acoustique/ Musique)* was being set up in Paris between 1970 and 1977 that Boulez – its founder and first director – adopted more clear-cut differentiations of material in *Rituel* (1974–5) and *Messagesquisse* (1976), moving on to the 'new thematicism' of *Dialogue de l'ombre double* (1985), *Anthèmes* (1991), *Incises* (1994/2001) and *Sur Incises* (1996–8).

Jonathan Goldman has shown that this new thematicism displays points of contact with serial thought; and it also suggests – through Boulez's characteristically binary, dialogic thinking – a continued modernism. Among the various binary oppositions that Boulez discussed in his Collège de France lectures (see below), system/accident and envelope/signal are especially resonant in relation to the serialism/modernism association. 'In the conjunction of accident and system, nothing survives intact of either element: on the one hand, accident is inconceivable within the system which provides its boundaries: on the other hand, system must reshape itself, reacting to the appearance of a foreign body.'[2] In addition: 'envelope, for Boulez, is a musical object perceived as a whole, simple and unitary, composed of many distinct but closely related elements … The Boulezian signal bursts out from nowhere with no regard to the surrounding acoustical context, without seeking integration with the surrounding sound-events. The signal has no direction, it neither continues what precedes it nor anticipates further developments' (38–9).

Boulez as lecturer

Boulez's fifty-year progression from memory-rejecting, athematic serialism to serially founded motivicism stands alongside a wealth of other post-1970 accommodations with the radical initiatives of earlier years, as well as a plethora of attempts to escape from the tainted associations of 'mechanical', 'mathematical' serial thought. Extensive documentary evidence for this change is provided by the lectures Boulez gave at the Collège de France in Paris between 1976 and 1995, published in 2005 as *Leçons de musique*. In these texts Boulez continued to underline the contrast in Schoenberg between the pervasive sense of liberation present for example in the post-tonal, pre-serial *Erwartung*, and the no-less-pervasive constraints of the twelve-tone *Von heute auf morgen*. Against his own ideal of a composer who aspires 'to create a rapport between hierarchy and free will' Boulez projects the image of Schoenberg as 'the man of disruption, who [nevertheless] prioritised the idea of continuity with the greatest passion' (494). Unlike Berg, whose genius 'is in that consistent suppleness of a discipline which creates superior ways of preserving the unpredictable … without risking incoherence or dislocation' (375), Boulez claims that, with Schoenberg, 'the evolution of his language is rooted in the desire to unify the work as strongly as possible, as inevitably as possible, by means of an extremely compact system of themes and motifs which pervade the texture, constraining it, providing its *raison d'être*, its coherence and its diversity' (367).

Boulez is unwilling to accept that Schoenberg might have allowed the unpredictable, the accidental, a constructive role in his music – at least once the 'academicism' of twelve-tone neo-classicism had taken hold in the mid-1920s. That academicism, it appears, was not just the cause or result of Schoenberg's 'desire to unify the work as strongly as possible'. In the later stages of *Leçons* Boulez claims that 'the grand utopianism of the [second] Viennese school, and especially of Schoenberg, was to regard vertical and horizontal as different deployments of a single dimension, organised according to the same generative principle' (646). This description sounds not unlike Boulez's own practice in *Le Marteau*, as outlined in chapter 11. But by the time of the Collège de France lectures he had come to feel that such unrealistic obsessions with unity, with a connectedness in which similarity had priority over difference, should be replaced by a dialogue between connections that are both close and distant. Better, it appears, to dramatise the opposition of vertical and horizontal. This does not mean that these dimensions are incompatible, but that the music acknowledges the necessary difference between them. So, how are constraints, systems, to manifest themselves in a non-academic, non-chaotic manner?

Style and idea in *Incises*

Boulez's music is all about creating impressions of spontaneity, of rendering connections between origins and consequences ambiguous. It is as if he imagined the composer as a magician initiating rituals which absorb and mystify audiences in real time: and one of the musician–magician's most powerful techniques is to play on the contrasting capacities for remembering and forgetting, to set off the rational and the instinctive against each other, in the listener as in the composer.

The piano piece *Incises* demonstrates Boulez's continued commitment to a methodology derived from 'classic' serial practice. It was assembled in two stages: the ten-page 1994 version has an inscription saying that it was written (as a test piece) for the Concours Umberto Micheli in Milan. The 2001 version (with the same inscription) adds another fourteen pages to the original. There is also the much larger work called *Sur Incises* (1966–8), dedicated to Paul Sacher on his ninetieth birthday, and scored for three pianos, three harps and three keyboard percussion players, which incorporates the music of the piano piece (or pieces). So we can be fairly confident that Boulez was already beginning to make plans for the Sacher tribute when the 1994 *Incises* was composed, since (like Carter's *A 6-Letter Letter*, discussed on p. 146) it involves prominent allusions to the 'Sacher' hexachord E flat [Es or 'S'], A, C, B [H], E and D [R or 'Re'], the hexachord first deployed by Boulez in *Messagesquisse* for seven cellos, written for Sacher's seventieth birthday in 1976.

Messagesquisse is playfully explicit in its use of the 'Sacher' hexachord (Ex. 13.1a), in textures that do little or nothing to hide the generative focus of the initial E flat, especially when this provides the fixed point for the matrix formed from successive rotations of the hexachord's interval classes. Ex. 13.1b shows two matrices: Matrix (A) rotates the interval classes in turn through E flat, while Matrix (B) transposes the same interval-class succession onto each pitch class of the 'Sacher' hexachord in turn. Ex. 13.1c is a short extract from the work's coda, in which rotations through E flat from Matrix (A) are woven together to produce a continuous *Gigue*-like line. (Rotation treats the pitches as a circular unit: so, 'b' (2–1) means using the notes of

S   A   C   H   E   R   0   1   2   4   5   7

Ex. 13.1a Boulez, *Messagesquisse*, ordered and unordered 'Sacher' hexachords

(a)	Eb	6	A♮	3	C♮	1	B♮	5	E♮	2	D♮	1			0	Eb	A♮	C♮	B♮	E♮	D♮
(b)	Eb	3	F♯	1	F♮	5	Bb	2	Ab	1	A♮	6			6	A♮	Eb	F♯	F♮	Bb	Ab
(c)	Eb	1	D♮	5	G♮	2	F♮	1	Gb	6	C♮	3			9	C♮	F♯	A♮	Ab	Db	B♮
(d)	Eb	5	Ab	2	Gb	1	G♮	6	Db	3	E♮	1			8	B♮	F♮	Ab	G♮	C♮	Bb
(e)	Eb	2	Db	1	D♮	6	Ab	3	B♮	1	A♯	5			1	E♮	Bb	Db	C♮	F♮	Eb
(f)	Eb	1	E♮	6	Bb	3	Db	1	C♮	5	F♯	2			11	D♮	Ab	B♮	Bb	Eb	Db

MATRIX (A)   MATRIX (B)

Ex. 13.1b Boulez, *Messagesquisse*, derived matrices from ordered version (A) by rotation (B) by transposition

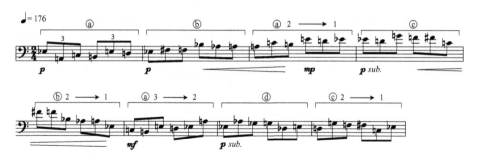

Ex. 13.1c Boulez, *Messagesquisse*, opening of final section (Cello 1 only)

the 'b' hexachord in the order 234561, and 'a' (3–2) indicates the 'a' hexachord ordered 345612.)

Incises also seems to have what Elliott Carter might call a 'tonic' collection, though not the obvious one, beginning from E flat. The 'tonic' collection is first made audible in the spread chord at the end of the improvisatory introduction: here left hand and right hand have separate Sacher hexachords: as normal-order pitch-class sets, these comprise, for the left hand, a version beginning on B and, for the right hand, a version beginning on C sharp (Ex. 13.2). There are three pitch classes

Ex. 13.2 Boulez, *Incises* (2001), chords with two forms of the 'Sacher' hexachord

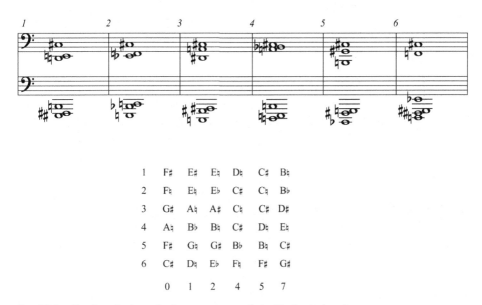

1	F♯	E♯	E♮	D♮	C♯	B♮
2	F♮	E♮	E♭	C♯	C♮	B♭
3	G♯	A♮	A♯	C♮	C♯	D♯
4	A♮	B♭	B♮	C♯	D♮	E♮
5	F♯	G♮	G♯	B♭	B♮	C♯
6	C♯	D♮	E♭	F♮	F♯	G♯
	0	1	2	4	5	7

Ex. 13.3 Boulez, *Incises*, closing sequence of six 'Sacher' chords

in common between these hexachords – C sharp, E flat/D sharp, and F sharp/G flat: and the placement of the left-hand C sharp as bass note signals an harmonic ('tonic') function that will be reinforced in the sustained chords of the piece's second part. Indeed, in Part Two's fourth and final version of this chord-based texture, the last six chords, all Sacher hexachords, are centred on C sharp, as their principal invariant pitch, though this now sounds at the top in each case (Ex. 13.3).

It is possible to argue that the overall form of *Incises* echoes that of *Messagesquisse*. The earlier work had four main sections which can be categorised generically as introduction, moto perpetuo, accompanied cadenza leading to solo cadenza and gigue. Sections one and three are slow, improvisatory: sections two and four are fast and motoric, with articulation and dynamics of particular importance in bringing variety to textures where rhythmic differentation is strictly reined in. In *Incises* the overall two-part division is reflected within each of the parts in turn. In Part One the opening section, marked 'freely, slowly, without dragging', has an improvisatory quality, while the ensuing Prestissimo is a typical Boulezian moto perpetuo, with no let-up until pauses are introduced in the concluding stages. Part Two makes this slow/fast, free/disciplined alternation the basis of a refrain or rondo form: the basic tempos are slow (quaver 46) and fast (crotchet 132). Perhaps the most important difference between the two parts is that, whereas in Part One the fast music in essentially monophonic, in Part Two it is homophonic.

In Part One's monophonic Prestissimo musical characterisation is clearly segmented in order to articulate the rhythmic flow, without falling into the dreaded naïvety (as Boulez would see it) of a Messiaen-style collage. Boulez's performance instructions draw attention to the most basic distinction: between groups of semiquavers, to be played very rhythmically, and groups of demisemiquavers, to be played less strictly, but as fast as possible. Both types of material can be marked as either legato or staccato, and in both cases the material ranges in length from a single semiquaver to fourteen: this last is the extreme, the loudest and longest single group, and another version of the Sacher hexachord (Ex. 13.4). The result is a dazzling kaleidoscope of permutations. Among the compositional controls used by Boulez in *Incises* are similar or identical pitch-class sets for groups with the same number of units: so, in the case of units with six demisemiquavers or six semiquavers, whether slurred or staccato, the Sacher hexachord is a prominent if not invariable feature. Where the hexachord is not present in pure form, it is possible to relate pitches and intervals to its sub-sets or derived sets – a consequence of the fact that, like most hexachords, the Sacher collection contains instances of all six interval classes.

The homophonic materials in the three fast sections of Part Two of *Incises* pursue comparable strategies: contrasting slurred and staccato articulations, continuous lines built from permutations of note-groups, initially of between one and four pitches only, later expanding considerably. In general, the Sacher hexachords might be thought to be exemplifying discipline and control within the freer manipulations that surround or succeed them. For example, in the mainly legato second 'vif' episode two [012457] collections – with three pitch classes (A, A flat, F) in common – are heard at the beginning (Ex. 13.5) but not – or at least not in such transparent guise – again. Throughout Part Two of *Incises*, it is in the slow, chordal refrains that the constraining authority of the hexachord is given full weight, contrasting with the

Ex. 13.4   Boulez, *Incises*: this extract centres on the fourteen-semiquaver group which uses the 'Sacher' hexachord A (0) G sharp (1) G (2) F (4) E (5) D (7)

Ex. 13.5   Boulez, *Incises*, opening of second 'vif' episode

derivable but freer linearity of the fast sections. In such ways, Boulez has continued to find fresh stimulus in aspects of serial thinking which seem to look back with a strong degree of scepticism on the more mechanistic processes he tried out in the early 1950s. By means of honouring one of the few musicians for whom he could feel unequivocal devotion, the Swiss conductor and patron Paul Sacher, Boulez seems in the end to have found it possible to acknowledge the technical if not the stylistic potential of Schoenberg's most seminal serial initiatives.

The later Stockhausen

Serial thinking is something that's come into our consciousness and will be there forever: it's relativity and nothing else. It just says: Use all the components of any given number of elements, don't leave out individual elements, use them all with equal importance and try to find an equidistant scale so that certain steps are no larger than others. It's a spiritual and democratic attitude toward the world. The stars are organized in a serial way . . . What we call serial music is based on a serial way of thinking. Every element that participates in a form at a given moment must have its own time and space to develop.

You don't suppress or make hierarchic forms in which certain elements are automatically subdued forever, as in the tonal system.[3]

In these comments, from conversations published in 1974, Stockhausen appeared to be attempting to resist the already potent trend to hierarchisation in contemporary composition. He sees serialism in visionary terms, not just as 'relativity' but as the ultimate model for a generative process in music – not too dissimilar from Boulez's celebrated (and scientifically, not spiritually, orientated) comments about a universe 'in continual expansion'.[4] Stockhausen came closer to those elusive practical details in his discussion of *Mantra* (1970) for two pianos and electronics, which he describes as

> a miniature of the way a galaxy is composed. When I was composing the work, I had no accessory feelings or thoughts; I knew only that I had to fulfill the mantra. And it demanded itself, it just started blossoming. As it was being constructed through me, I somehow felt that it must be a very true picture of the way the cosmos is constructed. I've never worked on a piece before in which I was so sure that every note I was putting down was right. And this was due to the integral systematization – the combination of the scalar idea with the idea of deriving everything from the One. It shines very strongly.[5]

It is tempting to dismiss such comments as more mystifying than mystical, yet they come only after Stockhausen had been rather more specific about his materials and how he saw their relation to traditional twelve-tone technique. First, he quoted the melodic idea of which the whole sixty-five-minute work is an expansion, explaining that 'the mantra itself has thirteen notes', coming back to its first pitch at the end: in Ex. 13.6a the Prime and Inversion of this are shown. In its compositional realisation (Ex. 13.6b) the upper stave of the Piano I part gives two statements of P-0, first a preliminary one compressed into a single bar, then an eight-bar melodic version. In the composer's words, 'the lower stave presents the same melody mirrored [that is, the I-0 form of the series] but in a permutated form. This is what I call the mantra ... and this formula is repeated all the time in different degrees of expansion and contraction. It's not varied, only *expanded*' (221–2).

From the very beginning of *Mantra* what the listener hears is affected fundamentally by the electronic process signalled in the lowest stave as shown for both instruments in Ex. 13.6b. As Jonathan Harvey explains, 'there are two sine-wave-producing oscillators for whom parts appear in the score. Their pitches are sent to a ring-modulator with the piano's sounds and ring modulated with them, the result being sent out into loudspeakers.'[6] As is often the case with

Ex. 13.6a   Stockhausen, *Mantra*, thirteen-tone series

Ex. 13.6b   Stockhausen, *Mantra*, opening

compositions involving the electronic modification of traditional instrumental sounds, the notated score provides only the basic material which the live performance process then 'interprets'. This does not affect the fact that *Mantra* is the result of serial thinking but, as with much radical music from the post-war decades, it distances the music as heard from its systematic background, as embodied in print.

Stockhausen is determined to distinguish his methods from those of the past: hence his rejection of the possibility that 'expansion' might also be a form of 'variation'.

> I don't use the mantra the way Webern or Beethoven would have in developing the original 'seed' formula – it has no thematic implications: . . . all the early twelve-tone composers presented the series as a *theme* to be developed. They transposed it, added sounds, showed it in mirror form, but they always had a thematic concept. And composers like Boulez, Pousseur, and myself criticized this when we were young, pointing out that though the serial concept might have given birth to a completely new musical technique – getting rid of thematic composition – composers like Schoenberg and Berg still couldn't get away from it. What I said then was that in traditional music you always see the same object – the theme or the motive – in a different light, whereas in the new music there are always new objects in the *same* light.[7]

For all *Mantra*'s radicalism, Robin Maconie is right to say that the work's primary significance is in 'the inauguration of a new era of melody-based serial composition, more approachable to the public and more confident in itself'.[8] Two factors – the avoidance of traditional motivic working and the consistent electronic manipulation of the piano sound – counter any suspicions that *Mantra* is a retreat from the avant-garde ideals of an evolutionary, tradition-rejecting music, even though, both here and in the later stages of *LICHT*, as discussed below, the music doesn't always avoid all contact with certain characteristics of tonality. Nor is there any reason why it should. As Jerome Kohl has emphasised, 'in the struggle for vitality, Stockhausen's compositions from the early 1950s quickly fell into a pattern of subverting their supposedly basic mechanisms with ad hoc, extra-systematic elements'[9]: but such a 'subversion' of serialism was, at the same time, an enrichment of it. Richard Toop demonstrated back in 1976 that Stockhausen's attitude to his materials changed markedly in the 1960s: 'as the serial method becomes more all-embracing, the number of materials that are stylistically "unsuitable" is reduced'[10]: and Toop identified various 'neo-tonal' elements in the works of those years, as well as procedures that 'are much more akin to traditional thematicism [that is, repetition and development] than to the typical results of serial distributions' (82). Stockhausen, it appears, had proved as susceptible as Boulez to the reintroduction of this aspect of tradition: and, again like Boulez, Stockhausen's serialism became more flexible as a result.

In Toop's diagnosis, 'by starting to write melodies that only *appear* to obey "conventional" criteria, Stockhausen ends up . . . by writing melodies which, for all their serial organisation, actually *do*' (85). *Trans* (1971), *Indianerlieder* (1972) and *Herbstmusik* (1974) all fit this formula, and Toop fixes on what he regards as 'a discrepancy between manner and matter' in the latter. 'One can't help questioning the necessity of a fairly complex serial system' when the result is 'innocuous and familiar' (90). At that time, then, it seemed possible, at least to admirers of Stockhausen's earlier music, that, in accepting rapprochements with tradition, he had simply lost his way.

Serialism *in excelsis*

If, in the early 1970s, Stockhausen himself recognised this circumstance as a crisis, his chosen way out was to embark on a large-scale project destined to occupy him for the next quarter-century. Seven years after the breakthrough represented by *Mantra*, he began *LICHT*, a seven-opera cycle – or, 'more accurately, mystery plays or passion plays, one for each day of the week'.[11]

Maconie's long narrative is the first serious attempt to deal with the strengths and weaknesses of *LICHT* as a whole, and it is clear from the outset that he is not prepared to detach the enterprise from all precedent:

> While the principle of determining the form and disposition of an entire composition from an initial series of intervallic relationships is fundamentally serialist and open-ended, and can be traced back at least as far in Stockhausen's oeuvre as the electronic *Studie I* [1953], the alternative approach of deriving an entire work from a closed system of melodic formulae dates more precisely from *Mantra*. Such a conception, distantly relating to the *ars nova* mass, or Bach's *Art of Fugue* – the conception, that is, of a large-scale, polyphonic masterwork based on a theme corresponding to the 'found object' of twentieth-century art, lays down a daunting challenge to the ingenuity of the composer to realize a universe of musical possibilities out of the barest of essential causes.

Maconie's conclusion is that *LICHT* is not always successful in meeting this challenge. And it is perhaps precisely because 'the distinctive poetic and aesthetic features of *LICHT* – its structure, its tight adherence to a limited repertoire of themes, its fantasy, even its serialist principles – conform ... to a very rich and ancient, one might even say timeless, body of conventions' (412) that its contents have to be judged of variable quality when placed in comparison with those conventions.

One challenge facing analysts of *LICHT* is whether its reliance on that 'barest of essential – serial – causes' is a hindrance or a help. Jerome Kohl has explained how each of the work's single-line formulas – for the three central characters of Michael, Eve and Lucifer – 'is composed of a twelve-tone row – save only that the last note of Lucifer's row is transferred to the end of Michael's formula, which means that Michael has thirteen tones' (Ex. 13.7a). Moreover, 'unity is accomplished through

214

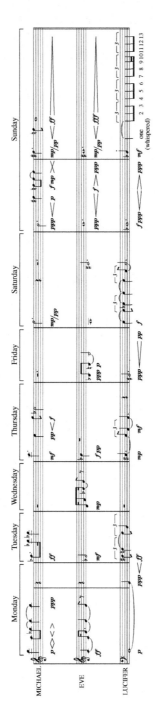

Ex. 13.7a Stockhausen, *LICHT*, the three formulas (nuclear formula)

Ex. 13.7b Stockhausen, *LICHT*, the trichordal invariants in the nuclear formula; see Kohl, 'Into the Middleground'

saturation of the [formula] with just two pairs of inversionally related trichord type, 014/034 and 015/045' (Ex. 13.7b). Kohl claims that 'while in principle everything within the operas is determined by (or perhaps better, derived from) the super-formula, there are some segments which fall outside of the formal plan it dictates'.[12] Given Stockhausen's liking for subversion, this is to be expected. As Maconie puts it: 'accepting the principle of total organization, Stockhausen pursued the idea of serial controls further than any composer before or since – and then, when the acoustic results were not sufficiently compelling or exciting, . . . he broke the rules, or sinned against the Webernian canon of divine perfection.'

Maconie sees the consequence of this – very germane to *LICHT* – as 'a statement of the human condition as necessarily imperfect, existing in an environment of constant change, unstable by nature and requiring expression for its very survival, hence incapable of attaining the stillness and tranquillity of an ideal perfection'.[13] Put this way, there is a strong contrast to the aura surrounding Stockhausen's earliest music: as Toop claims, around 1951–2 'he had developed an almost para-noidly critical attitude to his own work, undoubtedly because of the religious fanaticism that lay at its root (the idea of "perfectly" ordered music as an image of

Divine Perfection)'.[14] In *LICHT*, by contrast, the inevitable weaknesses inherent in such a grandiose project might be seen as necessary consequences of aspiring to perfection in circumstances which have made its attainment impossible.

The work is perhaps at its best, as in Scene 4 of *Samstag* – 'Lucifer's Farewell' – where Stockhausen rises most imaginatively to the restrictive challenges of the formula, which here 'has left him with almost nothing to work with apart from half a dozen pitches, a few pulsations, and rising and falling major third glissandi. Out of this unpromising material he has conjured a rite of purgation and transformation of genuine power and, for once, a work from which all cynical, ironic, or trivial matter has been excluded.'[15] As for *LICHT* as a whole: how often will it be heard and seen as such? The practical challenges to performance are immense, and with those challenges comes the further difficulty of deciding whether the cycle embodies the apotheosis of serial thought, by way of the supremacy of German music of which Schoenberg spoke, or simply confirms its vulnerability – its ability to survive only when its purity is subverted.

Kurtág

By birth date, György Kurtág (b. 1926) belongs with the pioneers of Cold War serialism. Yet the particular circumstances of his early life meant that he came to prominence as a composer only after 1973, by which time most of those pioneers had retrenched or retreated to varying degrees. Unlike Ligeti, Kurtág did not leave Hungary in 1956, though he was able to spend a year in Paris (1957–8), following the approved route of study with Messiaen and the Schoenberg pupil Max Deutsch, and hearing, among much else, the most recent works of Boulez (the then-current version of the Third Piano Sonata) and Stockhausen (*Klavierstücke X* and *XI*). Works of his were heard at Darmstadt in 1960 and 1968, though they made little impression, perhaps reflecting Kurtág's own uncertainties: he has said that it was contact with the psychologist Marianne Stein during his Paris year which was more significant for his musical development, since she recommended the kind of focus on extreme, intense basic materials and their possible connections which became the hallmark of his mature style: the opposite extreme from the seven-opera elaboration of a serial formula offered by *LICHT*.

During his Paris year Kurtág is said to have copied out 'all the principal works of Webern' to facilitate the close study which was so crucial an influence on the compositions which followed. To initiate this phase, 'his String Quartet Op. 1 [1959] shares features of Webern's opp. 5 and 9. All six movements typify his newly discovered concentration of expression, the principle of "completing" the twelve-note space is used frequently, and the work opens with an allusion to Webern (the first four notes of Op. 28). The third and fifth movements use a twelve-note row; although Kurtág experimented with dodecaphonic procedures during this period, a row is usually little more than the starting point for a movement.'[16] Webernian serialism was especially attractive to Kurtág because of the way it offset – even jarred with – other quite different tendencies. In the Op. 1 quartet he was able to show degrees of affinity between the later Webern's more 'classical' style and aspects of Bartók and Stravinsky. But it was only when he gave full rein to his own intensification of the kind of economical expressionism found in many of Webern's pre-twelve-tone vocal pieces that his own style came fully into focus.

Kurtág's most memorable and distinctive early work, *The Sayings of Péter Bornemisza* (1963–8), a 'concerto' for soprano and piano, is actually rather atypical in its length – forty minutes – and its 'large-scale, four-part symphonic structure'.[17] Yet there is also a sense of expression being compressed into much smaller frames in the cycle's twenty-four distinct movements, so it is no surprise to find a Webernian twelve-tone series among the work's materials. Rachel Beckles Willson suggests a network of allusions: 'Webern's String Trio Op. 20 begins with the same two tetrachords, and his Concerto Op. 24 and Variations Op. 30 share the first tetrachord, which also constitutes the first chord of Kurtág's String Quartet Op. 1. The row of Webern's Concerto Op. 24 is a fourfold statement of a trichord that combines a major third with a semitone, and which occurs three times in the row of 'Confession' (Ex. 13.8).[18]

As this example indicates, Kurtág's appropriation of Webernian techniques took particular advantage of their origins in the free, quasi-motivic use of trichord or tetrachordal cells in the pre-twelve-tone works. For Kurtág's most economical use of such elements we can turn to the *Einige Sätze aus den Sudelbüchern Georg Christoph Lichtenbergs*, Op. 37 (1996), tiny and mainly monodic movements consistently concerned with their constituent trichords or tetrachords: for example, one way of analysing the twenty-syllable, twenty-note 'Die Kartoffeln' is as a succession of trichords culminating in a [0,1,2,6] tetrachord (Ex. 13.9).[19] Kurtág begins with nine different pitches: repeats A in a different register before the tenth pitch, G sharp; repeats G, C sharp, F sharp and C, all in the registers used earlier; adds the eleventh note, B flat; then repeats F and A (a second time) before adding the twelfth note, E natural, and ending with a repeat of E flat.

Ex. 13.8   Kurtág, *The Sayings of Péter Bornemisza*, twelve-tone series used in first movement

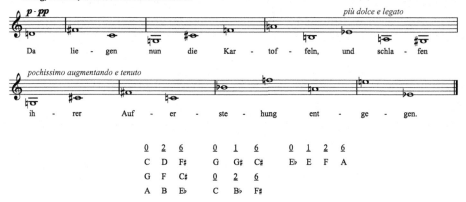

Ex. 13.9   Kurtág, *Einige Sätze aus den Sudelbüchern Georg Christoph Lichtenbergs*, 'Die Kartoffeln'

On the face of it, such simple monodies are scarcely conclusive evidence of a thoroughgoing commitment to serial thinking: yet what could be the intentionally ironic juxtaposition of compositional system with textual absurdity might be intended to demonstrate the impossibility of meaningful text/music synthesis. After all, no contemporary composer is likely to be more sensitive than Kurtág to the ironies of rootedness in a society (Hungary) which has proved such a fruitful source of personal and professional tension during his lifetime.

Chapter 14

European repercussions: V

The contemporary scene

One of the most fundamental themes in musical aesthetics and criticism concerns what can be heard of how a composition is conceived. The more information that emerged about 'total' serialisation after 1945, the more pertinent this issue became, and there are particularly striking comments about it in an essay by Xenakis, first published in 1955. The title refers to the 'crisis' created by serial music, and Xenakis sees the problem, the essential contradiction confronting the listener, as follows: 'linear polyphony destroys itself by its very complexity; what one hears is in reality nothing but a mass of notes in various registers. The enormous complexity prevents the audience from following the intertwining of the lines and has, as a macroscopic effect, an irrational and fortuitous dispersion of sounds over the whole extent of the sonic spectrum. There is consequently a contradiction between the polyphonic linear system and the heard result, which is surface or mass.'[1]

Despite such arguments, there has never been widespread acceptance of the assertion that serialism is justified, compositionally, only if serial techniques themselves, not just their musical consequences, can be aurally identified, in real-time performance. The alternative view, put forward with particular force by Ernst Krenek, claims that 'the reception of serial music requires less intellectual effort than earlier music did, general opinion to the contrary notwithstanding'.[2] This is because serial music – at least of the *Structures Ia* kind – cannot normally be heard in terms of such traditional structural elements as harmonic function or thematic process. Had integral serial music acquired even as much prominence and stability within musical life after 1950 as 'free atonality' did after 1910, so that it could be regarded as coexisting with tonality, then the Krenek argument might have won wider support. To a significant extent, however, composers have conceded the point by attempting to explore ways of using those 'traditional structural elements' in serial works: essentially what Schoenberg, Berg and Webern had done, before 1950.

Scandinavia: Nørgård

It will have become clear that the diffusion of serial thinking in European music after 1945 was far-reaching, and partial surveys of these compositional developments often bring serialism into their frames of reference. For example, Tim Howell's study of Finnish music after Sibelius notes at an early stage that Erik Bergman (1911–2006) 'was credited as the first composer in Finland to use the serial method and this was hugely influential upon subsequent generations'.[3] Howell's narrative then proceeds to outline how that influence worked, and continues to work. However, for a single example of a significant contribution to serial thinking in Scandinavia, I have chosen the Danish composer Per Nørgård (b. 1932), because of the special originality and distinctiveness of his style.

Nørgård devised something called the 'infinity series' which, far from aspiring to an endless, ideal equality between compositional components, attempted to revive the principle of hierarchy and, with it, the audible distinction between harmonic basics and melodic proliferations. Beginning in the 1960s, Nørgård pioneered what was in effect a kind of **fractal** modality, in which traditional, functional harmonic hierarchies were replaced by patterns which articulated comparable features while interacting on all structural levels. As one commentator has observed, 'Nørgård's interest in hierarchies was ... shared by many other thinkers in the humanities and the sciences at the end of the sixties. This was the period leading up to a major "paradigm shift" when holistic philosophy was formulated as a possible successor to the former reductionist, atomist modes of thinking.'[4] Such 'holistic philosophy' can be conceived as an anti-modernist, or post-modernist, initiative. But in music, at least, one of its effects has been to intensify the opposition, and often the interaction, between its synthesising ambitions and a reinvigorated modernism.

The musical result of Nørgård's increasing interest in hierarchies is less a matter of assembling twelve-tone aggregates, after the Babbitt model, than of gradually evolving pitch fields which are **heterophonic**. 'By the beginning of the 1970s, Per Nørgård had ... found hierarchical infinity systems in the fields of melody, rhythm and harmony – used for the first time, but not integrated, in the opera *Gilgamesh* (1971–2)' (83). Erling Kullberg can even claim that 'the guaranteed harmony that results from the system ... makes Nørgård's music more comprehensible than much other contemporary music' (91). Relative closeness to traditional modes of musical thought can be troubling as well as attractive, however. For Julian Anderson, Nørgård's 'recourse to familiar consonance ... is distinctly suspect. Indeed, I suspect that one of the main reasons some of Nørgård's most typical music still has a rare ability to disturb and perplex is his willingness to take historical associations on board in a totally straightforward, guilt-free way to a degree still unusual in music.'[5]

Anderson is able to compare Nørgård to Bartók and Sibelius at one extreme, and to such radical contemporaries as Scelsi, Ligeti, Grisey and Murail at the other, concluding that 'it is Nørgård's perpetual awareness of the unexpected, of the potential catastrophe just around the corner, and of the sheer fragility of coherent individual expression in an increasingly chaotic world which imbues his music with a forceful personal message not found in any other composer writing today' (166). Crucially, this quality is closely tied to his 'investigations of the auditory system, and his use of perceptual criteria as central arbiters in his compositional technique', as a reaction to the degree to which 'the question of the listeners' perception of the resultant music had been largely bypassed by modernist composers' of the late 1950s and early 1960s (161).

Anderson regards a short piano piece by Nørgård called *Grooving* (1967) as typical of his ability to allow time for the musical materials to be perceived as they unfold. '*Grooving* suggests a way in which non-tonal music could acquire a sense of predictability, surprise and contrast which many felt was lacking in total serialism. The form of the piece is straightforward enough – abbreviated ternary form with a short coda – but it is expressed harmonically by means of a gradual partitioning of the twelve notes of the chromatic scale' (148). At the opening of *Grooving* (Ex. 14.1a), the modal centre is E, and the initial pitch collection is the chromatic tetrachord E, F, F sharp, G, to which other tones within the octave – B flat and B above, C and D flat below, are soon added. Ex. 14.1b, 1c show later stages in the evolution of this initial collection of pitch classes and rhythmic patterns, the E remaining stable as a centre while the other tones change register. Anderson's detailed discussion of *Grooving* is illuminating, conveying a clear sense of the degree to which Nørgård's concern with accessibility has not led him into trying to replicate traditionally tonal formal and textural procedures in ways which could easily seem parodistic. But it remains to be seen whether his influence will extend to the degree that admirers like Anderson clearly feel that it should.

British serialism after 1950

Peter Maxwell Davies (b. 1934) emerged onto a British compositional scene in which serialism was very much a fringe phenomenon, with Lutyens and Searle overshadowed by Vaughan Williams, Walton, Britten and Tippett. Maxwell Davies shared with most other radically minded composers of the generation that came to musical maturity around 1950 the conviction that the last thing serial compositions should provide was explicit, surface successions of the twelve tones, which were little more than extensions of old-style thematic procedures. This was in part the result of a general aversion to the classic-romantic sediment in the style of Schoenberg's

Ex. 14.1a   Nørgård, *Grooving*, opening

Ex. 14.1b   Nørgård, *Grooving*, later stage

Ex. 14.1c   Nørgård, *Grooving*, later stage

twelve-tone works. Writing about his years of study in Manchester in the early
1950s, when Maxwell Davies and Harrison Birtwistle were fellow students,
Alexander Goehr comments: 'it is odd that Schoenberg's influence should have
come through his essays and not through his music. The situation was that we very
rarely heard any Schoenberg, and that everybody (except me) seemed to dislike it

intensely. Schoenberg's ideas were liked, the twelve-note technique was liked, but not actually his music. Richard Hall [their most enlightened and influential teacher in Manchester] disliked it strongly, as did most of the other students in the class.'

One wonders to what extent even those 'ideas' were understood and truly appreciated, especially as Goehr goes on to mention Krenek and Hauer as of more practical significance. Krenek's theories provided 'a way of deriving an artificial modality out of twelve-tone hexachords which made it possible to write a modified twelve-tone music in such a way that amateur recorder players could play it ... Hauer was another composer Richard Hall was interested in and whom he rather resembled, sharing a number of his preoccupations.'[6] The possibility of comparing the early experiences of the Manchester students with those of the Eimert-influenced Stockhausen can be noted: and in Maxwell Davies' case it is not too far-fetched to project a long-term working-out of the tension between ideas about modality deriving from Krenek or Hauer and formal principles and textural characteristics closer to Schoenberg, Berg and – ultimately – Mahler.

Maxwell Davies: before 1970

That working-out gained a crucial component of its complexity and sophistication from the kind of experience of a more 'classical' Schoenbergian method that can be detected in Maxwell Davies' Five Pieces for Piano Op. 2 No. 1 (1955–6) and the *St Michael Sonata* for seventeen wind instruments (1957)[7]: and the first of the Op. 2 Pieces demonstrates awareness of the potential in twelve-tone music for dialogues between symmetry and hierarchy of the kind found as early as the Schoenberg Piano Suite discussed in chapter 3. Gradually assembling his pair of twelve-tone series (P-0 and I-0: Ex. 14.2a) in the initial nine-bar period, Davies first deploys the first five notes only of P-0 (right hand) and I-0 (left hand) to assert the priority of E as centre, heard in three different octave positions, and the unambiguous 'root' of the harmony (Ex. 14.2b, bars 1–3). When the first full statement of the twelve-tone series begins with the right hand's E in bar 3, the texture becomes more complex. But the essential point is the subordination of I-0's final white-note trichord (D, C, G) as an inner voice within the phrase's 'perfect' cadence (bars 8–9), a cadence made all the more stable by the transfer of the 'dominant seventh' G sharp/F sharp from left hand (bar 8) to right hand (bar 9).

It was in 1957, while working on the Op. 2 Pieces, that Maxwell Davies made his only visit to the Darmstadt summer school. His twelve-tone Clarinet Sonata was performed, but the composer later spoke dismissively of the Darmstadt ethos as lacking relevance to his own already quite clearly defined objectives. The most

Ex. 14.2a   Maxwell Davies, Five Pieces for Piano, Op. 2 No. 1, twelve-tone series (P-0/I-0)

Ex. 14.2b   Maxwell Davies, Five Pieces for Piano, Op. 2 No. 1, bars 1–9

lasting and fruitful evidence of a European dimension in his early evolution as a serial composer probably stemmed from his studies with Goffredo Petrassi in Rome (1957–8),[8] and from his awareness of the intensely lyrical post-tonal manner which Luigi Nono had derived from Dallapiccola – who, in turn, had derived it from Berg (who had derived it from Mahler). The most lasting evidence of an English dimension which embraces sources of broader European content is in Davies' fascination with medieval and Tudor polyphony, and the extent to which his music works with transformations of Gregorian chant. The result is a serial technique which occasionally juxtaposes and often synthesises post-Bergian expressionism with material whose origins in chant-like melody is sometimes made explicit, sometimes suppressed.

The most extended published accounts of the nature and evolution of Davies' chant-derived serialism can be found in articles by Peter Owens and Richard McGregor, both of whom acknowledge the pioneering work of David Roberts.[9] Roberts describes Davies' *Alma Redemptoris Mater* (1957) for wind sextet, as 'the earliest of his published compositions to incorporate material from a medieval source',[10] and in this respect it is the prelude to such substantial achievements from the earlier phase of Davies' career as the opera *Taverner* (1962–8) and its orchestral offshoots, the two *Fantasias on Taverner's 'In nomine'* (1962, 1964) as well as the 'motet for orchestra' *Worldes Blis* (1966–9).

Davies' view of serialism at this stage of his career is well summarised in comments on the *St Michael* sonata, which was completed in 1957, the same year as *Alma Redemptoris Mater*: 'a basic shape (hardly a series) consciously underlies the design in large form and in detail of the whole work, containing features common to and determined by the various plainchant fragments'. Davies adds that 'as the series is always basically harmonic, the exact sequence of its notes is not fixed as in twelve-tone practice but is determined by the rhythmic proportions of intervals in combination with harmonic and melodic considerations of overall phrase length and contour'.[11] These remarks, dating from 1959, suggest that Davies was unaware of the degree to which earlier serialists, even Schoenberg, had loosened that 'fixed' order in their 'twelve-tone practice'. The remarks nevertheless confirm the importance he attached from an early stage to the kind of flexibility and multiplicity that would reach a new level of sophistication when he began to transform chant materials into serial matrices that took the form of magic squares.

Magic squares and serial structures

Davies' consistent recourse to magic squares from the mid-1970s onwards confirms his Webern-like delight in the kind of mystical speculations concerning music which have been less central to human thought since medieval times. As David Roberts comments, citing W. S. Andrews' *Magic Squares and Cubes* (New York, 1960), 'a magic square consists of a series of numbers so arranged in a square, that the sum of each row and column and of both the corner diagonals shall be the same amount'. In the case of *Ave Maris Stella* (1975) Davies takes the magic square of the moon, whose rows and columns each sum to 369. As Roberts cites it, the 'P-0' line of this square consists of the sequence 37, 78, 29, 70, 21, 62, 13, 54, 5. Davies arrives at his own sequence of 1, 6, 2, 7, 3, 8, 4, 9, 5 – which he uses at the beginning of the work to determine durations in quavers – by 'repeatedly subtracting 9 from each cell until only the integers 1 through 9 remain'.[12] He then attaches a nine-tone pitch series to the numbers.

Davies' fascination with elaborate transformational techniques is clearest in the way he generates ordered pitch-class series from chant melodies which include many pitch repetitions. In the case of *Ave Maris Stella*, the work's nine-tone series (Ex. 14.3b) begins with the same three pitches as the chant (Ex. 14.3a), but then diverges. Ex. 14.3c shows the magic-square matrix on which *Ave Maris Stella* is based: the top horizontal line presents a permutation of the nine-tone series shown in Ex. 14.3b. Finally, Ex. 14.3d shows the cello melody from the opening section. This follows the first three horizontal lines from the matrix, each pitch with the appropriate duration in quavers: C sharp as 1, F [E sharp] as 6, and so on. Also, a

a

Ex. 14.3a   Opening of plainsong hymn, 'Ave Maris Stella'

b

Ex. 14.3b   Maxwell Davies, *Ave Maris Stella*, nine-tone series

C♯	F	C	E	B	G♯	A	F♯	D
1	6	2	7	3	8	4	9	5
A	G♯	C	G	B	F♯	D♯	E	C♯
6	2	7	3	8	4	9	5	1
D♯	B	A♯	D	A	C♯	G♯	F	F♯
2	7	3	8	4	9	5	1	6
G	E	C	B	D♯	A♯	D	A	F♯
7	3	8	4	9	5	1	6	2
G	G♯	F	C♯	C	E	B	D♯	A♯
3	8	4	9	5	1	6	2	7
D♯	C	C♯	A♯	F♯	F	A	E	G♯
8	4	9	5	1	6	2	7	3
A♯	F	D	D♯	C	G♯	G	B	F♯
4	9	5	1	6	2	7	3	8
D	F♯	C♯	A♯	B	G♯	E	D♯	G
9	5	1	6	2	7	3	8	4
G♯	D♯	G	D	B	C	A	F	E
5	1	6	2	7	3	8	4	9

Ex. 14.3c   Maxwell Davies, *Ave Maris Stella*, magic square of pitch classes and durations

transposition down one semitone of the nine-tone series shown in Ex. 14.3b can be traced as the top left to bottom right diagonal of the matrix, from C sharp to E, underlining the fact that the composer can take as many different routes through the matrix as he desires, not only the basic horizontal and vertical ones.

Ex. 14.3d   Maxwell Davies, *Ave Maris Stella*, bars 1–15, cello only

As Roberts says, '*Ave Maris Stella* is quite literally an exploration of this matrix: various pathways through it [diagonal or spiral as well as horizontal and vertical] give rise to the musical material'. Roberts also emphasises the aesthetic conse- quences of what might easily appear to be an arid intellectual exercise, a substitute for inspiration rather than a stimulus for it. *Ave Maris Stella* is indeed 'an amazing work ... packed with textural and gestural invention and having an uncanny sense of formal balance'.[13] In turning to magic-square design, Davies was able to reinvigorate his already well-tried integration of modal and serial elements, and to embark on his most ambitious phase of large-scale composition – at the heart of which are the series of symphonies, concertos and string quartets (the Symphony No. 1 dates from 1973–6).

Maxwell Davies since the 1970s

A particularly clear perspective on the degree to which serialism and non-serialism interact in Davies' work, and of how the combination of stricter and freer approaches to serialism itself are managed, can be found in Richard McGregor's outline analysis of the ballet *Salome* (1978). McGregor actually describes hetero- geneous elements as 'contradictions', and writes that 'the compositional contra- dictions inherent in *Salome* were played out in the works of the 1980s', which display three levels of structural approach:

> At one end of the spectrum are chamber works such as *Image, Reflection,*
> *Shadow* (1982), a tightly structured and fully set-derived work with a plethora

of magic square-based manipulations, very much the successor to *Ave Maris Stella*. The symphonies fall within this general area of working ... The next level encompasses many of the concerto-type works of the '80s where the set material is extensively explored, but in these pieces there is clearly an element of freedom in the execution and working out of musical material. Then there are the lighter works which generally do not use set-based material at all but, significantly, begin to contribute extensively to the background materials for the more complex works, principally the symphonies.[14]

It is indeed in the symphonies and their successors, the series of ten 'Naxos' string quartets, that Davies' modern-classic synthesis of chant-derived serial materials with harmonic processes focusing on the symmetrical [0,3,6,9] division of the octave comes to complete fulfilment: and that synthesis involves a complex conception of hierarchy within the traditional symphonic formal designs to which he alludes as richly as he does to tonality – and to post-tonal serialism. Thus far, the published studies of Richard McGregor and Nicholas Jones, using available sketch materials and interviews with the composer, have reached furthest into the satisfactory explication of these complex, intense compositions, and in so doing they help to confirm the sense in which the 'fulfilment' they represent includes the working-out of those possibilities first outlined by Davies in his very earliest surviving pieces.[15]

From Manchester to Cambridge

Michael Hall has suggested that it was Alexander Goehr's 13-minute *Fantasia for orchestra*, Op. 4, composed in 1954 and first performed at Darmstadt in 1956, that 'led the way' in British explorations of a viable contemporary serialism by a generation significantly younger than that of Lutyens and Searle.[16] Goehr (b. 1932) has told the story of how, soon after being appointed Professor of Music at Cambridge in 1976,

I received a note from a well-known musician there who asked whether from now on only compositions or exercises using 12-note techniques would be acceptable in examinations. The fact that the question was asked at all, apart from some kind of intended insult, expressed the gap between what I was held to stand for and what was going on there. The public perception of me, inasmuch as there was one, was still of a hardline serialist in the Paris–Darmstadt–Princeton mode. Of course, anyone who had had any dealings with me knew this was miles from the truth. There was some irony in the fact that 1976 was precisely when I abandoned 12-note working and turned to modality and figured-bass techniques!

An editorial footnote to this comment states that 'the third string quartet (1976) was Goehr's last work to use the personal form of modal 12-note techniques he had been using since the early 1960s. *Psalm IV* (1976), his next work, eschewed 12-note considerations in favour of a radically simplified modality.'[17] However, neither this statement, nor Goehr's own, can be taken wholly at face value, since in the same volume Aaron Einbond instances the much later cantata *The Death of Moses* (1992) as an example of Goehr's 'mature compositional practice' which combines '12-note thinking with modal and tonal practices'. Einbond (building on a previously published discussion between Goehr and Christopher Wintle) goes on to claim that 'by examining the way Goehr incorporates Schoenberg's music into the fifth and sixth movements of his cantata, we can not only uncover the logic of his tonal and 12-note thinking, but we can see that it bears a resemblance to Schoenberg's own 12-note procedures'.[18]

Goehr invites this specific comparison by deriving an important harmonic progression from the first and fourth trichords of Schoenberg's *Moses und Aron* series (Ex. 14.4a). Ex. 14.4b shows four different versions of the x-y chord progression, and Ex. 14.4c shows the same eight chords in the context of a short extract from the fifth movement of *The Death of Moses*, where Moses attempts to explain his linguistic problems to the Almighty. The bass line added to the chords as they punctuate Moses' eloquent arioso serves to suggest aspects of the E major orientation which Goehr has indicated on a sketch for the passage, reproduced by Einbond (222). Nevertheless, according to the terms used earlier in this book, it might be felt that E major is only present as a suspended tonality, or as a point of reference for the music's pantonality: any single tonal identity is more apparent than real.

This is music that is comfortable with ambiguity, presenting that ambiguity against a strongly delineated historical background – cantata form, arioso style, Schoenbergian trichordal partitioning. Goehr has always resisted the kind of thinking which sought to deny that 'in Schoenberg's dodecaphonic composition, repetitions and note-patterns serve to make the music comprehensible to an ear steeped in eighteenth- and nineteenth-century music'.[19] The conviction that such music nevertheless failed to create a truly perceptible and functioning harmonic process has often been articulated – for example, by Goehr's pupil George Benjamin (b. 1960), in terms that echo Xenakis' plaint, quoted at the beginning of this chapter:

if you use a series in an orthodox fashion, like Schoenberg and some of his successors, the problem is that the twelve notes move so quickly across a texture that there is no form of audible harmony. That means that the music has become almost entirely horizontal, the vertical aspect often being without any kind of control. The lines may perhaps be

Ex. 14.4a   Schoenberg, *Moses und Aron*, twelve-tone series

Ex. 14.4b   Goehr, *The Death of Moses*, chord forms x and y

Ex. 14.4c   Goehr, *The Death of Moses*, extract from movement 5

interesting but the vertical rules are only negative, 'against'; there are no rules 'for'. Besides, if the ear is constantly saturated with twelve notes repeating quickly across all registers it perceives only a harmonic chaos of limited interest. Chaos is only interesting if it is intended. This means there is no harmonic background, and thus there is no harmonic *rhythm*.

For Benjamin, this builds to a general anathema: 'the problem with serial music is first and foremost a lack of poetry, of meaning, of harmonic control. But there is also a loss of speed and energy, everything that comes from mastery of harmony. These are terrible losses.'[20] Nevertheless, in the discussion of his piano work *Shadowlines* (2001) which follows these remarks, Benjamin concedes that not all processes deriving from serial principles need to be discarded in order for perceptible harmonic identities and processes to be established. Evidently, for a significant number of present-day composers, Milton Babbitt's assertion from 1964 (quoted earlier) must be questioned: 'the formal systems – of which the tonal system and the twelve-tone system are, respectively, instances – are, under no conceivable principle of correspondence, equivalent; they are so different in structure as to render the possibility of a work being an extended instance of both unthinkable'.[21] Rather, by building bridges which span tonality, modality, and serial thinking, productive compatibilities and contrasts are not only conceivable, but practicable. The aim is to use difference positively, to frame fields of activity that can generate coherent musical results.

Birtwistle

'Birtwistle is not a serialist, but the concerns of serialism have nonetheless left their mark on his music.'[22] Born, like Maxwell Davies, in 1934, and a Manchester student at the same time as Davies and Goehr, Harrison Birtwistle was evidently exposed to comparable ideas and influences. Equally obviously, his reactions were distinctive, his long-term development quite different to that of either of his more Schoenbergianly attuned colleagues. Jonathan Cross points out that Birtwistle's 'only thoroughgoing serial composition', a score 'steeped in twelve-note practices' (49), is the *Three Sonatas for Nine Instruments* (1960), which the composer withdrew after one rehearsal and has never been performed, though he did not destroy it, and it can now be studied in the Sacher Stiftung, Basel.

The 'mark' of serialism on Birtwistle's music is nevertheless pervasive. David Beard believes that it 'represents a productive misreading of serialism, most obviously the kinds of serial technique practised by both Stravinsky and Webern', and notes that, in discussing his 'breakthrough' piece *Tragoedia* (1965) 'the composer was primarily concerned to explain how the piece is based on a twelve-note expanding chromatic wedge around B, partitioned into four groups each of six pitch-classes'.[23] 'Misreading' perhaps implies a willingness to think of serialism as more to do with unordered collections than with ordered twelve-tone series. Nevertheless, generating pitch structures from wedge shapes, which tend to provide all-interval series forms, linked Birtwistle to avant-garde contemporaries, notably

Nono and Stockhausen, and the symmetrical qualities of such basic materials have been a decisive factor in promoting the presence of harmonic centres crucial to most of Birtwistle's major compositions.[24] This confirms the validity of Cross' claim that 'though [after the 1960 *Sonatas*] he never again attempted a wholehearted twelve-note composition, the serial legacy continues to resonate through Birtwistle's music' (54).

Ferneyhough

Brian Ferneyhough (b. 1943) is as anxious as George Benjamin to think of the word 'serial' in a critical light. In an early interview (1977) he declared that 'what I have against the term "serial" is certainly partially dictated by the cliché which the word has become. In a sense, it means all and nothing. Music is in every case a more or less ordered object; whether the methods employed call for some form of pre-ordering or emerge only in the course of actual composition by so-called intuitive processes is scarcely very interesting.'[25] This is a telling observation, implicitly acknowledging the possibility that twelve-tone serialism, together with its integral and freer aftermaths, raise the prospect of interpreting features of ordering in earlier musics in terms of serial processes. Nor is Ferneyhough distancing himself from all aspects of serial thought, and such technical commentaries on his music as have been published so far usually find it hard to do without serial concepts.

Twelve-tone backgrounds can be productive for composers whose aim is not to preserve the kind of harmonic rhythm and hierarchic relations found most directly within tonality, but to derive complex post-tonal invention from a systematic, and in some ways simple, nucleus. In Richard Toop's analyses of two works by Ferneyhough from 1981 – *Lemma-Icon-Epigram* for piano, and *Superscriptio* for piccolo – it is possible to trace some of the ways in which a twelve-tone series generates the explosive pitches, durations and dynamics of the musical surface.[26]

As with several of the analyses I have referred to in these pages, Toop's would scarcely have been possible without access to sketches, drafts and the composer's own comments. *Superscriptio* begins with an explicit twelve-tone statement, which is shown in abstract form in Ex. 14.5a, then as part of the score in Ex. 14.5b. P-0 is followed by I-3 and P-5 – transposition levels which relate to the first three pitches of P-0 itself. Series intersection is another Second Viennese School technique used by Ferneyhough: the D sharp which ends the I-3 statement functions simultaneously as the first pitch of P-5. Nevertheless, from the perspective of the piece as a whole, Toop emphasises that 'this series is not simply a set of pitches that can be transposed, inverted, retrograded, etc. It is also a sequence of intervals which can be read alternately in basic and inverted directions; moreover, both as pitch series and as

Ex. 14.5a   Ferneyhough, *Superscriptio*, twelve-tone series

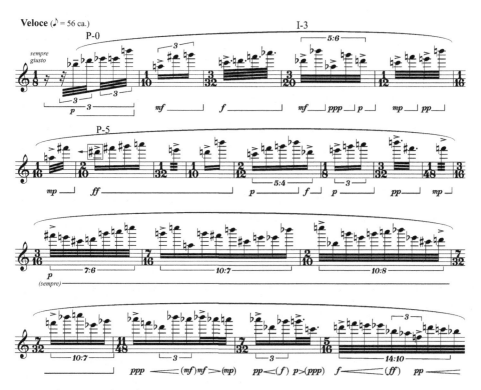

Ex. 14.5b   Ferneyhough, *Superscriptio*, opening

interval series, it can be interlocked with up to four other forms of itself to produce new pitch configurations.'[27]

Toop's analysis illustrates the results of these proliferations, whose effect is similar to Boulez's multiplication technique or Babbitt's aggregate- and array-based polyphony: they transform the original linear series rather than simply transfer it to the musical surface, as Schoenberg and Webern did. Another transformative technique of Ferneyhough's which has points of contact with serialism is his use of the 'Random Funnel series': this is discussed by Ross Feller in his short study of the *Trittico per*

5	9	4	6	8	1	2	7	3
7	1	4	5	9	2	6	3	8
6	1	3	2	8	4	7	9	5
6	4	3	8	1	5	7	9	2
8	6	3	1	5	4	7	9	2
6	9	3	2	5	1	7	8	4
9	1	3	2	5	6	7	8	4
2	1	3	9	5	6	7	8	1
9	2	3	4	5	6	7	8	1
1	2	3	4	5	6	7	8	9

Ex. 14.6 Ferneyhough, *Trittico per Gertrude Stein*, Random Funnel series with nine numbers; see Feller, 'Random Funnels', p. 33

Gertrude Stein for double bass (1989).[28] Ex. 14.6, a 'Random Funnel series with 9 numbers', might look like a serial matrix, but there is a major difference between it and the examples given above in that only the horizontal lines give permutations of the nine different integers. The vertical lines contain many repetitions, of fewer than nine different numbers: it follows that a 'Random Funnel' matrix is very different from a magic square.

As Ross Feller explains, 'the Random Funnel process [a computer-generated algorithm] generates a series of numbers via a linear, funnel-shaped random procedure', and in *Trittico per Gertrude Stein* 'Ferneyhough employed Random Funnel procedures in structuring various parameters including meter, tempo, rhythm, and pitch'. Feller gives several examples, referring to sketches, of how this process works in practice. Ferneyhough himself has referred to Random Funnel procedures as a means of ensuring

> the progressive erosion or distortion of elements … For each work I establish a series of grids which, beginning with a random ordering of the required values, progressively assign individual digits to their correct position in the final 'normative order' – usually in order of increasing or decreasing magnitude. Apart from being almost universally applicable to any quantifiable musical phenomenon (and thus highly amenable to the all-important task of musical 'punning') such complex but ultimately highly directional operations are a powerful tool in balancing basically simple fundamental operations against the significant level of complexity which emerges when relatively small numbers of such 'lines of force' impinge obliquely upon each other. I usually spend a considerable amount of time preparing the versions of such tables which, for any given set of values, will be employed in a particular compositional situation. One important factor is, obviously, the number of permutations required to move from a totally random to a particular normative ordering of the elements; another is the degree to which the specifics of any

given series may be usefully reflected in subsequent interlocking or nesting procedures making for larger-scale dispositional coherence.[29]

After this expansive statement – using words like 'set' and 'series' – of how the grand design of a composition might proceed, Ferneyhough rapidly counters any impression of control-freakery with this claim: 'I would not say that I was a notably systematic composer. Most of my time is spent finding ways of allowing my natural tendencies to disorder to find useful channels of expression commensurate with my (perhaps unrealistic) vision of the high compaction of abstract and concrete aspects which a work needs to embody in order to make it more than just one more thing in the world to trip over.' But Ferneyhough's early admission that 'what interests me is always the "shadow zone" between the totally ordered and that which lends that ordering significance'[30] nevertheless seems to confirm the importance of those elements of serial thought which Toop's analyses reveal. And his 1992 comment about preferring various types of 'loose context' to 'the serial production of uniquely specific solutions to radically isolated and self-enclosed problems'[31] reinforces the fact that his compositional thinking derives from a critique of systematic precedents rather than from a wholesale discounting of such precedents. For this reason, the hyper-expressionistic intensity of musical expression, as evident in both *Superscriptio* and the *Trittico per Gertrude Stein*, seems all the more potent for the ordered, directional, post-twelve-tone, permutational background from which it emerges.

Knussen

Oliver Knussen (b. 1952) and Julian Anderson (b. 1967) are like-minded composers, and a two-article study of the former by the latter provides an outline of something approximating to a mainstream early twenty-first-century musical language, freely serial rather than systematically twelve-tone, yet continuing the search for positive interactions between older and newer, traditional and innovatory, that was Schoenberg's own concern in the early 1920s.

Anderson concentrates on works by Knussen written since the late 1980s, though pointing out that many of their 'methods of harmonic and melodic generation had been evolving since the 1970s'. As Anderson then shows, 'it is in the personal methods adopted by Stravinsky in his late serial works that we find the key to Knussen's technique',[32] even though Knussen's sound-world is just as likely to bring Berg to mind, not least because Knussen uses Stravinskian rotational methods (themselves derived from Krenek) to validate a stronger degree of post-tonal pitch centricity than Stravinsky himself tended to admit to his own serial pieces. To this extent, there is even a degree of analogy with the kind of centricity admitted by Boulez in his compositions from the mid-1970s onwards.

Anderson traces the role of these techniques through a group of Knussen's works beginning with the *Flourish with Fireworks* (1988) and ending with the Violin Concerto (2001–2). Just as, with the *Whitman Settings* (1993), 'it says much for the viable results of Knussen's harmonic methods that the inevitability of its conclusion is clearly audible, even if one is unaware of the music's pitch structure' (13), so at the end of *Songs without Voices* (1991–2) 'the sense of harmonic closure … is a remarkable achievement in a post-tonal idiom'.[33] Anderson refers to Knussen's 'personal reinvention' of tonality, 'in the light of … harmonic habits such as the use of the all-interval tetrachord (0146) and its inversion (0256)' (33): evidence of Knussen's informed admiration for Elliott Carter, even if the musical result is very different. Simple instances can be found in the second of the *Two Organa* (1994), in which a pitch transliteration of the name of the conductor Reinbert de Leeuw (Ex. 14.7a) generates themes and harmonies to which the all-interval tetrachords are central. Ex. 14.7b shows a melody formed from the succession P-0, I-2, P-0, which puts the pitch repetitions inherent in the series to good use. Ex. 14.7c shows the six different pitch classes of the series, then the six different chords that series generates. The top line of the matrix shown in Ex. 14.7d gives a permutation of the six-tone series, then successive rotations of its interval classes (6, 4, 3, 2, 3, 4) through the fixed tone E. The six horizontal lines of the matrix correspond to the six chords of Ex. 14.7c, each of which has E as bass note.

Anderson explains that for Knussen's Horn and Violin Concertos (1994 and 2002), 'there are few charts of rotation or transposed inversion … Indeed the sketching method appears to have been quite different from earlier works. Instead of elaborate pre-compositional mapping of harmonic and melodic syntax, the sketches comprise mainly the plotting of formal schemes' (33). To some extent, this represents the kind of retreat from serialism in its purest, most rigorous forms which is not admired by those who hear dangers in the return to more romantic, more improvisatory idioms. But it also suggests the inherent adaptability of a way of musical thinking that has evolved by means of the specific technical challenges and possibilities it provides, as well as through the confrontations between system and spontaneity that it engenders.

An ending

That this chapter can contain two such different British-born composers as Brian Ferneyhough and Oliver Knussen confirms that the view of serialism and serial thinking adopted in this book is nothing if not diverse. For Steve Reich to proclaim

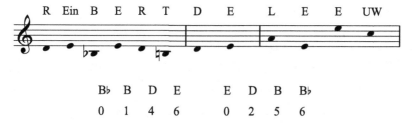

Ex. 14.7a   Knussen, *Two Organa*, twelve-element series using six different tones

Ex. 14.7b   Knussen, *Two Organa*, melodic line

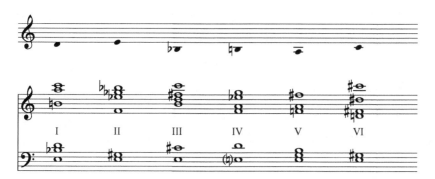

Ex. 14.7c   Knussen, *Two Organa*, chord forms derived from six-tone series

I	E	6	B♭	4	D	3	B♮	2	A	3	C	4
II	E	4	G♯	3	F	2	E♭	3	G♭	4	B♭	6
III	E	3	C♯	2	B	3	D	4	F♯	6	C	4
IV	E	2	D	3	F	4	A	6	E♭	4	G	3
V	E	3	G	4	B	6	F	4	A	3	F♯	2
VI	E	4	G♯	6	D	4	F♯	3	D♯	2	C♯	3

Ex. 14.7d   Knussen, *Two Organa*, matrix for generation of chord forms

in the London *Evening Standard* (9 August 2006), during his seventieth birthday year, that 'serialism is dead!' might indeed be true if the concept is associated only with a few years of intransigent experimentalism from the post-war avant-garde and its foreshadowings in Schoenberg and Webern against which Reich reacted so vehemently as a student. But from its earliest years, when the twelve-tone method showed itself able to relate to aspects of neo-classicism on the one hand (Schoenberg's Piano Suite) and late-romanticism on the other (Berg's Violin Concerto) serialism of one kind of another has proved to be a constant presence within the wider dialogue between the progressive and the conservative that has shaped music since 1900 as it extended, exploded and reinstated tonality with a resourcefulness and flexibility paralleled by the resourceful and flexible employment of serial techniques themselves. To the extent that this *Introduction* has at times threatened to turn into a survey of post-1900 music as a whole, the comprehensive relevance of serial thinking, even to composers who wouldn't dream of labelling themselves 'serialists', is clear: and there are many others who could have been included in a less selective survey. It seems more than likely that historians of music since 2000 will find it no less difficult to exclude serialism from their terminology, as composers continue to see no reason to exclude it from their thought.

Notes

Preface

1. Bryan Hyer, 'Tonality', in *The New Grove Dictionary of Music and Musicians* (hereafter: *The New Grove*), 2nd edn., eds. Stanley Sadie and John Tyrrell (London: Macmillan, 2001), xxv, p. 594.

1 Introducing the *Introduction*

1. Arnold Schoenberg, '"Schoenberg's Tone-Rows" (1936)', in *Style and Idea*, ed. Leonard Stein, trans. Leo Black (London: Faber & Faber, 1975), p. 213.
2. Anton Webern, *The Path to the New Music*, ed. Willi Reich, trans. Leo Black (Bryn Mawr, PA: Presser, 1963), p. 51.
3. Paul Lansky and George Perle, 'Twelve-note composition', in *The New Grove*, 2nd edn., eds. Stanley Sadie and John Tyrrell (London: Macmillan, 2001), xxvi, p. 1. For a fuller discussion of this example, and the work to which it refers, see George Perle, *Serial Composition and Atonality*, 4th edn. (Berkeley, Los Angeles and London: University of California Press, 1977), pp. 41–3.
4. Joseph N. Straus, *Introduction to Post-Tonal Theory*, 3rd edn. (Englewood Cliffs, NJ: Prentice Hall, 2005), p. 182.
5. For a 'Simplified Set List' showing all possible versions of pitch-class sets containing between three and nine elements, see Straus, *Introduction to Post-Tonal Theory*, pp. 261–4.
6. Milton Babbitt is fully discussed, and referenced, in chapter 8.
7. For a thorough explanation of the distinctions between normal form and prime form pitch-class sets, see Straus, *Introduction to Post-Tonal Theory*, pp. 1–11.
8. Allen Forte, 'Pitch-Class Set Analysis Today', *Music Analysis*, 4/2 (March–July 1985), p. 40.
9. Richard Taruskin, *The Oxford History of Western Music*, 6 vols. (New York: Oxford University Press, 2005), i, p. 207.
10. Stephen Walsh, *Stravinsky: The Second Exile. France and America, 1934–1971* (London: Jonathan Cape, 2006), pp. 281–2.

2 Schoenberg's path to the twelve-tone method

1. See Bryan Simms, *The Atonal Music of Arnold Schoenberg, 1908–1923* (New York: Oxford University Press, 2000), pp. 89–99.

2. George Perle, *Serial Composition and Atonality*, 4th edn. (Berkeley, Los Angeles and London: University of California Press, 1977), p. 40.

3. James M. Baker, *The Music of Alexander Scriabin* (New Haven and London: Yale University Press, 1986), p. 144.

4. Allen Forte, 'The Magical Kaleidoscope: Schoenberg's First Atonal Masterwork. Op. 11, No. 1', *Journal of the Arnold Schoenberg Institute*, 5 (1981), pp. 127–68; Will Ogdon, 'How Tonality Functions in Schoenberg's Op. 11, No. 1', *ibid.*, pp. 169–81.

5. See the discussion of Babbitt in chapter 8.

6. Allen Forte introduced pitch-class set theory and analysis in *The Structure of Atonal Music* (New Haven and London: Yale University Press, 1973). For useful commentary, including exercises for students, see Joseph N. Straus, *Introduction to Post-Tonal Theory*, 3rd edn. (Englewood Cliffs, NJ: Prentice Hall, 2005).

7. Simms, *The Atonal Music of Arnold Schoenberg*, p. 60. Further page references in text.

8. Joseph H. Auner, 'In Schoenberg's Workshop: Aggregates and Referential Collections in *Die glückliche Hand*', *Music Theory Spectrum*, 18/1 (Spring 1996), pp. 84–5.

9. See the discussion of Schoenberg's Op. 19 No. 6 in Jonathan Dunsby and Arnold Whittall, *Music Analysis in Theory and Practice* (London: Faber Music, 1988), pp. 116–22, 140–1, 158–61.

10. Jennifer Shaw, 'Androgyny and the Eternal Feminine in *Die Jakobsleiter*', in *Political and Religious Ideas in the Works of Arnold Schoenberg*, eds. Charlotte M. Cross and Russell A. Berman (New York: Garland, 2000), p. 83.

11. Arnold Schoenberg, 'On Twelve-Tone Composition and Tonality' [*c.* 1923], in *A Schoenberg Reader*, ed. Joseph H. Auner (New Haven and London: Yale University Press, 2003), pp. 174–5.

12. O. W. Neighbour, 'Schoenberg, Arnold' in *The New Grove*, 2nd edn., eds. Stanley Sadie and John Tyrrell (London: Macmillan, 2001), xxii, p. 580.

13. Arnold Schoenberg, 'Composition with Twelve Tones (2)', in *Style and Idea*, ed. Leonard Stein, trans. Leo Black (London: Faber & Faber, 1975), p. 247.

14. Ethan Haimo, *Schoenberg's Serial Odyssey: The Evolution of his Twelve-Tone Method, 1914–1928* (Oxford: Clarendon Press, 1990), pp. 64, 68.

15. John Covach, 'Twelve-tone Theory', in *The Cambridge History of Western Music Theory*, ed. Thomas Christensen (Cambridge: Cambridge University Press, 2002). All quotations from pp. 604–7.

16. Monika Lichtenfeld, 'Hauer, Josef Matthias', *The New Grove*, 2nd edn., eds. Stanley Sadie and John Tyrrell (London: Macmillan, 2001), xi, p. 135. For illustration and discussion of an early example of Hauer's method, in *Nomos* Op. 19 (1919), see Richard Taruskin, *The Oxford History of Western Music*, 6 vols. (New York: Oxford University Press, 2005), iv, pp. 680–7. For analysis of examples from Hauer's *Zwölftonspiele*, see John R. Covach, 'The *Zwölftonspiel* of Josef Matthias Hauer', *Journal of Music Theory*, 36/1 (Spring 1992), pp. 149–84.

17. Arnold Schoenberg, 'Hauer's Theories' [1923], in *Style and Idea*, ed. Leonard Stein, trans. Leo Black (London: Faber & Faber, 1975), p. 212.

18. Roberto Gerhard, *Gerhard on Music. Selected Writings*, ed. Meirion Bowen (Aldershot: Ashgate, 2000), p. 103. Further page references in text.

3 Serialism in close-up

1. Arnold Schoenberg, *Structural Functions of Harmony*, 2nd edn., ed. Leonard Stein (New York: Norton, 1969), p. 19.

2. Ethan Haimo, *Schoenberg's Serial Odyssey: The Evolution of his Twelve-Tone Method, 1914–1928* (Oxford: Clarendon Press, 1990), p. 85.

3. Jonathan W. Bernard, 'Chord, Collection, and Set in Twentieth-Century Theory', in *Music Theory in Concept and Practice*, eds. James M. Baker, David W. Beach and Jonathan W. Bernard (Rochester, NY: University of Rochester Press, 1997), p. 27.

4. First used in print by Schoenberg in 1911 in *Harmonielehre*. See *Theory of Harmony*, trans. Roy E. Carter (London: Faber & Faber, 1978), p. 323.

5. For an interpretation of this canon which emphasises the comic potential of any post-tonal treatment of a traditionally tonal form, hitherto dependent on traditional rules of voice-leading, see Richard Taruskin, *The Oxford History of Western Music*, 6 vols. (New York: Oxford University Press, 2005), iv, pp. 691–9.

4 Schoenberg in the 1920s

1. Ethan Haimo, *Schoenberg's Serial Odyssey: The Evolution of his Twelve-Tone Method, 1914–1928* (Oxford: Clarendon Press, 1990), p. 70.

2. Bryan R. Simms, *The Atonal Music of Arnold Schoenberg, 1908–1923* (New York: Oxford University Press, 2000), p. 217.

3. Kathryn Bailey, *'Composing with Tones': A Musical Analysis of Schoenberg's Op. 23 Pieces for Piano* (London: Royal Musical Association, 2001), p. 122.

4. Haimo, *Schoenberg's Serial Odyssey*, p. 80.

5. Haimo, *Schoenberg's Serial Odyssey*, p. 91.

6. Simms, *The Atonal Music of Arnold Schoenberg*, p. 188.

7. Bailey, 'Composing with Tones', p. 100.

8. Arnold Schoenberg, 'Composition with Twelve Tones (1)', in *Style and Idea*, ed. Leonard Stein, trans. Leo Black (London: Faber & Faber, 1975), p. 224.

9. Arnold Schoenberg, 'Problems of Harmony', in *Style and Idea*, ed. Leonard Stein, trans. Leo Black (London: Faber & Faber, 1975), p. 284.

10. Arnold Schoenberg, 'Composition with Twelve Tones (1)', in *Style and Idea*, ed. Leonard Stein, trans. Leo Black (London: Faber & Faber, 1975), p. 227. Further page references in text.

11. Arnold Schoenberg, 'Foreword to *Three Satires for Mixed Chorus*, Op. 28', in *A Schoenberg Reader*, ed. Joseph Auner (New Haven and London: Yale University Press, 2003), p. 187.

12. 'Two Statements on the Third String Quartet', in *A Schoenberg Reader*, ed. Joseph Auner (New Haven and London: Yale University Press, 2003), p. 198.

13. Carl Dahlhaus, *Schoenberg and the New Music*, trans. Derrick Puffett and Alfred Clayton (Cambridge: Cambridge University Press, 1987), pp, 75, 76, 77.

14. Arnold Schoenberg, 'Schoenberg's Tone Rows', in *Style and Idea*, ed. Leonard Stein, trans. Leo Black (London: Faber & Faber, 1975), p. 213.

15. *Arnold Schoenberg Letters*, ed. Erwin Stein, trans. Eithne Wilkins and Ernst Kaiser (London: Faber & Faber, 1964), pp. 164–5.

16. John Covach, 'Schoenberg's "Poetics of Music", the Twelve-Tone Method, and the Musical Idea', in *Schoenberg and Words: The Modernist Years*, eds. Charlotte M. Cross and Russell A. Berman (New York: Garland, 2000), pp. 315–16. Further page references in text.

17. See Arnold Whittall, *Exploring Twentieth-Century Music: Tradition and Innovation* (Cambridge: Cambridge University Press, 2003), pp. 9, 13.

5 Alban Berg: reverence and resistance

1. George Perle, *The Operas of Alban Berg, I: Wozzeck* (Berkeley, Los Angeles and London: University of California Press, 1980), p. 10.

2. Anthony Pople, 'The Musical Language of *Wozzeck*', in *The Cambridge Companion to Berg*, ed. Anthony Pople (Cambridge: Cambridge University Press, 1997), pp. 145–64.

3. Patricia Hall, 'Compositional Process in *Wozzeck* and *Lulu*: A Glimpse of Berg's Atonal Method', in *The Cambridge Companion to Berg*, ed. Anthony Pople (Cambridge: Cambridge University Press, 1997), p. 186.

4. *The Berg–Schoenberg Correspondence: Selected Letters*, eds. Juliane Brand, Christopher Hailey and Donald Harris (London: Macmillan, 1987), p. 346.

5. *Schoenberg, Berg, Webern: The String Quartets. A Documentary Study*, ed. Ursula Rauchhaupt (Hamburg: DGG, 1971), p. 89.

6. Arnold Schoenberg, 'Opinion or Insight?', in *Style and Idea*, ed. Leonard Stein, trans. Leo Black (London: Faber & Faber, 1975), p. 263.

7. *The Berg–Schoenberg Correspondence*, p. 348.

8. *The Berg–Schoenberg Correspondence*, p. 349.

9. Arved Ashby, 'Of *Modell-Typen* and *Reihenformen*: Berg, Schoenberg, F. H. Klein and the Concept of Row Derivation', *Journal of the American Musicological Society*, 48 (1995), p. 73. Further page references in text.

10. Neil Boynton, 'Compositional Technique 1923–6: The Chamber Concerto and the *Lyric Suite*', in *The Cambridge Companion to Berg*, ed. Anthony Pople (Cambridge: Cambridge University Press, 1997), pp. 191, 192, 193.

11. *The Berg–Schoenberg Correspondence*, p. 349.

12. George Perle, *The Operas of Alban Berg, II: Lulu* (Berkeley, Los Angeles and London: University of California Press, 1989), p. 5.

13. Perle, *The Operas of Alban Berg, II*, p. 6.

14. One of Schoenberg's transitional works, the *Serenade* Op. 24 (1920–3), contains a setting of a Petrarch sonnet, each of whose fourteen lines has eleven syllables. Schoenberg's entirely syllabic setting uses 154 pitches – twelve complete statements of a twelve-tone series, plus ten notes of a thirteenth statement. At the same time as the voice has the ninth and tenth notes of the thirteenth statement, the violin and viola play the eleventh and twelfth.

15. Craig Ayrey, 'Tonality and the Series: Berg', in *Models of Musical Analysis: Early Twentieth-Century Music*, ed. Jonathan Dunsby (Oxford: Blackwell, 1993), pp. 109, 111.

16. Dave Headlam, *The Music of Alban Berg* (New Haven and London: University of Yale Press, 1996), p. 11. Further page references in text.

17. Perle, *The Operas of Alban Berg, II*, p. 25.

18. Perle, *The Operas of Alban Berg, II*, pp. 22–3.

19. Pierre Boulez, *Conversations with Célestin Deliège* (London: Eulenberg, 1976), p. 24.

20. Pierre Boulez, 'Alban Berg', in *Stocktakings from an Apprenticeship*, trans. Stephen Walsh (Oxford: Clarendon Press, 1991), p. 255.

21. Perle, *The Operas of Alban Berg, II*, p. 85.

22. Douglas Jarman, *Alban Berg: Lulu* (Cambridge: Cambridge University Press, 1991), pp. 100–1.

23. Anthony Pople, 'In the Orbit of *Lulu*: The Late Works', in *The Cambridge Companion to Berg*, ed. Anthony Pople (Cambridge: Cambridge University Press, 1997) p. 210.

24. Patricia Hall, *A View of Berg's Lulu* (Berkeley, Los Angeles and London: University of California Press, 1996), p. 99.

25. Pople, *The Cambridge Companion to Berg*, p. 219.
26. Anthony Pople, *Berg: Violin Concerto* (Cambridge: Cambridge University Press, 1991), pp. 79–80.
27. Ex. 5.12a is from Pople, 'In the Orbit of *Lulu*', p. 212. Ex. 5.12b is from Pople, *Berg: Violin Concerto*, p. 82.
28. Douglas Jarman, 'Secret Programmes', in *The Cambridge Companion to Berg*, ed. Anthony Pople (Cambridge: Cambridge University Press, 1997), pp. 167–9.

6 Anton Webern: discipline and licence

1. See in particular Kathryn Bailey, *The Life of Webern* (Cambridge: Cambridge University Press, 1998), and Julian Johnson, *Webern and the Transformation of Nature* (Cambridge: Cambridge University Press, 1999).
2. See the facsimile edition with Webern's markings, provided for Peter Stadlen, who gave the first performance of Op. 27 (Vienna: Universal Edition, No. 16845, 1979).
3. Anne C. Shreffler, '"Mein Weg geht jetzt vorüber": The Vocal Origins of Webern's Twelve-Tone Composition', *Journal of the American Musicological Society*, 47 (1994), p. 276. Further page references in text.
4. Johnson, *Webern*, p. 166.
5. Kathryn Bailey, *The Twelve-Note Music of Anton Webern* (Cambridge: Cambridge University Press, 1991), p. 33. Further page references in text.
6. Johnson, *Webern*, p. 201.
7. Johnson, *Webern*, p. 211.
8. Anton Webern, *The Path to the New Music*, ed. Willi Reich, trans. Leo Black (Bryn Mawr, PA: Presser, 1963), p. 54.
9. Kathryn Bailey, 'Symmetry as Nemesis: Webern and the First Movement of the Concerto, Opus 24', *Journal of Music Theory*, 40 (1996), p. 246.
10. Arnold Whittall, *Musical Composition in the Twentieth Century* (Oxford: Oxford University Press, 1999), p. 207.
11. Anton Webern, *Letters to Hildegard Jone and Josef Humplik*, ed. Josef Polnauer, trans. Cornelius Cardew (Bryn Mawr, PA: Presser, 1967), p. 10.
12. Johnson, *Webern*, p. 77.
13. Johnson, *Webern*, p. 215.
14. Arnold Whittall, *Exploring Twentieth-Century Music: Tradition and Innovation* (Cambridge: Cambridge University Press, 2003), p. 30.
15. For accounts of twelve-tone canons by Webern, see Jonathan Dunsby and Arnold Whittall, *Music Analysis in Theory and Practice* (London: Faber Music, 1987), pp. 192–200, and Arnold Whittall, 'Webern and Multiple Meaning', *Music Analysis*, 6/1 (October 1987), pp. 333–53.

16. Pierre Boulez, *Conversations with Célestin Deliège* (London: Eulenberg, 1976), p. 24.
17. William E. Benjamin, 'Abstract Polyphonies: The Music of Schoenberg's Nietzschean Moment', in *Political and Religious Ideas in the Works of Arnold Schoenberg*, eds. Charlotte M. Cross and Russell A. Berman (New York: Garland, 2000), p. 33.

7 The later Schoenberg

1. Richard Taruskin, *The Oxford History of Western Music*, 6 vols. (New York: Oxford University Press, 2005), iv, p. 741.
2. Taruskin, *The Oxford History of Western Music*, iv, p. 703.
3. William E. Benjamin, 'Abstract Polyphonies: The Music of Schoenberg's Nietzschean Moment', in *Political and Religious Ideas in the Works of Arnold Schoenberg*, eds. Charlotte M. Cross and Russell A. Berman (New York: Garland, 2000), p. 30.
4. Edward D. Latham, 'The Prophet and the Pitchman: Dramatic Structure and its Musical Elucidation in *Moses und Aron*, Act 1, Scene 2', in *Political and Religious Ideas in the Works of Arnold Schoenberg*, eds. Charlotte M. Cross and Russell A. Berman (New York: Garland, 2000), p. 134–5.
5. Latham, 'The Prophet', p. 134.
6. Joseph Auner, 'Schoenberg and his Public in 1930: The Six Pieces for Male Chorus, Op. 35', in *Schoenberg and his World*, ed. Walter Frisch (Princeton: Princeton University Press, 1999), pp. 88, 89. See also Joseph Auner, 'Composing on Stage: Schoenberg and the Creative Process as Public Performance', *19th Century Music*, xxix/1 (Summer 2005), pp. 64–93.
7. For a concise, technically informed discussion of this work, see Stephen Davison, '*Von heute auf morgen*: Schoenberg as Social Critic', in *Political and Religious Ideas in the Works of Arnold Schoenberg*, eds. Charlotte M. Cross and Russell A. Berman (New York: Garland, 2000), pp. 85–110.
8. The term 'combinatorial' appears to have been first applied to twelve-tone music by Milton Babbitt. See citations from 1950 and 1955 in the *Collected Essays of Milton Babbitt*, eds. Stephen Peles with Stephen Dembski, Andrew Mead and Joseph N. Straus (Princeton: Princeton University Press, 2003), pp. 13, 15. 41, 46–7.
9. The most detailed analysis of twelve-tone areas and motivic identities in *Moses und Aron* is in Pamela C. White, *Schoenberg and the God-Idea: The Opera* Moses und Aron (Ann Arbor: UMI Research Press, 1985). However, White's proposal that the inversion form in the A-0 combinatorial pair should be termed 'I-0' rather than I-3 has not been widely adopted.
10. Babbitt, *Collected Essays*, p. 234.

11. White, *Schoenberg and the God-Idea*, pp. 160–1. See White's Appendix 2 for an illustrated listing of the opera's *Leitmotive*, and Appendix 3 for a full analysis of motives and twelve-tone areas.

12. For the twelve-tone basis of this passage, see White, *Schoenberg and the God-Idea*, Appendix 3.

13. Bluma Goldstein, 'Schoenberg's *Moses und Aron*: A Vanishing Biblical Nation', in *Political and Religious Ideas in the Works of Arnold Schoenberg*, eds. Charlotte M. Cross and Russell A. Berman (New York: Garland, 2000), p. 187.

14. See, for example, Michael Cherlin, 'Dialectical Opposition in Schoenberg's Music and Thought', *Music Theory Spectrum*, 22/2 (Fall 2000), pp. 157–76.

15. David Isadore Lieberman, 'Schoenberg Rewrites his Will: *A Survivor from Warsaw*, Op. 46', in *Political and Religious Ideas in the Works of Arnold Schoenberg*, eds. Charlotte M. Cross and Russell A. Berman (New York: Garland, 2000), pp. 212, 216–17, 218.

16. Naomi André, 'Returning to a Homeland: Religious and Political Context in Schoenberg's *Dreimal tausend Jahre*', in *Political and Religious Ideas in the Works of Arnold Schoenberg*, eds. Charlotte M. Cross and Russell A. Berman (New York: Garland, 2000), p. 281.

17. 'I do not attach so much importance to being a musical bogy-man as to being a natural continuer of properly understood good old tradition!' *Arnold Schoenberg Letters*, ed. Erwin Stein, trans. Eithne Wilkins and Ernst Kaiser (London: Faber & Faber, 1964), p. 100.

18. *Arnold Schoenberg Letters*, p. 200.

19. *Schoenberg, Berg, Webern: The String Quartets. A Documentary Study*, ed. Ursula Rauchhaupt (Hamburg: DGG, 1971), p. 58. Further page references in text.

20. Letter to Arthur Locke, cited in Josef Rufer, *The Works of Arnold Schoenberg*, trans. Dika Newlin (London: Faber & Faber, 1962), p. 141.

21. See Silvina Milstein, *Arnold Schoenberg: Notes, Sets, Forms* (Cambridge: Cambridge University Press, 1992); Timothy L. Jackson, 'Review of Silvina Milstein, *Arnold Schoenberg: Notes, Sets, Forms*', *Journal of Musicological Research*, 15 (1995), pp. 285–311; Richard Kurth, 'Suspended Tonalities in Schoenberg's Twelve-Tone Compositions', *Journal of the Arnold Schoenberg Center*, 3 (2001), pp. 239–66; Kurth, 'Moments of Closure: Thoughts on the Suspension of Tonality in Schoenberg's Fourth Quartet and Trio', in *Music of My Future: The String Quartets and Trio*, eds. Reinhold Brinkmann and Christoph Wolff (Cambridge, MA: Harvard University Press, 2000), pp. 139–60; Robert Pascall, 'Theory and Practice: Schönberg's American Pedagogical Writings and the First Movement of the Fourth String Quartet, Op. 37', *Journal of the Arnold Schoenberg Center*, 4 (2002), pp. 229–44; Pascall, 'Arnold Schönberg and Radical Guardianship', in *Experiencing Tradition: Essays of Discovery*, eds. Hinrich Siefken and Anthony Bushell (York: Sessions, 2003), pp. 179–85.

22. J. Peter Burkholder, 'Schoenberg the Reactionary', in *Schoenberg and his World*, ed. Walter Frisch (Princeton: Princeton University Press, 1999), pp. 185–6.

23. Schoenberg, 'National Music', in *Style and Idea*, ed. Leonard Stein (London: Faber & Faber, 1975), p. 174.

24. Arnold Whittall, 'Fulfilment or Betrayal? Twentieth-Century Music in Retrospect', *Musical Times* (Winter 1999), pp. 11–21.

25. Martha M. Hyde, 'Neoclassic and Anachronistic Impulses in Twentieth-Century Music', *Music Theory Spectrum*, 18/2 (Fall 1996), p. 228.

26. Jackson, 'Review of Silvina Milstein', p. 289.

27. Kurth, 'Moments of Closure', p. 146.

28. Kurth, 'Moments of Closure', pp. 149–50.

29. Michael Cherlin, 'Schoenberg and *Das Unheimliche*', *Journal of Musicology*, xi/3 (1993), p. 359.

30. Roger Scruton, *The Aesthetics of Music* (Oxford: Clarendon Press, 1997), p. 256.

31. Hans Keller, *Essays on Music*, ed. Christopher Wintle (Cambridge: Cambridge University Press, 1994), p. 190.

32. See in particular Milton Babbitt, *Words about Music*, eds. Stephen Dembski and Joseph N. Straus (Madison, WI: University of Wisconsin Press, 1987), pp. 19–24.

33. As cited by Ben Earle, 'Taste, Power, and Trying to Understand Op. 36: British Attempts to Popularize Schoenberg', *Music & Letters*, 84/4 (November 2003), p. 633.

34. Earle, 'Taste', p. 609.

35. Arnold Whittall, *Exploring Twentieth-Century Music: Tradition and Innovation* (Cambridge: Cambridge University Press, 2003), p. 84.

36. Robert Pascall, 'Arnold Schönberg and Radical Guardianship', in *Experiencing Tradition: Essays of Discovery*, eds. Hinrich Siefken and Anthony Bushell (York: Sessions, 2003), pp. 182–3.

37. The classic analysis of combinatoriality and form in the *Phantasy* is David Lewin, 'A Study of Hexachord Levels in Schoenberg's Violin Fantasy', in *Perspectives on Schoenberg and Stravinsky*, eds. Benjamin Boretz and Edward T. Cone (Princeton: Princeton University Press, 1968), pp. 78–92.

8 American counterpoints: I

1. Ulrich Mosch, ' "Taking Sound in Hand": Wolfgang Rihm and Varèse', in *Edgard Varèse: Composer, Sound Sculptor, Visionary*, eds. Felix Meyer and Heidy Zimmermann (Woodbridge: Boydell & Brewer, 2006), p. 434, quoting Varèse in 1965.

2. Theo Hirsbrunner, 'Varèse and La Jeune France', in *Edgard Varèse: Composer, Sound Sculptor, Visionary*, eds. Felix Meyer and Heidy Zimmermann (Woodbridge: Boydell & Brewer, 2006), p. 205.

3. Denise von Glahn, 'The Conceptual Origins of *Déserts*', in *Edgard Varèse: Composer, Sound Sculptor, Visionary*, eds. Felix Meyer and Heidy Zimmermann (Woodbridge: Boydell & Brewer, 2006), p. 304.

4. Jonathan W. Bernard, 'Varèse's Space, Varèse's Time', in *Edgard Varèse: Composer, Sound Sculptor, Visionary*, eds. Felix Meyer and Heidy Zimmermann (Woodbridge: Boydell & Brewer, 2006), p. 153, n. 14.

5. Chou Wen-chung, 'Converging Lives: Sixteen Years with Varèse', in *Edgard Varèse: Composer, Sound Sculptor, Visionary*, eds. Felix Meyer and Heidy Zimmermann (Woodbridge: Boydell & Brewer, 2006), p. 359.

6. Kyle Gann, '"Magnificent – in a Mysterious Way": Varèse's Impact on American Music', in *Edgard Varèse: Composer, Sound Sculptor, Visionary*, eds. Felix Meyer and Heidy Zimmermann (Woodbridge: Boydell & Brewer, 2006), p. 431.

7. Joseph N. Straus, *The Music of Ruth Crawford Seeger* (Cambridge: Cambridge University Press, 1995), pp. 73–6.

8. Austin Clarkson, 'Wolpe, Stefan', *The New Grove*, 2nd edn., eds. Stanley Sadie and John Tyrrell (London: Macmillan, 2001), xxvii, p. 516.

9. Ernst Krenek, *Studies in Counterpoint* (New York: Schirmer, 1940), pp. viii, 1.

10. Frederik Prausnitz, *Roger Sessions: How a 'Difficult' Composer Got That Way* (New York: Oxford University Press, 2002), p. 260. Further page references in text.

11. Howard Pollack, *Aaron Copland: The Life and Work of an Uncommon Man* (London: Faber & Faber, 2000), p. 445.

12. Pollack, *Aaron Copland*, p. 462.

13. Dave Headlam, 'Introduction', in George Perle, *The Right Notes: Twenty-Three Selected Essays on Twentieth-Century Music* (Stuyvesant, NY: Pendragon, 1995), p. xii.

14. Ernst Krenek, 'Serialism', in *Dictionary of Twentieth-Century Music*, ed. John Vinton (London: Thames & Hudson, 1974), p. 673.

15. Paul Lansky, 'Perle, George', in *The New Grove*, 2nd edn., eds. Stanley Sadie and John Tyrrell (London: Macmillan, 2001), xix, pp. 438–41.

16. Milton Babbitt, *Words about Music*, eds. Stephen Dembski and Joseph N. Straus (Madison, WI: University of Wisconsin Press, 1987), pp. 5–6.

17. Milton Babbitt, *Collected Essays*, ed. Stephen Peles, with Stephen Dembski, Andrew Mead and Joseph N. Straus (Princeton: Princeton University Press, 2003), p. 338.

18. Steve Reich, *Writings on Music: 1965–2000*, eds. Paul Hillier (New York: Oxford University Press, 2002), pp. 186–7.

19. See pp. 111, 125.

20. Bryan Simms, 'Review of Babbitt, *Collected Essays*', *Music & Letters*, 86/1 (February 2005), p. 157.

21. Simms, 'Review of Babbitt, *Collected Essays*', pp. 157–8.

22. Roger Scruton, *The Aesthetics of Music* (Oxford: Clarendon Press, 1997), p. 471.

23. Babbitt, *Collected Essays*, p. 463. Further page references in text.

24. Richard Barrett, 'Tracts for our Times?', *Musical Times* (Autumn 1998), p. 23.

25. Babbitt, *Words about Music*, p. 28.

26. Paul Griffiths, *Modern Music and After: Directions since 1945* (Oxford: Oxford University Press, 1995), pp. 64–5.

27. 'Mod'. is short for modulus, a term in mathematics indicating a constant multiplier. 'Mod. 12' means that, for numbers greater than 11, 12 – or multiples of 12 – can be subtracted to ensure that all numbers fit into the range of 0 to 11.

28. Andrew Mead, *An Introduction to the Music of Milton Babbitt* (Princeton: Princeton University Press, 1994), p. 177. Further page references in text.

29. Joseph Dubiel, 'Three Essays on Milton Babbitt (Part Two)', *Perspectives of New Music*, 29/1 (1991), p. 113.

30. Elaine Barkin and Martin Brody, 'Babbitt, Milton', *The New Grove*, 2nd edn., eds. Stanley Sadie and John Tyrrell (London: Macmillan, 2001), ii, p. 287.

31. Richard Taruskin, *The Oxford History of Western Music*, 6 vols. (New York: Oxford University Press, 2005), v, p. 156. Further page references in text.

32. Martin Brody, '"Music for the Masses": Milton Babbitt's Cold War Music Theory', *Musical Quarterly*, 77/2 (1993), p. 168.

33. Taruskin, *The Oxford History of Western Music*, v, pp. 162–3. Further page references in text.

9   American counterpoints: II

1. Igor Stravinsky, *Themes and Conclusions* (London: Faber & Faber, 1972). For discussion of Robert Craft's authorship, see Stephen Walsh, *Stravinsky: The Second Exile. France and America, 1934–1971* (London: Jonathan Cape, 2006), pp. 559–60.

2. Milton Babbitt, *Collected Essays*, ed. Stephen Peles, with Stephen Dembski, Andrew Mead and Joseph N. Straus (Princeton: Princeton University Press, 2003), p. 166.

3. For Babbitt on Schenker, see *Words about Music*, eds. Stephen Dembski and Joseph N. Straus (Madison, WI: University of Wisconsin Press, 1987), and Babbitt, *Collected Essays*.

4. See Arnold Schoenberg, *Theory of Harmony*, trans. Roy E. Carter (London: Faber & Faber, 1978) and *Structural Functions of Harmony*, 2nd edn., ed. Leonard Stein (New York: Norton, 1969).

5. Igor Stravinsky, *Poetics of Music*, trans. Arthur Knodel and Ingolf Dahl (New York: Vintage, 1947), p. 39.

6. Richard Taruskin, *Stravinsky and the Russian Traditions*, 2 vols. (Berkeley and Los Angeles: University of California Press, 1996), p. 1675.

7. Joseph N. Straus, *Stravinsky's Late Music* (Cambridge: Cambridge University Press, 2001), p. 81.

8. For a full account of this relationship, see Walsh, *Stravinsky*.

9. Robert Craft, *Stravinsky: Glimpses of a Life* (London: Lime Tree, 1992) pp. 16–17.

10. Allen Forte, *The Harmonic Organization of The Rite of Spring* (New Haven and London: Yale University Press, 1978), pp. 19, 28.

11. See Pieter van den Toorn, *The Music of Igor Stravinsky* (New Haven and London: Yale University Press, 1983), and Taruskin, *Stravinsky and the Russian Traditions*.

12. See for example Allen Forte, 'Debussy and the Octatonic', *Music Analysis* 10/1–2 (1991), and *The Atonal Music of Anton Webern* (New Haven and London: Yale University Press, 1998).

13. Joseph N. Straus, 'Stravinsky the Serialist', in *The Cambridge Companion to Stravinsky*, ed. Jonathan Cross (Cambridge: Cambridge University Press, 2003), p. 153.

14. Stephen Walsh, *Stravinsky*, p. 370.

15. Joseph N. Straus, *Stravinsky's Late Music*, p. 66.

16. Straus, 'Stravinsky the Serialist', p. 150. Further page references in text.

17. See reference in chapter 7, n. 21.

18. Michael Nyman, *Experimental Music: Cage and Beyond*, 2nd edn. (Cambridge: Cambridge University Press, 1999).

19. John Cage, interviewed by Peter Dickinson in 1987 and printed in *CageTalk: Dialogues with and about John Cage*, ed. Peter Dickinson (Rochester, NY and Woodbridge: University of Rochester Press, 2006), p. 31. See also Michael Hicks, 'John Cage's Studies with Schoenberg', *American Music*, 8/2 (Summer 1990), pp. 124–40.

20. Brenda Ravenscroft, 'Re-construction: Cage and Schoenberg', *Tempo*, 235 (January 2006), p. 14.

21. Virgil Thomson, interviewed by Peter Dickinson in 1987, in *CageTalk: Dialogues with and about John Cage*, ed. Peter Dickinson (Rochester, NY and Woodbridge: University of Rochester Press, 2006), p. 116.

22. Kyle Gann, *The Music of Conlon Nancarrow* (Cambridge: Cambridge University Press, 1995), p. 241.

23. Keith Potter, *Four Musical Minimalists* (Cambridge: Cambridge University Press, 2000), pp. 10–11. Further page references in text.

24. K. Robert Schwarz, *Minimalists* (London: Phaedon, 1996), pp. 56–7.

25. Stephen Peles, 'Serialism and Complexity', in *The Cambridge History of American Music*, ed. David Nicholls (Cambridge: Cambridge University Press, 1998), pp. 509–10. Further page references in text.

26. Peles, 'Serialism and Complexity', p. 509, quoting Babbitt, 'Some Aspects of Twelve-Tone Composition' (1955), in Milton Babbitt, *Collected Essays*, ed. Stephen Peles with Stephen Dembski, Andrew Mead and Joseph N. Straus (Princeton: Princeton University Press, 2003), p. 40.

27. Peles, 'Serialism and Complexity', p. 511. Further page reference in text.

28. Elliott Carter, *Collected Essays and Lectures, 1937–1995*, ed. Jonathan W. Bernard (Rochester, NY and Woodbridge: University of Rochester Press, 1997), p. 7. Further page references in text.

29. Andrew Mead, 'Twelve-Tone Composition and the Music of Elliott Carter', in *Concert Music, Rock, and Jazz since 1945: Essays and Analytical Studies*, eds. Elizabeth West Marvin and Richard Hermann (Rochester, NY and Woodbridge: University of Rochester Press, 1995).

30. David Schiff, 'Elliott Carter's Harmony Book', *Tempo*, 224 (April 2003), pp. 54–5.

31. Andrew Mead, 'Twelve-Tone Composition', in *Concert Music, Rock, and Jazz since 1945: Essays and Analytical Studies*, eds. Elizabeth West Marvin and Richard Hermann (Rochester, NY: and Woodbridge: University of Rochester Press, 1995), p. 67.

32. Tina Koivisto, 'Syntactical Space and Registral Spacing in Elliott Carter's *Remembrance*', *Perspectives of New Music*, 42/2 (Summer 2004), p. 158.

33. Schiff, 'Elliott Carter's Harmony Book', p. 53.

34. David Schiff, *The Music of Elliott Carter* (London: Faber & Faber, 1998), p. 106.

35. Schiff, 'Elliott Carter's Harmony Book', p. 54.

36. For this term, see under 'aleatory technique' in Charles Bodman Rae, *The Music of Lutosławski*, 3rd edn. (London: Omnibus Press, 1999).

37. Carter first used these terms in his *esprit rude/esprit doux* (rough breathing/smooth breathing) for flute and clarinet, written in 1984 for Pierre Boulez's sixtieth birthday (1985).

10 European repercussions: I

1. For consideration of twelve-tone, serial and pitch-class set aspects of Bartók's music, see George Perle, *Serial Composition and Atonality* 4th edn. (Berkeley, Los Angeles and London: University of California Press, 1977); Milton Babbitt, *Collected Essays*, ed. Stephen Peles, with Stephen Dembski, Andrew Mead and Joseph N. Straus (Princeton: Princeton University Press, 2003); Paul Wilson, *The Music of Béla Bartók* (New Haven and London: Yale University Press, 1992). See also Ivan F. Waldbauer, 'Analytical Responses to Bartók's Music: Pitch Organization', in *The Cambridge Companion to Bartók*, ed. Amanda Bayley (Cambridge: Cambridge University Press, 2001), pp. 215–30.

2. *Britten on Music*, ed. Paul Kildea (Oxford: Oxford University Press, 2003), pp. 228–9.

3. Among important accounts of Britten's musical language, see Peter Evans, *The Music of Benjamin Britten* (Oxford: Oxford University Press, 1996); Philip Rupprecht, *Britten's Musical Language* (Cambridge: Cambridge University Press, 2001).

4. See Elisabeth Lutyens, *A Goldfish Bowl* (London: Cassell, 1972); Meirion and Susie Harries, *A Pilgrim Soul: The Life and Work of Elisabeth Lutyens* (London: Michael Joseph, 1989).

5. See Jennifer Doctor, *The BBC and Ultra-Modern Music, 1922–1936* (Cambridge: Cambridge University Press, 1999); William Glock, *Notes in Advance: An Autobiography in Music* (Oxford: Oxford University Press, 1991).

6. Peter J. Schmelz, 'Shostakovich's "Twelve-Tone" Compositions and the Politics and Practice of Soviet Serialism', in *Shostakovich and his World*, ed. Laurel E. Fay (Princeton: Princeton University Press, 2004), p. 303. Further page references in text. See also Peter J. Schmelz, 'Andrey Volkonsky and the Beginnings of Unofficial Music in the Soviet Union', *Journal of the American Musicological Society*, 58/1 (Spring 2005), pp. 139–207.

7. Adrian Thomas, *Polish Music since Szymanowski* (Cambridge: Cambridge University Press, 2005), p. 23.

8. Steven Stucky, *Lutosławski and his Music* (Cambridge: Cambridge University Press, 1981), p. 108.

9. Thomas, *Polish Music*, p. 95. Further page references in text.

10. Stucky, *Lutosławski*, p. 114.

11. Thomas, *Polish Music*, pp. 96–7.

12. Martina Homma, 'Lutosławski's Studies in Twelve-Tone Rows', in *Lutosławski Studies*, ed. Zbigniew Skowron (Oxford: Oxford University Press, 2001), p. 210.

13. Thomas, *Polish Music*, p. 107.

14. Anthony Sellors, 'Dallapiccola, Luigi', *Opera Grove*, ed. Stanley Sadie (London: Macmillan, 1992), iii, pp. 1095–6.

15. Reginald Smith Brindle, 'Italian Contemporary Music', in *European Music in the Twentieth Century*, ed. Howard Hartog (Harmondsworth: Penguin, 1961), p. 199.

16. Peter Evans, 'Music of the European Mainstream: 1940–60', in *The New Oxford History, X. The Modern Age: 1980–1960*, ed. Martin Cooper (London: Oxford University Press, 1974), pp. 420–1.

17. Theodor W. Adorno, 'Neue Musik heute', in *Gesammelte Schriften*, xviii (Frankfurt am Main: Suhrkamp Verlag, 1984), p. 130. My translation.

18. Raymond Fearn, *The Music of Luigi Dallapiccola* (Rochester, NY and Woodbridge: University of Rochester Press, 2003), p. 129. Further page references in text.

19. Luigi Dallapiccola, 'On the Twelve-Tone Road' [1951], in *Music Survey: New Series 1949–1952*, eds. Donald Mitchell and Hans Keller (London: Faber Music/Faber & Faber, 1981), p. 330.

20. Friedrich Spangemacher, 'Schönberg as Role Model: On the Relationship between Luigi Nono and Arnold Schönberg', in *Luigi Nono: The Suspended Song*, ed. Stephen Davismoon, *Contemporary Music Review*, 18/1 (1999), pp. 34–5.

21. For an introduction to some aspects of the contributions of Leibowitz and Sartre to musical culture at the time, see Mark Carroll, *Music and Ideology in Cold-War Europe* (Cambridge: Cambridge University Press, 2003).

22. Rossana Dalmonte, 'Maderna, Bruno', in *The New Grove*, 2nd edn., eds. Stanley Sadie and John Tyrrell (London: Macmillan, 2001), xv, p. 534.

23. Christopher Fox, 'Luigi Nono and the Darmstadt School: Form and Meaning in the Early Works (1950–1959)', in *Luigi Nono: Fragments and Silence*, ed. Stephen Davismoon, *Contemporary Music Review*, 18/2 (1999), p. 111. Further page references in text.

24. Carola Nielinger, ' "The Song Unsung": Luigi Nono's *Il canto sospeso*', *Journal of the Royal Musical Association*, 131/1 (2006), pp. 98–9. Further page references in text.

25. Fox, 'Luigi Nono', p. 124.

26. Heinz-Klaus Metzger, *Muzik wozu: Literatur zu Noten* (Frankfurt am Main: Suhrkamp Verlag, 1980), pp. 120–1. Cited in Nielinger, ' "The Song Unsung" ', p. 92.

11 European repercussions: II

1. There are many accounts of Messiaen's modal system. For a basic introduction see Robert Sherlaw Johnson, *Messiaen* (London: Dent, 1975), pp. 16–17. Messiaen's own most elaborate discussion is in his *Traité de rythme, de couleur, et d'ornithologie*, 7 vols. (Paris: Leduc, 1994–2005). See also Allen Forte, 'Olivier Messiaen as Serialist', *Music Analysis*, 21/2 (March 2002), pp. 3–34.

2. For some discussion of Leibowitz and his work, see Mark Carroll, *Music and Ideology in Cold-War Europe* (Cambridge: Cambridge University Press, 2003).

3. Alexander Goehr, *Finding the Key: Selected Writings*, ed. Derrick Puffett (London: Faber & Faber, 1998), p. 55.

4. Goehr, *Finding the Key*, p. 54.

5. Pierre Boulez, 'Trajectories', in *Stocktakings from an Apprenticeship*, trans. Stephen Walsh (Oxford: Clarendon Press, 1991), p. 199.

6. Boulez, *Stocktakings from an Appenticeship*, p. 212.

7. See *The Boulez-Cage Correspondence*, trans. Robert Samuels (Cambridge: Cambridge University Press, 1993); *Pierre Boulez, John Cage: Correspondance et documents*, eds. Jean-Jacques Nattiez and Robert Piencikowski (Mainz and London: Schott, 2002).

8. Ben Parsons, 'Arresting Boulez: Post-War Modernism in Context', *Journal of the Royal Musical Association*, 129/1 (2004), p. 173.

9. Ben Parsons, 'Sets and the City: Serial Analysis, Parisian Reception, and Pierre Boulez's *Structures Ia*', *Current Musicology*, 76 (Fall 2003), p. 63.

10. Richard Taruskin, *The Oxford History of Western Music*, 6 vols. (New York: Oxford University Press, 2005), v, p. 170. Further page references in text.

11. Paul Griffiths, *Boulez* (Oxford: Oxford University Press, 1978), p. 28.

12. Pierre Boulez, *Stocktakings from an Apprenticeship*, trans. Stephen Walsh (Oxford: Clarendon Press, 1991), pp. 149–50. Further page references in text.

13. Boulez's own discussion of techniques relevant to *Le Marteau* is in *Boulez on Music Today*, trans. Susan Bradshaw and Richard Rodney Bennett (London: Faber & Faber, 1971), pp. 35–143. See also 'Possibly . . . ', in *Stocktakings from an Apprenticeship*, trans. Stephen Walsh (Oxford: Clarendon Press, 1991), pp. 111–40. The most extensive sketch-and source-based discussion of *Le Marteau* as a serial work is in Pierre Boulez, *Le Marteau sans maître: Facsimile of the Draft Score and the First Fair Copy of the Full Score*, ed. Pascal Decroupet (Mainz and London: Schott, 2005). In my discussion I have relied primarily on two sources: Stephen Heinemann, 'Pitch-class Set Multiplication in Theory and Practice', *Music Theory Spectrum*, 20/1 (Spring, 1998), pp. 72–96, and Ciro Scotto, 'Reevaluating Complex Pitch-Class Set Multiplication and its Relationship to Transpositional Combination in Boulez's *Le Marteau sans maître*', paper presented at Royal Holloway, London, 19 November 2005.

14. Lev Koblyakov, *Pierre Boulez: A World of Harmony* (Chur: Harwood, 1990).

15. Robin Maconie, *Other Planets: The Music of Karlheinz Stockhausen* (Lanham, MA: Scarecrow Press, 2005), p. 23. Further page references in text.

16. Stephen Truelove, 'The Translation of Rhythm into Pitch in Stockhausen's *Klavierstück XI*', *Perspectives of New Music*, 36/1 (1998), pp. 189–220. On this piece, see also Richard Toop, *Six Lectures from the Stockhausen Courses Kürten 2002* (Kürten: Stockhausen-Verlag, 2005), pp. 33–6.

17. Richard Toop, 'Stockhausen's *Klavierstück VIII (1954)*', *Miscellanea Musicologica*, 10 (1979), p. 93. Further page references in text.

18. M.J. Grant, *Serial Music, Serial Aesthetics: Compositional Theory in Post-War Europe* (Cambridge: Cambridge University Press, 2001), p. 164.

19. Grant, *Serial Music*, p. 163.

20. Robin Maconie, *The Music of Stockhausen* (Oxford: Clarendon Press, 1990), p. 93.

21. Jonathan Harvey, *The Music of Stockhausen: An Introduction* (London: Faber & Faber, 1975), p. 56. Further page references in text.

22. Richard Toop, '"O alter Duft": Stockhausen and the Return to Melody', *Studies in Music*, 10 (1976), pp. 79–97.

23. Maconie, *Other Planets*, p. 184.

12 European repercussions: III

1. Bálint András Varga, *Conversations with Iannis Xenakis* (London: Faber & Faber, 1996), pp. 38–9.

2. James Harley, *Xenakis: His Life in Music* (New York and London: Routledge, 2004), p. 6. Further page references in text.

3. 'Stochastic' is a mathematical term which Xenakis associates with composing according to principles of probability. Computer programs can be used to determine the distribution of large numbers of pitches in passages of especially dense texture, where the overall effect matters more than the individual details.

4. Peter Hoffmann, 'Xenakis, Yannis', *The New Grove*, 2nd edn., eds. Stanley Sadie and John Tyrrell (London: Macmillan, 2001), xxvii, p. 608.

5. Harley, *Xenakis*, p. 42. Further page reference in text.

6. Pelog is one of the two tuning systems for the Javanese gamelan.

7. Richard Toop, *György Ligeti* (London: Phaidon, 1999), p. 63.

8. First published in German as 'Pierre Boulez: Entscheidung und Automatik in der *Structure Ia*', *Die Reihe* 4 (Vienna: Universal, 1958), pp. 38–63. English trans. by Leo Black, 'Pierre Boulez: Decision and Automation in *Structure Ia*', *Die Reihe* 4 (Bryn Mawr, PA: Presser, 1960), pp. 36–62.

9. Richard Steinitz: *Györgi Ligeti: Music of the Imagination* (London: Faber & Faber, 2003), p. 58. Further page references in text.

10. *Ligeti in Conversation* (London: Eulenberg, 1983), p. 125. Further page references in text.

11. Steinitz, *Györgi Ligeti*, p. 90. Further page references in text.

12. Luciano Berio, *Remembering the Future* (Cambridge, MA: Harvard University Press, 2006), pp. 20–1.

13. Luciano Berio, *Two Interviews*, ed. and trans. David Osmond-Smith (London: Calder & Boyars, 1985), p. 106.

14. David Osmond-Smith, *Berio* (Oxford: Oxford University Press, 1991), p. 3. Further page references in text.

15. Berio, *Two Interviews*, p. 53. Further page references in text.

16. Osmond-Smith, *Berio*, p. 10. Further page references in text.

17. Berio, *Two Interviews*, p. 154. Further page references in text.

18. Osmond-Smith, *Berio*, p. 25. Further page references in text.

19. Björn Heile, *The Music of Mauricio Kagel* (Aldershot: Ashgate, 2006), p. 4. Further page references in text.

20. See discussion in chapter 4, pp. 58–60.

21. Heile, *The Music of Mauricio Kagel*, p. 25. Further page references in text.

13 European repercussions: IV

1. Pierre Boulez, 'Conférence sur *Anthèmes* 2' (Paris, 21 October 1997). Translated in Jonathan Goldman, *Understanding Pierre Boulez's Anthèmes (1991): 'Creating a Labyrinth out of another Labyrinth'*, MA, University of Montreal (2001), p. 79.

2. Jonathan Goldman, 'Introduction' to Pierre Boulez, *Leçons de Musique*, ed. Jean-Jacques Nattiez (Paris: Bourgois, 2005), p. 33. Further page references (to the lectures themselves) in text. All translations are mine.

3. *Stockhausen: Conversations with the Composer*, ed. Jonathan Cott (London: Robson Books, 1974), pp. 102–3.

4. Pierre Boulez, 'Series', in *Stocktakings from an Apprenticeship*, trans. Stephen Walsh (Oxford: Clarendon Press, 1991), p. 236.

5. *Stockhausen: Conversations with the Composer*, ed. Cott, p. 242. Further page references in text.

6. Jonathan Harvey, *The Music of Stockhausen: An Introduction* (London: Faber & Faber, 1975), p. 126.

7. *Stockhausen: Conversations with the Composer*, ed. Cott, p. 224.

8. Robin Maconie, *Other Planets: The Music of Karlheinz Stockhausen* (Lanham, MA: Scarecrow Press, 2005), pp. 332–3.

9. Jerome Kohl, 'Into the Middleground: Formula Syntax in Stockhausen's *LICHT*', *Perspectives of New Music*, 28/2 (1989–90), p. 264.

10. Richard Toop, '"O alter Duft": Stockhausen and the Return to Melody', *Studies in Music*, 10 (1976), p. 81. Further page references in text.

11. Maconie, *Other Planets*, p. 403. Further page references in text.

12. Kohl, 'Into the Middleground', pp. 267, 276.

13. Maconie, *Other Planets*, p. 442.

14. Toop, '"O alter Duft"', p. 80.

15. Maconie, *Other Planets*, p. 454.

16. Rachel Beckles Willson, 'Kurtág, György', *The New Grove*, 2nd edn., eds. Stanley Sadie and John Tyrrell (London: Macmillan, 2001), xiv, p. 45.

17. Beckles Willson, 'Kurtág', p. 46.

18. Rachel Beckles Willson, *György Kurtág: The Sayings of Péter Bornemisza, Op. 7* (Aldershot: Ashgate, 2004), p. 72.

19. See Arnold Whittall, 'Plotting the Path, Prolonging the Moment: Kurtág's Settings of German', in *Perspectives on Kurtág*, eds. Rachel Beckles Willson and Alan E. Williams, *Contemporary Music Review*, 20, 2/3 (2001), pp. 103, 107.

14 European repercussions: V

1. Iannis Xenakis, *Formalized Music: Thought and Mathematics in Music*, rev. edn. (Stuyvesant, NY: Pendragon, 1990), p. 8.

2. Ernst Krenek, 'Serialism', in *Dictionary of Twentieth-Century Music*, ed. John Vinton (London: Thames & Hudson, 1974), p. 673.

3. Tim Howell, *After Sibelius: Studies in Finnish Music* (Aldershot: Ashgate, 2006), p. 58.

4. Erling Kullberg, 'Beyond Infinity: On the Infinity Series – The DNA of Hierarchical Music', in *The Music of Per Nørgård*, ed. Anders Beyer (Aldershot: Ashgate/Scolar, 1996), p. 77. Further page references in text.

5. Julian Anderson, 'Perception and Deception: Aspects of Per Nørgård's "Hierarchical" Methods and Parallel Developments in Recent Central European Music', in *The Music of Per Nørgård*, ed. Anders Beyer (Aldershot: Ashgate/Scolar, 1996), pp. 154–5. Further page references in text.

6. Alexander Goehr, *Finding the Key: Selected Writings*, ed. Derrick Puffett (London: Faber & Faber, 1998), pp. 34–5.

7. David Roberts, 'Review of Griffiths, *Peter Maxwell Davies*', *Contact*, 24 (Spring 1982), p. 25.

8. Enzo Restagno has stressed that Petrassi's 'relationship with 12-tone technique was never one of complete conformity'. Restagno emphasises 'the freedom of Petrassi's use of 12-tone technique', and notes that Berg 'was Petrassi's favourite of the Second Viennese School composers'. Enzo Restagno, 'Petrassi, Goffredo', *The New Grove*, 2nd edn., eds. Stanley Sadie and John Tyrrell (London: Macmillan, 2001), xix, 500–1.

9. Peter Owens, 'Revelation and Fallacy: Observations on Compositional Technique in the Music of Peter Maxwell Davies', *Music Analysis* 13/2–3 (July–October 1994), p. 164; '*Worldes Blis* and its Satellites', in *Perspectives on Peter Maxwell Davies*, ed. Richard McGregor (Aldershot: Ashgate, 2000), pp. 23–50 – see also the two essays by McGregor himself in the same collection; David Roberts, *Techniques of Composition in the Music of Peter Maxwell Davies*: PhD, Birmingham University (1985).

10. David Roberts, '*Alma Redemptoris Mater*', in *Perspectives on Peter Maxwell Davies*, ed. Richard McGregor (Aldershot: Ashgate, 2000), p. 2.

11. Cited in Owens, 'Revelation and Fallacy', p. 162.

12. David Roberts, 'Review of Maxwell Davies Scores', in *Contact*, 19 (Summer 1978), p. 28.

13. Roberts, 'Review', pp. 28–9.

14. Richard McGregor, 'Stepping Out: Maxwell Davies's *Salome* as a Transitional Work', *Tempo*, 236 (April 2006), p. 7.

15. See Nicholas Jones, 'Peter Maxwell Davies's "Submerged Cathedral": Architectural Principles in the Third Symphony', *Music & Letters*, 81/3 (August 2000), pp. 402–32; 'Dominant Logic: Peter Maxwell Davies's Basic Unifying Hypothesis', *The Musical Times* (Spring 2002), pp. 37–45; 'Playing the "Great Game"?: Maxwell Davies, Sonata Form, and the *Naxos* Quartet No. 1', *The Musical Times* (Autumn 2005), pp. 71–81.

16. Michael Hall, *Harrison Birtwistle* (London: Robson Books, 1984), p. 8.

17. *Sing, Ariel: Essays and Thoughts for Alexander Goehr's Seventieth Birthday*, ed. Alison Latham (Aldershot: Ashgate, 2003), p. 35.

18. Aaron Einbond, 'Twelve-Note Roots: The Fifth and Sixth Movements of *The Death of Moses*', in *Sing, Ariel: Essays and Thoughts for Alexander Goehr's Seventieth Birthday*, ed. Alison Latham (Aldershot: Ashgate, 2003), p. 218.

19. Goehr, *Finding the Key*, p. 8.

20. *George Benjamin*, eds. Risto Nieminen and Renaud Machart (London: Faber & Faber, 1997), pp. 14–15.

21. Milton Babbitt, *Collected Essays*, ed. Stephen Peles, with Stephen Dembski, Andrew Mead and Joseph N. Straus (Princeton: Princeton University Press, 2003), p. 166.

22. Jonathan Cross, *Harrison Birtwistle: Man, Mind, Music* (London: Faber & Faber, 2000), p. 35. Further page references in text.

23. David Beard, 'The Endless Parade: Competing Narratives in Recent Birtwistle Studies', *Music Analysis*, 23/1 (March 2004), p. 103.

24. For further analytical perspectives on Birtwistle, see Arnold Whittall, 'Modernist Aesthetics, Modernist Music: Some Analytical Perspectives', in *Music Theory in Concept and Practice*, eds. James M. Baker, David W. Beach and Jonathan W. Bernard (Rochester, NY: University of Rochester Press, 1997), pp. 157–80; *Exploring Twentieth-Century Music: Tradition and Innovation* (Cambridge: Cambridge University Press, 2003), pp. 145–66.

25. Brian Ferneyhough, 'Interview with Andrew Clements (1977)', in *Brian Ferneyhough: Collected Writings*, eds. James Boros and Richard Toop (Amsterdam: Harwood, 1995), p. 214.

26. Richard Toop, 'Lemma–Icon–Epigram', *Perspectives of New Music*, 28/2 (1990), pp. 52–101; 'Prima la parole: On the Sketches for Brian Ferneyhough's *Carceri d'Invenzione* I–III', *Perspectives of New Music*, 32/1 (1994), pp. 154–75; 'On *Superscriptio*: An Interview with Brian Ferneyhough and an Analysis', *Contemporary Music Review*, 13/1 (1995), pp. 3–17.

27. Toop, 'On *Superscriptio*', p. 8.

28. Ross Feller, 'Random Funnels in Brian Ferneyhough's *Trittico per Gertrude Stein*', *Mitteilungen der Paul Sacher Stiftung*, 10 (March 1997), p. 33. See also Ross Feller, 'E-Sketches: Brian Ferneyhough's Use of Computer-Assisted Compositional Tools', in *A Handbook to Twentieth-Century Sketches*, eds. Patricia Hall and Friedemann Sallis (Cambridge: Cambridge University Press, 2004), pp. 176–88.

29. Brian Ferneyhough, 'Interview with Jean-Baptiste Barrière', in *Brian Ferneyhough: Collected Writings*, eds. James Boros and Richard Toop (Amsterdam: Harwood, 1995), p. 407.

30. Ferneyhough, 'Interview with Andrew Clements (1977)', p. 214.

31. 'A Verbal Crane Dance: Interview with Ross Feller', in *Brian Ferneyhough: Collected Writings*, eds. James Boros and Richard Toop (Amsterdam: Harwood, 1995), p. 460.

32. Julian Anderson, 'Harmonic Practices in Oliver Knussen's Music since 1988 I', *Tempo*, 221 (July 2002), p. 2. Further page references in text.

33. Julian Anderson, 'Harmonic Practices in Oliver Knussen's Music since 1988 II', *Tempo*, 223 (January 2003), p. 22. Further page references in text.

Bibliography

Adorno, Theodor W. 'Neue Musik heute', in *Gesammelte Schriften*, xviii (Frankfurt am Main: Suhrkamp Verlag, 1984), 124–33

Anderson, Julian, 'Perception and Deception: Aspects of Per Nørgård's "Hierarchical" Methods and Parallel Developments in Recent Central European Music', in *The Music of Per Nørgård*, ed. Anders Beyer (Aldershot: Ashgate/Scolar, 1996), 147–66

'Harmonic Practices in Oliver Knussen's Music since 1988 I', *Tempo*, 221 (July 2002), 2–13; 'Harmonic Practices in Oliver Knussen's Music since 1988 II', *Tempo*, 223 (January 2003), 16–45

André, Naomi, 'Returning to a Homeland: Religious and Political Context in Schoenberg's *Dreimal tausend Jahre*', in *Political and Religious Ideas in the Works of Arnold Schoenberg*, eds. Charlotte M. Cross and Russell A. Berman (New York: Garland, 2000), 259–88

Arnold, Stephen, 'Peter Maxwell Davies', in *British Music Now*, ed. Lewis Foreman (London: Elek, 1975), 71–85

Ashby, Arved, 'Of *Modell-Typen* and *Reihenformen*: Berg, Schoenberg, F. H. Klein and the Concept of Row Derivation', *Journal of the American Musicological Society*, 48 (1995), 67–105

Auner, Joseph H., 'In Schoenberg's Workshop: Aggregates and Referential Collections in *Die Glückliche Hand*', *Music Theory Spectrum*, 18/1 (1996), 77–105

'Schoenberg and his Public in 1930: The Six Pieces for Male Chorus, Op. 35', in *Schoenberg and his World*, ed. Walter Frisch (Princeton: Princeton University Press, 1999), 85–125

(ed.), *A Schoenberg Reader* (New Haven and London: Yale University Press, 2003)

'Composing on Stage: Schoenberg and the Creative Process as Public Performance', *19th Century Music*, xxix/1 (Summer 2005), 64–93

Ayrey, Craig, 'Tonality and the Series: Berg', in *Models of Musical Analysis: Early Twentieth-Century Music*, ed. Jonathan Dunsby (Oxford: Blackwell, 1993), 81–113

Babbitt, Milton, *Words about Music*, eds. Stephen Dembski and Joseph N. Straus (Madison, WI: University of Wisconsin Press, 1987)

Collected Essays, ed. Stephen Peles with Stephen Dembski, Andrew Mead and Joseph N. Straus (Princeton: Princeton University Press, 2003)

Bailey, Kathryn, *The Twelve-Note Music of Anton Webern* (Cambridge: Cambridge University Press, 1991)

'Symmetry as Nemesis: Webern and the First Movement of the Concerto, Opus 24', *Journal of Music Theory*, 40 (1996), 245–310

The Life of Anton Webern (Cambridge: Cambridge University Press, 1998)

'Composing with Tones': A Musical Analysis of Schoenberg's Op. 23 Pieces for Piano* (London: Royal Musical Association, 2001)

Baker, James M., *The Music of Alexander Scriabin* (New Haven and London: Yale University Press, 1986)

Barkin, Elaine and Martin Brody, 'Babbitt, Milton', *The New Grove Dictionary of Music and Musicians* (hereafter: *The New Grove*), 2nd edn., eds. Stanley Sadie and John Tyrrell (London: Macmillan, 2001), ii, 283–9

Barrett, Richard, 'Tracts for our Times?', *Musical Times* (Autumn 1998), 21–4

Beard, David, 'The Endless Parade: Competing Narratives in Recent Birtwistle Studies', *Music Analysis*, 23/1 (March 2004), 89–127

Beckles Willson, Rachel, 'Kurtág, György', *The New Grove*, 2nd edn., eds. Stanley Sadie and John Tyrrell (London: Macmillan, 2001), xiv, 45–9

György Kurtág: The Sayings of Péter Bornemisza, Op. 7 (Aldershot: Ashgate, 2004)

Benjamin, William E., 'Abstract Polyphonies: The Music of Schoenberg's Nietzschean Moment', in *Political and Religious Ideas in the Works of Arnold Schoenberg*, eds. Charlotte M. Cross and Russell A. Berman (New York: Garland, 2000), 1–39

Berio, Luciano, *Two Interviews*, ed. and trans. David Osmond-Smith (London: Calder & Boyars, 1985)

Remembering the Future (Cambridge, MA: Harvard University Press, 2006)

Bernard, Jonathan W., 'Chord, Collection, and Set in Twentieth-Century Theory', in *Music Theory in Concept and Practice*, eds. James M. Baker, David W. Beach and Jonathan W. Bernard (Rochester, NY: University of Rochester Press, 1997), 11–51

'Varèse's Space, Varèse's Time', in *Edgard Varèse: Composer, Sound Sculptor, Visionary*, eds. Felix Meyer and Heidy Zimmermann (Woodbridge: Boydell & Brewer, 2006), 149–55

Beyer, Anders (ed.), *The Music of Per Nørgård* (Aldershot: Ashgate/Scolar, 1996)

Boulez, Pierre, *Boulez on Music Today*, trans. Susan Bradshaw and Richard Rodney Bennett (London: Faber & Faber, 1971)

Conversations with Célestin Deliège (London: Eulenberg, 1976)

Stocktakings from an Apprenticeship, trans. Stephen Walsh (Oxford: Clarendon Press, 1991)

Leçons de musique, ed. Jean-Jacques Nattiez (Paris: Bourgois, 2005)

Le Marteau sans maître: Facsimile of the Draft Score and the First Fair Copy of the Full Score, ed. Pascal Decroupet (Mainz and London: Schott, 2005)

Bowen, Meirion (ed.), *Gerhard on Music: Selected Writings* (Aldershot: Ashgate, 2000)

Boynton, Neil, 'Compositional Technique 1923–6: The Chamber Concerto and the *Lyric Suite*', in *The Cambridge Companion to Berg*, ed. Anthony Pople (Cambridge: Cambridge University Press, 1997), 189–203

Brand, Juliane, Christopher Hailey and Donald Harris (eds.), *The Berg–Schoenberg Correspondence: Selected Letters* (London: Macmillan, 1987)

Brody, Martin, ' "Music for the Masses": Milton Babbitt's Cold War Music Theory', *Musical Quarterly*, 77/2 (1993), 161–92

Burkholder, J. Peter, 'Schoenberg the Reactionary', in *Schoenberg and his World*, ed. Walter Frisch (Princeton: Princeton University Press, 1999), 162–91

Carroll, Mark, *Music and Ideology in Cold-War Europe* (Cambridge: Cambridge University Press, 2003)

Carter, Elliott, *Collected Essays and Lectures, 1937–1995*, ed. Jonathan W. Bernard (Rochester, NY and Woodbridge: University of Rochester Press, 1997)

    Harmony Book, ed. Nicholas Hopkins and John F. Link (New York: Carl Fischer, 2002)

Cherlin, Michael, 'Schoenberg and *Das Unheimliche*', *Journal of Musicology*, xi/3 (1993), 357–73

    'Dialectical Opposition in Schoenberg's Music and Thought', *Music Theory Spectrum*, 22/2 (Fall 2000), 157–76

Clarkson, Austin, 'Wolpe, Stefan', *The New Grove*, 2nd edn., eds. Stanley Sadie and John Tyrrell (London: Macmillan, 2001), xxvii, 515–17

Cott, Jonathan (ed.), *Stockhausen: Conversations with the Composer* (London: Robson Books, 1974)

Covach, John, 'The *Zwölftonspiel* of Josef Matthias Hauer', *Journal of Music Theory*, 36/1 (Spring 1992), 149–84

    'Schoenberg's "Poetics of Music", the Twelve-Tone Method, and the Musical Idea', in *Schoenberg and Words: The Modernist Years*, eds. Charlotte M. Cross and Russell A. Berman (New York: Garland, 2000), 309–46

    'Twelve-tone Theory', in *The Cambridge History of Western Music Theory*, ed. Thomas Christensen (Cambridge: Cambridge University Press, 2002)

Craft, Robert, *Stravinsky: Glimpses of a Life* (London: Lime Tree, 1992)

Cross, Charlotte M. and Russell A. Berman (eds.), *Political and Religious Ideas in the Works of Arnold Schoenberg* (New York: Garland: 2000)

    (eds.) *Schoenberg and Words: The Modernist Years* (New York: Garland, 2000)

Cross, Jonathan, *Harrison Birtwistle: Man, Mind, Music* (London: Faber & Faber, 2000)

Dahlhaus, Carl, *Schoenberg and the New Music*, trans. Derrick Puffett and Alfred Clayton (Cambridge: Cambridge University Press, 1987)

Dallapiccola, Luigi, 'On the Twelve-Tone Road' (1951), in *Music Survey: New Series, 1949–1952*, eds. Donald Mitchell and Hans Keller (London: Faber Music/Faber & Faber, 1981), 318–32

Dalmonte, Rossana, 'Maderna, Bruno', *The New Grove*, 2nd edn., eds. Stanley Sadie and John Tyrrell (London: Macmillan, 2001), xv, 532–6

Davison, Stephen, '*Von heute auf morgen*: Schoenberg as Social Critic', in *Political and Religious Ideas in the Works of Arnold Schoenberg*, eds. Charlotte M. Cross and Russell A. Berman (New York: Garland, 2000), 85–110

Decroupet, Pascal, 'Floating Hierarchies: Organisation and Composition in Works by Pierre Boulez and Karlheinz Stockhausen during the 1950s', in *A Handbook to Twentieth-Century Musical Sketches*, eds. Patricia Hall and Friedemann Sallis (Cambridge: Cambridge University Press, 2004), 146–60

Dickinson, Peter (ed.), *CageTalk: Dialogues with and about John Cage* (Rochester, NY and Woodbridge: University of Rochester Press, 2006)

Doctor, Jennifer, *The BBC and Ultra-Modern Music, 1922–1936* (Cambridge: Cambridge University Press, 1999)

Dubiel, Joseph, 'Three Essays on Milton Babbitt (Part Two)', *Perspectives of New Music* 29/1 (1991), 90–123

Dunsby, Jonathan (ed.), *Models of Musical Analysis: Early Twentieth-Century Music* (Oxford: Blackwell, 1993)

Dunsby, Jonathan and Arnold Whittall, *Music Analysis in Theory and Practice* (London: Faber Music, 1987)

Earle, Ben, 'Taste, Power, and Trying to Understand Op. 36: British Attempts to Popularize Schoenberg', *Music & Letters*, 84/4 (2003), 608–43

Einbond, Aaron, 'Twelve-Note Roots: The Fifth and Sixth movements of *The Death of Moses*', in *Sing, Ariel: Essays and Thoughts for Alexander Goehr's Seventieth Birthday*, ed. Alison Latham (Aldershot: Ashgate, 2003)

Evans, Peter, 'Music of the European Mainstream, 1940–60', in *The New Oxford History of Music, X. The Modern Age: 1890–1960*, ed. Martin Cooper (London: Oxford University Press, 1974), 387–502

The Music of Benjamin Britten (Oxford: Oxford University Press, 1996)

Fearn, Raymond, *The Music of Luigi Dallapiccola* (Rochester, NY and Woodbridge: University of Rochester Press, 2003)

Feller, Ross, 'Random Funnels in Brian Ferneyhough's *Trittico per Gertrude Stein*', *Mitteilungen der Paul Sacher Stiftung*, 10 (March 1997), 32–8

'E-sketches: Brian Ferneyhough's use of Computer-Assisted Compositional Tools', in *A Handbook to Twentieth-Century Musical Sketches*, eds. Patricia Hall and Friedemann Sallis (Cambridge: Cambridge University Press, 2004), 176–88

Ferneyhough, Brian, *Collected Writings*, eds. James Boros and Richard Toop (Amsterdam: Harwood, 1995)

Forte, Allen, *The Structure of Atonal Music* (New Haven and London: Yale University Press, 1973)

The Harmonic Organization of The Rite of Spring (New Haven and London: Yale University Press, 1978)

'The Magical Kaleidoscope: Schoenberg's First Atonal Masterwork. Opus 11, No. 1', *Journal of the Arnold Schoenberg Institute*, 5 (1981), 127–68

'Pitch-Class Set Analysis Today', *Music Analysis*, 4/2 (March–July 1985), 29–58

'Debussy and the Octatonic', *Music Analysis*, 10/1–2 (1991), 125–69

The Atonal Music of Anton Webern (New Haven and London: Yale University Press, 1998)

'Olivier Messiaen as Serialist', *Music Analysis*, 21/2 (March 2002), 3–34

Fox, Christopher, 'Luigi Nono and the Darmstadt School: Form and Meaning in the Early Works (1950–1959)', in *Luigi Nono: Fragments and Silence*, ed. Stephen Davismoon, *Contemporary Music Review*, 18/2 (1999), 111–30

Frisch, Walter (ed.), *Schoenberg and his World* (Princeton: Princeton University Press, 1999)

Gann, Kyle, *The Music of Conlon Nancarrow* (Cambridge: Cambridge University Press, 1995)

'"Magnificent – in a Mysterious Way": Varèse's Impact on American Music', in *Edgard Varèse: Composer, Sound Sculptor, Visionary*, eds. Felix Meyer and Heidy Zimmermann (Woodbridge: Boydell & Brewer, 2006), 426–32

Gerhard, Roberto, *Gerhard on Music: Selected Writings*, ed. Meirion Bowen (Aldershot: Ashgate, 2000)

Glahn, Denise von, 'The Conceptual Origins of *Déserts*', in *Edgard Varèse: Composer, Sound Sculptor, Visionary*, eds. Felix Meyer and Heidy Zimmermann (Woodbridge: Boydell & Brewer, 2006), 298–308

Glock, William, *Notes in Advance: An Autobiography in Music* (Oxford: Oxford University Press, 1991)

Goehr, Alexander, *Finding the Key: Selected Writings*, ed. Derrick Puffett (London: Faber & Faber, 1998)

Goldman, Jonathan, *Understanding Pierre Boulez's Anthèmes (1991): 'Creating a Labyrinth out of another Labyrinth'*, MA, University of Montreal (2001)

'Introduction' to Pierre Boulez, *Leçons de Musique*, ed. Jean-Jacques Nattiez (Paris: Bourgois, 2005)

Goldstein, Bluma, 'Schoenberg's *Moses und Aron*: A Vanishing Biblical Nation', in *Political and Religious Ideas in the Works of Arnold Schoenberg*, eds. Charlotte M. Cross and Russell A. Berman (New York: Garland, 2000), 159–92

Grant, M. J., *Serial Music, Serial Aesthetics: Compositional Theory in Post-War Europe* (Cambridge: Cambridge University Press, 2001)

Griffiths, Paul, *Boulez* (Oxford: Oxford University Press, 1978)

Peter Maxwell Davies (London: Robson Books, 1982)

Modern Music and After: Directions since 1945 (Oxford: Oxford University Press, 1995)

Haimo, Ethan, *Schoenberg's Serial Odyssey: The Evolution of his Twelve-Tone Method, 1914–1928* (Oxford: Clarendon Press, 1990)

Hall, Michael, *Harrison Birtwistle* (London: Robson Books, 1984)

Hall, Patricia, *A View of Berg's Lulu* (Berkeley, Los Angeles and London: University of California Press, 1996)

'Compositional Process in *Wozzeck* and *Lulu*: A Glimpse of Berg's Atonal Method', in *The Cambridge Companion to Berg*, ed. Anthony Pople (Cambridge: Cambridge University Press, 1997), 180–8

Harley, James, *Xenakis: His Life in Music* (New York and London: Routledge, 2004)

Harries, Meirion and Susie Harries, *A Pilgrim Soul: The Life and Work of Elisabeth Lutyens* (London: Michael Joseph, 1989)

Harvey, Jonathan, *The Music of Stockhausen: An Introduction* (London: Faber & Faber, 1975)

Headlam, Dave, 'Introduction', in George Perle, *The Right Notes: Twenty-Three Selected Essays on Twentieth-Century Music* (Stuyvesant, NY: Pendragon, 1995)

The Music of Alban Berg (New Haven and London: Yale University Press, 1996)

Heile, Björn, *The Music of Mauricio Kagel* (Aldershot: Ashgate, 2006)

Heinemann, Stephen, 'Pitch-class Set Multiplication in Theory and Practice', *Music Theory Spectrum*, 20/1 (Spring 1998), 72–96

Hicks, Michael, 'John Cage's Studies with Schoenberg', *American Music*, 8/2 (Summer 1990), 124–40

Hirsbrunner, Theo, 'Varèse and La Jeune France', in *Edgard Varèse: Composer, Sound Sculptor, Visionary*, eds. Felix Meyer and Heidy Zimmermann (Woodbridge: Boydell & Brewer, 2006), 202–10

Hoffmann, Peter, 'Xenakis, Yannis', in *The New Grove*, 2nd edn., eds. Stanley Sadie and John Tyrrell (London: Macmillan, 2001), xxvii, 605–13

Homma, Martina, 'Lutosławski's Studies in Twelve-Tone Rows', in *Lutosławski Studies*, ed. Zbigniew Skowron (Oxford: Oxford University Press, 2001), 194–210

Howell, Tim, *After Sibelius: Studies in Finnish Music* (Aldershot: Ashgate, 2006)

Hyde, Martha M., 'Neoclassic and Anachronistic Impulses in Twentieth-Century Music', *Music Theory Spectrum*, 18/2 (Fall 1996), 200–35

Hyer, Brian, 'Tonality', in *The New Grove*, 2nd edn., eds. Stanley Sadie and John Tyrrell (London: Macmillan, 2001), xxv, 583–94

Jackson, Timothy L., 'Review of Silvina Milstein, *Arnold Schoenberg: Notes, Sets, Forms*', *Journal of Musicological Research*, 15 (1995), 285–311

Jarman, Douglas, *Alban Berg: Lulu* (Cambridge: Cambridge University Press, 1991)

'Secret Programmes', in *The Cambridge Companion to Berg*, ed. Anthony Pople (Cambridge: Cambridge University Press, 1997), 167–79

Johnson, Julian, *Webern and the Transformation of Nature* (Cambridge: Cambridge University Press, 1999)

Jones, Nicholas, 'Peter Maxwell Davies's "Submerged Cathedral": Architectural Principles in the Third Symphony', *Music & Letters*, 81/3 (2000), 402–32

'Dominant Logic: Peter Maxwell Davies's Basic Unifying Hypothesis', *The Musical Times* (Spring 2002), 37–45

'Playing the "Great Game"?: Maxwell Davies, Sonata Form, and the *Naxos* Quartet No. 1', *The Musical Times* (Autumn 2005), 71–81

Keller, Hans, *Essays on Music*, ed. Christopher Wintle (Cambridge: Cambridge University Press, 1994)

Kildea, Paul (ed.), *Britten on Music* (Oxford: Oxford University Press, 2003)

Koblyakov, Lev, *Pierre Boulez: A World of Harmony* (Chur: Harwood, 1990)

Kohl, Jerome, 'Into the Middleground: Formula Syntax in Stockhausen's *LICHT*', *Perspectives of New Music*, 28/2 (1989–90), 262–91

Koivosto, Tina, 'Syntactical Space and Registral Spacing in Elliott Carter's *Remembrance*', *Perspectives of New Music*, 42/2 (Summer 2004), 158–89

Krenek, Ernst, *Studies in Counterpoint* (New York: Schirmer, 1940)

'Serialism', in *Dictionary of Twentieth-Century Music*, ed. John Vinton (London: Thames & Hudson, 1974)

Kullberg, Erling, 'Beyond Infinity: On the Infinity Series – The DNA of Hierarchical Music', in *The Music of Per Nørgård*, ed. Anders Beyer (Aldershot: Ashgate/Scolar, 1996), 71–93

Kurth, Richard, 'Moments of Closure: Thoughts on the Suspension of Tonality in Schoenberg's Fourth Quartet and Trio', in *'Music of My Future': The Schoenberg Quartets and Trio*, eds. Reinhold Brinkmann and Christoph Wolff (Cambridge, MA: Harvard University Press, 2000), 139–60

'Suspended Tonalities in Schoenberg's Twelve-Tone Compositions', *Journal of the Arnold Schoenberg Center*, 3 (2001), 239–66

Lansky, Paul and George Perle, 'Twelve-note Composition', in *The New Grove*, 2nd edn., eds. Stanley Sadie and John Tyrrell (London: Macmillan, 2001), xxvi, 1–11

Latham, Alison (ed.), *Sing, Ariel: Essays and Thoughts for Alexander Goehr's Seventieth Birthday* (Aldershot: Ashgate, 2003)

Latham, Edward D., 'The Prophet and the Pitchman: Dramatic Structure and its Musical Elucidation in *Moses und Aron*, Act 1, Scene 2', in *Political and Religious Ideas in the Works of Arnold Schoenberg*, eds. Charlotte M. Cross and Russell A. Berman (New York: Garland, 2000), 131–58

Lewin, David, 'A Study of Hexachord Levels in Schoenberg's Violin Fantasy', in *Perspectives on Schoenberg and Stravinsky*, eds. Benjamin Boretz and Edward T. Cone (Princeton: Princeton University Press, 1968), 78–92

Lichtenfeld, Monika, 'Hauer, Josef Matthias', in *The New Grove*, 2nd edn., eds. Stanley Sadie and John Tyrrell (London: Macmillan, 2001), xi, 134–7

Lieberman, David Isadore, 'Schoenberg Rewrites his Will: *A Survivor from Warsaw*, Op. 46', in *Political and Religious Ideas in the Works of Arnold Schoenberg*, eds. Charlotte M. Cross and Russell A. Berman (New York: Garland, 2000), 193–229

Ligeti, György, 'Pierre Boulez: Decision and Automation in *Structure Ia*', trans. Leo Black, *Die Reihe* 4 (Bryn Mawr, PA: Presser, 1960), 36–62

Ligeti in Conversation (London: Eulenberg, 1983)

Lutyens, Elisabeth, *A Goldfish Bowl* (London: Cassell, 1972)

Maconie, Robin, *The Music of Stockhausen* (Oxford: Clarendon Press, 1990)

Other Planets: The Music of Karlheinz Stockhausen (Lanham, MA: Scarecrow Press, 2005)

McGregor, Richard (ed.), *Perspectives on Peter Maxwell Davies* (Aldershot: Ashgate, 2000)

'Stepping Out: Maxwell Davies's *Salome* as a Transitional Work', *Tempo*, 236 (April 2006), 2–12

Mead, Andrew, *An Introduction to the Music of Milton Babbitt* (Princeton: Princeton University Press, 1994)

'Twelve-Tone Composition and the Music of Elliott Carter', in *Concert Music, Rock, and Jazz since 1945: Essays and Analytical Studies*, eds. Elizabeth West Marvin and Richard Hermann (Rochester, NY and Woodbridge: University of Rochester Press, 1995)

Messiaen, Olivier, *Traité de rythme, de couleur, et d'ornithologie*, 7 vols. (Paris: Leduc, 1994–2005)

Metzger, Heinz-Klaus, *Musik wozu: Literatur zu Noten* (Frankfurt am Main: Suhrkamp Verlag, 1980)

Meyer, Felix and Heidy Zimmermann (eds.), *Edgard Varèse: Composer, Sound Sculptor, Visionary* (Woodbridge: Boydell & Brewer, 2006)

Milstein, Silvina, *Arnold Schoenberg: Notes, Sets, Forms* (Cambridge: Cambridge University Press, 1992)

Mosch, Ulrich, ' "Taking sound in Hand": Wolfgang Rihm and Varèse', in *Edgard Varèse: Composer, Sound Sculptor, Visionary*, eds. Felix Meyer and Heidy Zimmermann (Woodbridge: Boydell & Brewer, 2006), 433–42

Nattiez, Jean-Jacques and Robert Piencikowski, *Pierre Boulez, John Cage: Correspondance et documents* (Mainz and London: Schott, 2002)

Neighbour, O. W., 'Schoenberg, Arnold' in *The New Grove*, 2nd edn., eds. Stanley Sadie and John Tyrrell (London: Macmillan, 2001), xxii, 577–604

Nielinger, Carola, ' "The Song Unsung": Luigi Nono's *Il canto sospeso*', *Journal of the Royal Musical Association*, 131/1 (2006), 83–150

Nieminen, Risto and Renaud Machart (eds.), *George Benjamin* (London: Faber & Faber, 1997)

Nyman, Michael, *Experimental Music: Cage and Beyond*, 2nd edn. (Cambridge: Cambridge University Press, 1999)

Ogdon, Will, 'How Tonality Functions in Schoenberg's Op. 11, No. 1', *Journal of the Arnold Schoenberg Institute*, 5 (1981), 169–81

Osmond-Smith, David, *Berio* (Oxford: Oxford University Press, 1991)

Owens, Peter, 'Revelation and Fallacy: Observations on Compositional Technique in the Music of Peter Maxwell Davies', *Music Analysis* 13/2–3 (July–October 1994), 161–202

   '*Worldes Blis* and its Satellites', in *Perspectives on Peter Maxwell Davies*, ed. Richard McGregor (Aldershot: Ashgate, 2000), 23–50

Parsons, Ben, 'Sets and the City: Serial Analysis, Parisian Reception, and Pierre Boulez's *Structures Ia*', *Current Musicology*, 76 (Fall 2003), 53–79

   'Arresting Boulez: Post-War Modernism in Context', *Journal of the Royal Musical Association*, 129/1 (2004), 161–76

Pascall, Robert, 'Theory and Practice: Schoenberg's American Pedagogical Writings and the First Movement of the Fourth String Quartet, Op. 37', *Journal of the Arnold Schoenberg Center*, 4 (2002), 229–44

   'Arnold Schoenberg and Radical Guardianship', in *Experiencing Tradition: Essays of Discovery*, eds. Hinrich Siefken and Anthony Bushell (York: Sessions, 2003), 179–85

Peles, Stephen, 'Serialism and Complexity', in *The Cambridge History of American Music*, ed. David Nicholls (Cambridge: Cambridge University Press, 1998), 496–516

Perle, George, *Serial Composition and Atonality*, 4th edn. (Berkeley, Los Angeles and London: University of California Press, 1977)

   The Operas of Alban Berg, I: Wozzeck (Berkeley, Los Angeles and London: University of California Press, 1980)

   The Operas of Alban Berg, II: Lulu (Berkeley, Los Angeles and London: University of California Press, 1989)

Pollack, Howard, *Aaron Copland: The Life and Work of an Uncommon Man* (London: Faber & Faber, 2000)

Pople, Anthony, *Berg: Violin Concerto* (Cambridge: Cambridge University Press, 1991)

   (ed.) *The Cambridge Companion to Berg* (Cambridge: Cambridge University Press, 1997)

   'The Musical Language of *Wozzeck*', in *The Cambridge Companion to Berg*, ed. Anthony Pople (Cambridge: Cambridge University Press, 1997), 145–64

   'In the Orbit of *Lulu*: The Late Works', in *The Cambridge Companion to Berg*, ed. Anthony Pople (Cambridge: Cambridge University Press, 1997), 204–26

Potter, Keith, *Four Musical Minimalists* (Cambridge: Cambridge University Press, 2000)

Prausnitz, Frederik, *Roger Sessions: How a 'Difficult' Composer Got That Way* (New York: Oxford University Press, 2002)

Rae, Charles Bodman, *The Music of Lutosławski*, 3rd edn. (London: Omnibus Press, 1999)

Rauchhaupt, Ursula (ed.), *Schoenberg, Berg, Webern: The String Quartets. A Documentary Study* (Hamburg: DGG, 1971)

Ravenscroft, Brenda, 'Re-construction: Cage and Schoenberg', *Tempo*, 235 (January 2006), 2–14

Reich, Steve, *Writings on Music: 1965–2000*, ed. Paul Hillier (New York: Oxford University Press, 2002)

Restagno, Enzo, 'Petrassi, Goffredo', *The New Grove*, 2nd edn., eds. Stanley Sadie and John Tyrrell (London: Macmillan, 2001), xix, 499–503

Roberts, David, 'Review of Maxwell Davies Scores', *Contact*, 19 (Summer 1978), 26–9

  'Review of Griffiths, *Peter Maxwell Davies*', *Contact*, 24 (Spring 1982), 23–5

  Techniques of Composition in the Music of Peter Maxwell Davies, PhD, Birmingham University (1985)

  'Alma Redemptoris Mater', in Richard McGregor (ed.), *Perspectives on Peter Maxwell Davies* (Aldershot: Ashgate, 2000), 1–22

Rufer, Josef, *The Works of Arnold Schoenberg*, trans. Dika Newlin (London: Faber & Faber, 1962)

Rupprecht, Philip, *Britten's Musical Language* (Cambridge: Cambridge University Press, 2001)

Samuels, Robert (trans.), *The Boulez–Cage Correspondence* (Cambridge: Cambridge University Press, 1993)

Schiff, David, *The Music of Elliott Carter* (London: Faber & Faber, 1998)

  'Elliott Carter's Harmony Book', *Tempo*, 224 (April 2003), 53–5

Schmelz, Peter J., 'Shostakovich's "Twelve-Tone" Compositions and the Politics and Practice of Soviet Serialism', in *Shostakovich and his World*, ed. Laurel E. Fay (Princeton: Princeton University Press, 2004), 303–54

  'Andrey Volkonsky and the Beginnings of Unofficial Music in the Soviet Union', *Journal of the American Musicological Association*, 58/1 (Spring 2005), 139–207

Schoenberg, Arnold, *Structural Functions of Harmony*, 2nd edn., ed. Leonard Stein (New York: Norton, 1969)

  Style and Idea, ed. Leonard Stein, trans. Leo Black (London: Faber & Faber, 1975)

  Theory of Harmony, trans. Roy E. Carter (London: Faber & Faber, 1978)

  The Musical Idea and the Logic, Technique, and Art of its Presentation, eds. and trans. Patricia Carpenter and Severine Neff (New York: Columbia University Press, 1995)

Schwarz, K. Robert, *Minimalists* (London: Phaedon, 1996)

Scotto, Ciro, 'Reevaluating Complex Pitch-Class Set Multiplication and its Relationship to Transpositional Combination in Boulez's *Le Marteau sans maître*', Unpublished paper (2005)

Scruton, Roger, *The Aesthetics of Music* (Oxford: Clarendon Press, 1997)

Sellors, Anthony, 'Prigioniero, Il', *The Grove Dictionary of Opera*, ed. Stanley Sadie (London: Macmillan, 1992), iii, 1095–6

Shaw, Jennifer, 'Androgyny and the Eternal Feminine in *Die Jakobsleiter*', in *Political and Religious Ideas in the Works of Arnold Schoenberg*, eds. Charlotte M. Cross and Russell A. Berman (New York: Garland, 2000), 61–83

Sherlaw Johnson, Robert, *Messiaen* (London: Dent, 1975)

Shreffler, Anne C., ' "Mein Weg geht jetzt vorüber": The Vocal Origins of Webern's Twelve-Tone Composition', *Journal of the American Musicological Society*, 47 (1994), 275–339

Simms, Bryan R., *The Atonal Music of Arnold Schoenberg, 1908–1923* (New York: Oxford University Press, 2000)

'Review of Babbitt, *Collected Essays*', *Music & Letters*, 86/1 (2005), 157–60

Smith Brindle, Reginald, 'Italian Contemporary Music', in *European Music in the Twentieth Century*, ed. Howard Hartog (Harmondsworth: Penguin, 1961), 189–210

Spangemacher, Friedrich, 'Schönberg as Role Model: On the Relationship between Luigi Nono and Arnold Schönberg', in *Luigi Nono: The Suspended Song*, ed. Stephen Davismoon, *Contemporary Music Review*, 18/1 (1999), 31–46

Stein, Erwin (ed.), *Arnold Schoenberg Letters*, trans. Eithne Wilkins and Ernst Kaiser (London: Faber & Faber, 1964)

Steinitz, Richard, *Györgi Ligeti: Music of the Imagination* (London: Faber & Faber, 2003)

Straus, Joseph N. *The Music of Ruth Crawford Seeger* (Cambridge: Cambridge University Press, 1995)

Stravinsky's Late Music (Cambridge: Cambridge University Press, 2001)

'Stravinsky the Serialist', in *The Cambridge Companion to Stravinsky*, ed. Jonathan Cross (Cambridge: Cambridge University Press, 2003), 149–74

Introduction to Post-Tonal Theory, 3rd edn. (Englewood Cliffs, NJ: Prentice Hall, 2005)

Stravinsky, Igor, *Poetics of Music*, trans. Arthur Knodel and Ingolf Dahl (New York: Vintage, 1947)

Themes and Conclusions (London: Faber & Faber, 1972)

Stucky, Steven, *Lutosławski and his Music* (Cambridge: Cambridge University Press, 1981)

Taruskin, Richard, *Stravinsky and the Russian Traditions*, 2 vols. (Berkeley and Los Angeles: University of California Press, 1996)

The Oxford History of Western Music, 6 vols. (New York: Oxford University Press, 2005)

Thomas, Adrian, *Polish Music since Szymanowski* (Cambridge: Cambridge University Press, 2005)

Toop, Richard, ' "O alter Duft": Stockhausen and the Return to Melody', *Studies in Music*, 10 (1976), 79–97

'Stockhausen's *Klavierstück VIII (1954)*', *Miscellanea Musicologica*, 10 (1979), 93–130

'Lemma–Icon–Epigram', *Perspectives of New Music*, 28/2 (1990), 52–101

'Prima la parole: On the Sketches for Brian Ferneyhough's *Carceri d'Invenzione I–III*', *Perspectives of New Music*, 32/1 (1994), 154–75

'On *Superscriptio*: An Interview with Brian Ferneyhough and an Analysis', *Contemporary Music Review*, 13/1 (1995), 3–17

György Ligeti (London: Phaidon, 1999)

Six Lectures from the Stockhausen Courses Kürten 2002 (Kürten: Stockhausen-Verlag, 2005)

Truelove, Stephen, 'The Translation of Rhythm into Pitch in Stockhausen's *Klavierstück XI*', *Perspectives of New Music*, 36/1 (1998), 189–220

van den Toorn, Pieter, *The Music of Igor Stravinsky* (New Haven and London: Yale University Press, 1983)

Varga, Bálint András, *Conversations with Iannis Xenakis* (London: Faber & Faber, 1996)

Waldbauer, Ivan F., 'Analytical Responses to Bartók's Music: Pitch Organization', in *The Cambridge Companion to Bartók*, ed. Amanda Bayley (Cambridge: Cambridge University Press, 2001), 215–30

Walsh, Stephen, *Stravinsky: The Second Exile. France and America, 1934–1971* (London: Jonathan Cape, 2006)

Webern, Anton, *The Path to the New Music*, ed. Willi Reich, trans. Leo Black (Bryn Mawr, PA: Presser, 1963)

Letters to Hildegard Jone and Josef Humplik, ed. Josef Polnauer, trans. Cornelius Cardew (Bryn Mawr, PA: Presser, 1967)

Wen-chung, Chou, 'Converging Lives: Sixteen Years with Varèse', in *Edgard Varèse: Composer, Sound Sculptor, Visionary*, eds. Felix Meyer and Heidy Zimmermann (Woodbridge: Boydell & Brewer, 2006), 348–60

White, Pamela C., *Schoenberg and the God-Idea: The Opera Moses und Aron* (Ann Arbor: UMI Research Press, 1985)

Whittall, Arnold, 'Webern and Multiple Meaning', *Music Analysis*, 6/1 (October 1987), 333–53

'Fulfilment or Betrayal? Twentieth-Century Music in Retrospect', *Musical Times* (Winter 1999), 11–21

'Plotting the Path, Prolonging the Moment: Kurtág's Settings of German', in *Perspectives on Kurtág*, eds. Rachel Beckles Willson and Alan E. Williams, *Contemporary Music Review*, 20 (2001), 89–107

Exploring Twentieth-Century Music: Tradition and Innovation (Cambridge: Cambridge University Press, 2003)

Wilson, Paul, *The Music of Béla Bartók* (New Haven and London: Yale University Press, 1992)

Xenakis, Iannis, *Formalized Music: Thought and Mathematics in Music*, rev. edn. (Stuvyesant, NY: Pendragon, 1990)

Glossary

This glossary includes the most important and frequently used technical terms found in this *Introduction*. These, or closely related forms of the same term, are printed in **bold** in the main text on their first occurrence. In some cases, further discussion is provided in the text itself.

AGGREGATE	A collection of all twelve pitch classes.
ALEATORY	Used to describe music associated with a significant element of chance or randomness. Lutosławski, Boulez, and many other composers after the late 1950s devised ways of providing degrees of performer choice ('Alea' is the Latin word for dice). The aim was to encourage a productive degree of spontaneity in musical interpretation, and also to demonstrate that a musical work need not take exactly the same form in every performance.
ALL-INTERVAL SERIES	A twelve-tone series devised to include single examples of each of the eleven different intervals available within the octave. See Ex. 5.4.
ALL-INTERVAL TETRACHORD	A collection of four pitch classes from which all six INTERVAL CLASSES can be derived.
ALL-TRICHORD HEXACHORD	A collection of six pitch classes from which all twelve possible TRICHORDS can be derived.
ARRAY	A succession of aggregates.
ATONALITY	(also FREE ATONALITY) The absence of tonality. Given the difficulty of providing conclusive evidence for this absence in musical compositions, POST-TONAL is often preferred. This implies that elements of tonality might persist even in music which is dominated by other features, like twelve-tone serialism.

COLLECTION   Often used as a synonym for SERIES or SET, and often qualified as 'ordered' or 'unordered'.

COMBINATORIALITY   A quality shared by some twelve-tone collections whereby the collection and one of its transformations combine to form a pair of aggregates. The P-0/I-5 combination often used by Schoenberg creates two aggregates, between the first hexachords of each, and the second hexachords of each, respectively. Twelve-tone theorists have refined the concept to distinguish between different orders of combinatoriality (see Babbitt, *Words about Music*, p. 193).

COMPLEMENTATION   As with COMBINATORIALITY, this signifies the separation of pitch-class collections into complementary sets, one set containing pitch classes absent from the other.

DERIVATION   The process, particularly important to Webern, whereby a twelve-tone series is generated by adding related versions to an ordered trichord or tetrachord. See Ex. 6.5.

DEVELOPING   Schoenberg's term for a process of small-scale but constant
VARIATION   thematic development and transformation (see Schoenberg, *The Musical Idea and the Logic, Technique, and Art of its Presentation*, p. 365).

DODECAPHONIC   Synonym for twelve-tone, or serial, in the domain of pitch only.

DYAD   A collection of two pitch classes.

FIBONACCI SERIES   A sequence of numbers in which each term sums the two preceding terms: thus, 1, 2, 3, 5, 8, 13 . . .

FRACTAL   A term in mathematics describing a curve with the property that any segment of it, if enlarged, has the same statistical character as the whole. The concept is widely known through the visual presentation of Mandelbrot sets. In a serial context, the term has been applied to procedures found in Ligeti and Nørgård (see chapters 12 and 14).

FUNCTION   This refers primarily to a feature of tonal harmony, in which chords other than tonic, dominant or subdominant are regarded as sharing the harmonic functions of those chords within the tonal system. Speaking of tonic, dominant or subdominant functions reinforces the idea that tonality is hierarchic, the tonic being more fundamental to tonality than the dominant, etc. A further function within tonal practice involves the tendency of dissonances to resolve onto consonances, and in this sense to be hierarchically subordinate to consonances.

HAUPTSTIMME	Leading voice or line, marked with a particular sign in compositions where the texture does not necessarily differentiate clearly between principal and subordinate lines. See Ex. 4.6.
HETEROPHONY	A type of polyphony in which all participating voices have the same or similar lines, each with a different rhythmic profile.
HEXACHORD	A collection of six pitch classes.
HEXACHORDAL COMPLEMENTATION	Making a feature of the potential for pairs of hexachords to contain six different pitch classes each, and thereby complete an AGGREGATE.
INTEGER NOTATION	The translation of pitch classes and/or interval classes into whole numbers, to facilitate the most economical presentation of information about the basic materials of post-tonal compositional materials: thus, C = 0, C sharp = 1 ... A sharp = 10, B = 11. In some sources, '10' is replaced by 't' for ten, '11' by 'e' for eleven.
INTEGRAL SERIALISM	The compositional use of series for such aspects as duration, dynamics and register, as well as pitch. Sometimes known as TOTAL (or 'TOTAL') SERIALISM. During the mid-twentieth century there was a tendency to restrict the term SERIALISM to such music, thereby distinguishing it from the earlier kind of TWELVE-TONE COMPOSITION, in which pitch alone was serialised.
INTERVAL CLASS [IC]	An abstraction convenient in analytical and theoretical discussion. Strictly speaking, 'interval class' is shorthand for 'unordered pitch-class interval'. Whereas there are eleven ordered pitch-class intervals (the ascending

distances between pairs of pitch classes within the octave) there are only six unordered pitch-class intervals, when distance is calculated by ascent or descent, whichever is the shorter: for example, the ordered pitch-class interval C to B is 11, but the unordered interval class between C and B is 1.

INTERVAL CYCLE   A collection of different pitch classes constructed from a sequence of the same interval class (1, 2, 3, 4, 5), or from the alternation of interval classes 6 and 5. See Ex. 5.7.

INVARIANTS   Sequences of pitch classes (sometimes termed SUB-SETS) which recur in different versions of a given series, or as SUB-SETS of different series.

INVERSION   In tonal inversion, a perfect fourth inverts to a perfect fifth, a major third to a minor sixth, etc. Post-tonal inversion is literal, with respect to interval-class distance: an ascending tritone (ic 6) becomes a descending tritone, an ascending perfect fourth (ic 5) a descending perfect fourth, etc.

INVERTED RETROGRADE (IR)   Retrograde inversion (RI) forms of a series reverse the pitch classes of inversion forms: RI-0 is simply I-0 in reverse. The INVERTED RETROGRADE (IR) begins with the last pitch class of a P or I series form and then proceeds through the interval classes of that series form, inverting them in turn, to produce a new pitch-class succession. See chapter 9 for an example from Stravinsky.

MAGIC SQUARE   In relation to music, a square consisting of rows of numbers arranged so that all the rows sum to the same total. See Ex. 14.3c.

MATRIX   A presentation of all the versions of a particular series in a form whereby Primes and Inversions, with their retrogrades, are combined into a single square. A MATRIX can employ pitch-class letter names or integers. See Ex. 1.6.

MODE   A scale or sequence of pitches whose intervallic content is used to determine its identity. Major or minor mode is synonymous with major or minor scale, and Messiaen's second 'mode of limited transposition' is also known as the octatonic scale.

MODERN-CLASSICISM   Post-tonal music that aspires to emulate a degree of unity and connectedness characteristic of the classical aesthetic, but without losing all assocation with the more fragmented structures proper to modernism.

MOMENTFORM   A concept of Stockhausen's which sought to focus maximum weight on the individual structural segments that make up larger wholes. By regarding each segment as self-contained and self-sufficient, Stockhausen was attempting to provide a definitive substitute for the cumulative, goal-directed formal designs of classical and romantic tradition.

MULTIPLICATION   A technique in which musical materials can be generated from the combination of multiple transpositional levels of the same series. See Chapter 11.

NEO-CLASSICISM   The allusion to earlier styles and techniques, in ways which dramatise the tensions between those allusions and more contemporary qualities.

NORMAL ORDER or   The 'unordered' representation of a pitch-class set: that is,
NORMAL FORM   the ordering that is the most compact in respect of interval-class succession. For a detailed explanation of how to establish the normal order of a set, see Straus, *Introduction to Post-Tonal Theory*, pp. 27–30.

OSTINATO   A persistently repeated phrase, usually short in duration. Some writers on serialism see an analogy between the ground bass ostinato familiar from baroque music and the constant unfoldings of series forms.

PANTONALITY   Schoenberg's term for the (theoretical) presence of all possible keys in a given compositional context. The term is most usefully considered in connection with the more manageable concepts of extended tonality and SUSPENDED TONALITY. See chapter 7.

PARAMETER   A term in physics and mathematics denoting a distinct class of some kind. In serial music, it refers to such specific elements, available for systematic organisation, as pitch, duration, or dynamic level.

PARTITIONING	The division of ordered series statements into identical or similar segments, or into distinct textural strands.
PERMUTATION	The reordering of elements extracted from an ordered series.
PITCH CLASS [PC]	The pitch class C stands for all possible Cs, in whatever octave position. It is used to distinguish the concept from PITCH, which is understood to specify a single registral location for the note in question. It is also used to counter the impression, created when a twelve-tone series is shown on a single treble stave, that these pitches are the only notes to be used.
PRIME FORM	By convention, the principal form of a series (P-0), and its transpositions (P-1, etc.).
POST-TONAL	Many theorists have come to prefer this term to ATONAL, arguing that it allows for the continued presence of elements which can be associated with aspects of tonal thinking, even when the predominant quality of a serial composition is not tonal in the traditional sense.
ROTATION	Using an ordered series, or segment of a series, in such a way that the sequence may begin and end with tones other than the first and last. Thus, the hexachord 123456 might be rotated as 345612, or 432165.
SERIES	An ordering of pitch classes.
SET	A collection of pitch classes arranged in relation to consistent ordering principles, such that all possible sets of 3 to 9 pitch classes total 208, rather than 362,877 (9 factorial minus 3) (see Forte, *The Structure of Atonal Music*, appendix 1, pp. 179–81). In this definition of SET, consistent ordering as the motive for compositional usage is not a defining attribute. In practice, however, references to 'ordered sets' are quite common in the technical literature.
SET CLASS	This term is useful in analysis to focus on the association of different presentations of the same pitch-class set. 'Webern uses set class 3–3 in his Bagatelle Op. 9 No. 5' means that at least two different manifestations of that set are present.

SIEVING	In serial technique, to sieve is to select systematically. See the discussions of Berg (chapter 5), Xenakis (chapter 12) and Peter Maxwell Davies (chapter 14).
SOURCE SET	The unordered pitch-class collection from which an ordered twelve-tone series can be derived.
SPECTRALISM	This term, apparently first used by the French composer Hugues Dufourt in 1979, denotes the derivation of musical materials from the acoustic properties of sound, as found in the overtones of the harmonic series and (in many cases) their electronic manipulation. As Dufourt and others have shown, this initiative is by no means incompatible with serialism.
SUB-SET	A component of a given series or set.
SUSPENDED TONALITY	Schoenberg used this term (*schwebende Tonalität*) in relation to his song 'Lockung', Op. 6 No. 7, in which 'the tonic, E flat, does not appear throughout the whole piece' (Schoenberg, *Structural Functions of Harmony*, p. 111). The concept has been elaborated by later theorists, in particular Richard Kurth. See chapter 7.
TETRACHORD	A collection of four pitch classes.
TIME-POINT SERIES	A series of integers which locates the position of pitch attacks within a particular durational grid. See Ex. 8.2.
TRANSPOSITION	Changing the pitch level of a particular collection or sequence of pitch classes, while preserving the interval content. In serial music, transposition levels are usually indicated by integer notation: thus, P-6 is P-0 transposed up or down by six semitones. This operation is often referred to as 't6' (that is, transposition by the specified interval).
TRICHORD	A collection of three pitch classes.
TROPE	A synonym for SET (or MODE), implying that the content of a collection, but not its order, is specified.

Index

Adorno, Theodor W. 112, 161
aggregate 34, 271, 273
aleatory 159, 271
all-interval series 168, 271
all-interval tetrachord 146, 148, 149, 236, 271
all-interval twelve-tone chord 146
all-trichord hexachord 146, 149, 271
Anderson, Julian 220–1, 235–6
array 127, 271
Ashby, Arved 68, 69
atonality 16, 19, 271, 275
Auner, Joseph 21, 102
Ayrey, Craig 72

Babbitt, Milton 9, 19, 28, 29, 100, 103, 117,
    119, 120, 122–34, 135, 144, 145, 148,
    164, 174, 175, 188, 220, 231, 233
    Composition for Four Instruments 126
    Post-Partitions 128–30
    A Solo Requiem 131
Bach, J.S. 31, 35, 101
Bailey, Kathryn 46, 47, 90–5
Baird, Tadeusz 157
Barrett, Richard 125
Bartók, Béla 190
    String Quartet No. 4 151
    Violin Concerto No. 2 151
Beard, David 231
Beckles Willson, Rachel 217
Beethoven, Ludwig van 93, 106, 108, 109, 110,
    114, 197, 212
Benjamin, George 229, 232
    Shadowlines 231

Benjamin, Walter 11
Berg, Alban 65–84, 85–6, 121, 152, 188, 204,
    212, 223, 235, 277
    Altenberg Lieder 65
    Chamber Concerto 70, 75, 79
    Lulu 65, 70, 78, 166
    Lyric Suite 67, 69, 71, 72, 75–8, 79–82, 79
    Schliesse mir die Augen beide 69, 71–2,
        80
    String Quartet, Op. 2, 65
    Violin Concerto 14, 71, 74, 79–84, 120, 160,
        238
    Der Wein 80
    Wozzeck, 65–6, 67, 68, 160
Bergman, Erik 220
Berio, Luciano 143, 193–8
    Allelujah I 196
    Allelujah II 196
    Chamber Music 194
    Cinque variazioni 194
    Due pezzi 194
    Harvard Lectures 194
    Nones 195
    O King 198
    'Points on the Curve to Find . . . ' 198
    Sequenza V 198
    Two Interviews 197
    Variazioni 194
    La vera storia 198
Bernard, Jonathan 34, 118
Birtwistle, Harrison 155, 222, 231–2
    Three Sonatas 231
    Tragoedia 231

Boulez, Pierre 16, 28, 40, 58, 79, 84, 85, 98, 100,
    121, 124, 130, 131, 144, 155, 164, 166,
    171–81, 185, 210, 236, 271
  Anthèmes 203
  Dialogue de l'ombre double 203
  Douze Notations 173
  Incises 203, 205–9
  Leçons de musique 204
  Le Marteau sans maître 176, 191, 192, 194,
    197, 203, 204
  Messagesquisse 203, 205, 208
  ' . . . Near and Far' 177
  Piano Sonata No. 3 216
  Pli selon pli 178, 203
  Rituel 203
  'Schoenberg is dead' 174
  Sonatine for flute and piano 173, 203
  Structures Ia 165, 172, 173, 175–7, 178, 190,
    195, 219
  Sur Incises 203, 205
Boynton, Neil 69
Brody, Martin 133

Cage, John 124, 141–2, 175, 201
  First Construction in Metal 141
Carter, Elliott 3, 131, 145–50, 206, 236
  A 6-Letter Letter 146, 205
  Concerto for Orchestra 148
  Double Concerto 148
  Gra 148–50
  Harmony Book 147
  Night Fantasies 148
  Piano Concerto 148
  Remembrance 147
  Sonata for Cello and Piano 147
  String Quartet No. 1 148
  String Quartet No. 2 148
  Variations for Orchestra 148
Char, René 178
Cherlin, Michael 109, 111, 113
Clark, Edward 153
collection 8, 272
combinatoriality 42, 103, 272
complementation 13, 272

Copland, Aaron 121
  Connotations 121
  Inscape 121
  Nonet 121
  Piano Fantasy 121, 145
  Piano Variations 121
Covach, John 24, 62
Cowell, Henry 117, 201
Craft, Robert 15, 135, 136
Crawford Seeger, Ruth 119
Cross, Jonathan 231, 232

Dahlhaus, Carl 61
Dallapiccola, Luigi 84, 100, 121, 124, 160–3,
    194, 224
  Canti di prigionia I 161
  Cinque frammenti di Saffo 162
  Goethe-Lieder 162
  Il prigioniero 121, 160, 161
  Ulisse 162
Darmstadt 134, 159, 164, 175, 182, 187, 188,
    194, 195, 216, 223, 228
Debussy, Claude 171, 178, 185
Demur, Guy 175
derivation 13, 272
Deutsch, Max 216
developing variation 20, 28, 38, 41
dodecaphonic 272
Dubiel, Joseph 132
Dufourt, Hugues 277
dyad 13, 272

Earle, Ben 112, 113
Eimert, Herbert 25, 181
Einbond, Aaron 229
emancipation of the dissonance 35, 41, 153, 176
Evans, Peter 161

Fearn, Raymond 161
Feller, Ross 233, 234
Ferneyhough, Brian 232–5, 236
  Lemma-Icon-Epigram 232
  Superscriptio 232, 235
  Trittico per Gertrude Stein 233–4, 235

Fibonacci series 187, 272
Forte, Allen 12, 18, 19, 125, 137, 275
Fox, Christopher 164, 166, 169
fractal 220, 272
Fuchs-Robettin, Hanna 75, 80
function 3, 18, 272

Gann, Kyle 119, 142
Gerhard, Roberto 27–9, 153, 155
   Concerto for Piano and Strings 27
   'Reminiscences of Schoenberg' 27
   'Schoenberg in Barcelona' 27
   'Tonality in Twelve-Tone music' 28
Glahn, Denise von 118
Glass, Philip 124, 142
Glock, William 155
Goehr, Alexander 155, 171, 222, 223, 228–9,
   231
   The Death of Moses 229
   Fantasia for Orchestra 228
   Psalm IV 229
   String Quartet No. 3 229
Goehr, Walter 153
Goeyvaerts, Karel 182
Goldman, Jonathan 203
Goldstein, Bluma 104
Górecki, Henryk 159
Grant, M.J. 184
Griffiths, Paul 130
Gropius, Manon 84

Haimo, Ethan 34, 45, 46
Hall, Michael 228
Hall, Patricia 66, 82
Hall, Richard 223
Harley, James 187–9
Harvey, Jonathan 185, 186, 210
Hauer, Josef-Matthias 22, 24–6, 68, 69, 87,
   181, 223
   Nomos 24, 25
   Zwölftonspiele 25
Hauptstimme 53, 273
Headlam, Dave 72–5, 76, 79
Heile, Bjørn 200–2

heterophony 273, 220
hexachord 273, 13
hexachordal complementation 273, 13
Hirsbrunner, Theo 118
Holliger, Heinz 146
Howell, Tim 220
Hyde, Martha 109

integer notation 2, 10, 65, 273
integral serialism 98, 119, 130, 134, 159, 175,
   200, 219, 273
interval class 11, 91, 271, 273
interval cycle 72, 122, 274
invariants 19, 41, 274
inversion 4, 274
inverted retrograde 139, 274
IRCAM 203
Ives, Charles 117

Jackson, Timothy L. 108, 110
Jarman, Douglas 80
Johnson, Julian 90, 94, 96
Jone, Hildegard 96, 99
Jones, Nicholas 228

Kagel, Mauricio 198–202
   Anagrama 201
   Aus Deutschland 201–2
   Die Erschöpfung der Welt 201
   Intermezzo 201, 202
   Kantrimusik 201
   Transición II 201
   String Quartet No. 3 202
   Variations 200
   Vox humana? 201
Keller, Hans 112, 152
Klein, Fritz Heinrich 68–70, 71, 75
Knussen, Oliver 235–6
   Flourish with Fireworks 236
   Horn Concerto 236
   Songs without Voices 236
   Two Organa 236
   Violin Concerto 236
   Whitman Settings 236

Koblyakov, Lev 181
Koenig, Gottfried-Michael 191
Kohl, Jerome 212, 213
Krenek, Ernst, 117, 119–20, 138, 219, 223, 235
  Lamentatio Jeremiae Prophetae 120
  Studies in Counterpoint 120
Kullberg, Erling 220
Kurtág, György 85, 100, 157, 216–18
  *Einige Sätze aus den Sudelbüchern Georg
      Christoph Lichtenbergs* 217
  The Sayings of Péter Bornemisza 217
  String Quartet No. 1 216, 217
Kurth, Richard 108, 110–12, 141, 277

Lansky, Paul 122
Latham, Edward 106
Leeuw, Reinbert de 236
Leibowitz, René 124, 164, 171, 175, 190
Lendvai, Ernö 190
Lewin, David 9
Lieberman, David Isadore 106
Ligeti, György 159, 189–93, 190, 216
  Apparitions 190, 192
  Chromatic Fantasy 190
  Études 192
  Monument 192
Lutosławski, Witold 149, 157–9, 271
  Funeral Music 157
Lutyens, Elisabeth 153

Maconie, Robin 181, 184, 185, 186, 212, 213,
    215
Maderna, Bruno 164, 194, 195, 196
  Serenata 196
magic square 225, 274
Mahler, Alma 82
Mahler, Gustav 79, 82, 94, 109, 115, 165, 223,
    224
Mallarmé, Stéphane 178
Martin, Frank 121
Martino, Donald 145
matrix 10, 274
Maxwell Davies, Peter 221–8, 231, 277

  Alma Redemptoris Mater 224, 225
  Ave Maris Stella 225–8
  Fantasias [I and 2] *on an 'In nomine' of John
      Taverner* 224
  Five Pieces for Piano, Op. 2 223
  Image, Reflection, Shadow 227
  'Naxos' string quartets 228
  St Michael 223, 225
  Salome 227
  Sonata for Clarinet and Piano 223
  Symphony No. 1 227
  Taverner 224
  Worldes Blis 224
McGregor, Richard 224, 227, 228
Mead, Andrew 131, 146, 148
Messiaen, Olivier 171–3, 182, 187, 208, 216
  Mode de valeurs et d'intensités 172, 195, 187
Metzger, Karl-Heinz 169
Milhaud, Darius 143
Milstein, Silvina 108, 274
mode 8, 277
modern-classicism 63, 79, 86, 196, 202, 228,
    275
modes of limited transposition 171
Moment form 119, 275
Morris, Robert 145
multiplication 13, 179–81, 275

Nancarrow, Conlon 142
Neighbour, O.W. 23
neo-classicism 40, 50, 79, 98, 122, 136, 198,
    204, 238, 275
Nielinger, Carola 168
Nono, Luigi 131, 163–9, 174, 177, 187, 194,
    224, 231
  Canti per tredici 166
  Il canto sospeso 166–9
  polifonica-monodia-ritmica 165
  Variazioni canoniche 164, 165
Nørgård, Per 220–1, 272
  Gilgamesh 220
  Grooving 221
normal order pitch-class set 8, 275

octatonic scale 137, 141
Ogdon, Will 18
Osmond-Smith, David 194, 195, 196, 198
ostinato 18, 140, 275
Owens, Peter 224

pantonality 47, 48, 66, 110, 229
Panufnik, Andrzej 157
    Tragic Overture 157
parameter 3, 275
Parsons, Ben 175
partitioning, 13, 276
Pascall, Robert 108, 109, 115
Peles, Stephen 144
Perle, George 17, 24, 65, 70, 72, 75, 78, 80, 121, 134
permutation 13, 276
Petrassi, Goffredo 224
Pfitzner, Hans 22
pitch class 3, 276
pitch-class set analysis 10, 19, 65
pitch-class set multiplication 181, 233
Pollack, Howard 121
Ponsonby, Robert 155
Potter, Keith 142, 143
post-tonal 1, 16, 271, 276
Pousseur, Henri 194, 212
    Rimes 196
Prausnitz, Frederik 121
prime form 4, 276

random funnel series 233, 234
Ravenscroft, Brenda 141
Reich, Steve 123–4, 142, 143–4, 236
    Music for String Orchestra 143
    Pitch Charts 143
Riegger, Wallingford 117
Riley, Terry 124
Roberts, David 224, 225, 227, 236
rotation 138, 205, 276
Ruggles, Carl 119

Sacher, Paul 146, 205
Sartre, Jean-Paul 164

Schenker, Heinrich 124, 135
Scherchen, Hermann 164, 187
Scheuchl, Marie 84
Schiff, David 147, 148
Schmelz, Peter J. 155–6
Schnittke, Alfred 155
Schoenberg, Arnold 12, 17–63, 70, 101–16, 117,
    121, 122–4, 153, 175, 177, 179, 181, 221,
    223, 225, 229, 235, 238, 272, 275, 277
in America 101–16
Canons in C major 67
Chamber Symphony No. 1 173
Chamber Symphony No. 2 105
'Composition with 12 Tones I' 51, 54
deviser of the twelve-tone technique 1–3
Dreimal tausend Jahre 107
Erwartung 17, 61, 204
Five Pieces for Piano, Op. 23 45, 47–9, 63,
    117
Four Pieces for Mixed Chorus, Op. 27 with
    Three Satires, Op. 28 50, 56–8, 66, 70
Die glückliche Hand 21
Harmonielehre 20, 69
interactions with Webern 85–90, 93, 100
Die Jakobsleiter 21, 22, 22–4, 46
and John Cage 141
Modern Psalms 116
Moses und Aron 61, 80, 102–6, 120, 182,
    229
Ode to Napoleon Bonaparte 106, 114, 164,
    174
'Opinion or Insight?' 67, 69, 71
*Phantasy for Violin with Piano
    Accompaniment* 116, 122
Piano Concerto 106, 113, 114
Piano Piece, Op. 33a 50
Pierrot lunaire 17, 194
Serenade, Op. 24 45, 46
Six Pieces for Male Chorus, Op. 35 102
Six Short Piano Pieces, Op. 19: No. 6 21
String Quartet No. 3 50, 61, 109
String Quartet No. 4 106, 107–12, 114, 122
String Trio 107, 114–15, 122, 145

Schoenberg, Arnold (cont.)
  Suite for Piano, Op. 25 2, 4, 10, 16, 17, 19,
    31–43, 45, 46, 87, 88, 90, 106, 117,
    204, 212, 223, 238
  Suite Op. 29 15, 50, 58–60, 70, 71, 87, 201
  A Survivor from Warsaw 106, 115, 160, 164
  Symphony (unfinished) 19, 21, 22–5, 23
  Theme and Variations for Wind Band 114,
    122
  Three Piano Pieces, Op. 11: No. 1 18–19
  Three Satires, Op. 10
  transition to serialism 17–32
  Variations for Orchestra, Op. 31 50, 62, 101,
    103
  Variations on a Recitative for Organ 114
  Verklärte Nacht 17, 54
  Violin Concerto 106, 113, 114, 122
  Von heute auf morgen 56, 61, 102, 120,
    204
  Wind Quintet, Op. 9, 50–6, 87, 197
Schubert, Franz 109
Schwarz, Robert 143
Scruton, Roger 111, 124, 125
Searle, Humphrey 153, 228
series 2, 3, 8, 272, 276
Serocki, Kazimierz 157
set 8, 272, 276, 277
set-class 11, 276
Sessions, Roger 120
Shaw, Jennifer 22
Shostakovich, Dmitri 151, 155–6
  String Quartet No. 12 156
Shreffler, Anne C. 86–90
sieving 82, 188, 189, 277
Simms, Bryan 19–20, 23, 46, 124, 125, 126
Skryabin, Aleksandr 8, 9, 18
Smith Brindle, Reginald 160
source set 9, 29, 277
spectralism 118, 277
Stein, Erwin, 152
Stein, Leonard 143
Steinitz, Richard 190, 192
stochastics 188

Stockhausen, Karlheinz 25, 119, 124, 125,
    181–6, 189–93, 191, 209–16, 223, 232
  Formel 182
  Gesang der Jünglinge 196
  Gruppen 181, 182, 184–6, 190
  Herbstmusik 212
  Indianerlieder 212
  Klavierstück VII 184
  Klavierstück VIII 182–4
  Klavierstück X 216
  Klavierstück XI 182
  Konkrete Etüde 182
  Kontakte 186
  Kontrapunkte 195
  Kreuzspiel 182
  Mantra 186, 210–12, 213
  LICHT 186, 212, 213–16, 216
  Punkte 182
  Refrain 186
  Sonatine 181
  Studie 1 213
  Trans 212
  Zyklus 186
Straus, Joseph 8, 119, 137, 138, 140
Strauss, Richard 22
Stravinsky, Igor 14–15, 18, 85, 100, 117, 124,
    135–41, 231, 235, 274
  Abraham and Isaac 137
  Agon 144, 145, 196
  Canticum Sacrum 145
  In memoriam Dylan Thomas 140
  Movements 135, 137
  Octet 56, 58
  Piano-Rag-Music 46
  The Rake's Progress 135, 136
  Requiem Canticles 137, 139
  The Rite of Spring 78, 58, 137
  Septet 140
  Three Shakespeare Songs 140
  Threni 135
sub-set 9, 274, 277
suspended tonality 48, 72, 110, 229, 275, 277
symmetry 94, 96, 99, 122, 137, 138

Taruskin, Richard 14, 101, 104, 132–4, 136, 137
tetrachord 13, 277
Thomas, Adrian 157, 159
Thomson, Virgil 142
time-point series 130, 277
Tippett, Michael 154
Toop, Richard 182, 186, 190, 212, 215, 232, 235
Toorn, Pieter van den 137
transposition 4, 277
transpositional combination 181
trichord 9, 271, 277
trope 22, 24, 277
Truelove, Stephen 182
twelve-tone tonality 121, 134

Varèse, Edgard 117, 118–19, 141, 165
    Déserts 118
    Octandre 118
Volkonsky, Andrey 155

Wagner, Richard 75, 103
Walsh, Stephen 14, 138
Webern, Anton 6–8, 17, 70, 80, 85–100, 101, 137, 138, 153, 177, 179, 191, 194, 212, 216, 231, 238, 272, 276
    Das Augenlicht, Op. 26 153, 161
    Bagatelles Op. 9 6–8, 10–13, 86
    Cantata No. 1 Op. 29 97–9, 100
    Cantata No. 2 Op. 31 85
    Concerto for Nine Instruments, Op. 24 9, 96, 217

Five Canons, Op. 16 88
Five Sacred Songs, Op. 15 87, 88
Kinderstück 87, 88, 90
Klavierstück 90
The Path to the New Music 94
String Quartet, Op. 28 86
String Trio, Op. 20 89, 92–3, 217
Symphony, Op. 21 85, 90, 94–6
Three Songs, Op. 18 87, 89, 92
Three Traditional Rhymes, Op. 17: No. 1 87, 88, 89, 90; No. 2 90, 91
Zwei Lieder for mixed chorus, Op. 19 92
Variations for orchestra, Op. 30 96, 217
Variations for piano, Op. 27 86, 96
Weill, Kurt 56
Weiss, Adolph 117
Wen-chung, Chou 118
White, Pamela 103
Wintle, Christopher 229
Wolpe, Stefan 119
Wood, Hugh 155
Wuorinen, Charles 144

Xenakis, Yannis 187–9, 219, 229, 277
    Herma 188
    Jonchaies 189
    Metastaseis 187
    Le Sacrifice 187, 188

Young, La Monte 143

Zemlinsky, Alexander von 75